MARKET PLACE AND ENTRANCE TO BAZAARS, BAGDAD.

*From a photograph in possession of the Author.*

# ARABISTAN:

OR

## THE LAND OF
## "THE ARABIAN NIGHTS."

BEING

TRAVELS THROUGH EGYPT, ARABIA, AND PERSIA,
TO BAGDAD.

BY

## WM. PERRY FOGG, A.M.

AUTHOR OF "ROUND THE WORLD LETTERS," ETC.

With an Introduction by

## BAYARD TAYLOR.

LONDON:
DARF PUBLISHERS LIMITED
1985

First Published .. .. 1875

New Impression .. .. 1985

ISBN 1 85077 023 9

Reprinted by A. Wheaton & Co. Ltd, Exeter

THIS VOLUME

IS RESPECTFULLY INSCRIBED TO

Steriker Finnis, Jun.,

MY "COMPAGNON DE VOYAGE;"

AND TO

The English Residents of Bagdad and Bassorah,

WHOSE UNBOUNDED KINDNESS AND

HOSPITALITY TO THEIR "AMERICAN COUSIN,"

WILL EVER BE HELD IN GRATEFUL REMEMBRANCE

BY THE AUTHOR

# INTRODUCTION

BY

BAYARD TAYLOR.

———•◦•———

I have read the proof-sheets of this work with a double interest:—First, from my long and familiar acquaintance with the Author: and, secondly, from the manifold charms which belong to the field of his travels.

Although *Arabistan*, or *Ikâr-Arabi*, as it is also called, has become accessible to the tourist within the last few years, it has only attracted such visitors as feel a special interest in both its antique and mediæval memories; and of these Mr. Fogg is, I believe, with but one exception only, the first American to make report of what he has seen. I find not only inherent proofs of his fidelity as an observer, in the narrative itself, but the circumstance that a portion of the ground he has traversed is also familiar to me, enables me to testify to it out of my own knowledge. From the manner in which he depicts the experiences of a traveler in Palestine and Egypt, I accept his picture of Bagdad, the Plains of the Euphrates, and the ruins of Babylon, as being equally honest and exact.

I therefore cheerfully accede to the desire of his publishers that I should contribute this introductory note.

The reader must not suppose that I have revised, or in any way edited, a work which was complete, in type, before I saw it. Every traveler should tell his own story in his own way. Especially where the field is so new and so fascinating as in the present case, the simple, unvarnished recital of one's own experiences and observations is all that is needed. If any further endorsement seems desirable, it can only be that which comes from knowledge of the Author's character; and I am sure that this, also, is superfluous.

The interest which all intelligent persons feel in the sites of the earliest Chaldean civilization, in the traces of the later Macedonian empire, and the latest splendors of the famous capital of the Caliphs, will sufficiently commend this volume to the public. My knowledge of the author, and of the circumstances under which his journey was made, must be my apology for an introduction which I would fain believe is unnecessary.

So many of our citizens have the time, means, and capacity for adding similar contributions to our knowledge of the world, and so few avail themselves of those advantages or recognize a higher duty than their own personal gratification, that this example deserves a general and grateful recognition.

BAYARD TAYLOR.

NEW YORK, July 1st, 1875.

# The Author's Preface.

————•◦•————

THE title of this volume, "ARABISTAN," signifies in Persian, "The Country of the Arabs." Egypt, Arabia, and Persia, are the scene of the "Thousand and One Stories," in many of which Haroun-al-Raschid, the Caliph of Bagdad, is the hero.

My motive in visiting these countries was not merely the pursuit of pleasure, but a desire to gratify a long-cherished wish, I might almost say a passion, to see, at least once in my lifetime, the strange and curious nations of the Orient, which have always had for me a strange fascination.

The excuse of ordinary travelers who write books, was not mine. I was not ordered abroad "by the doctors," but started in perfect health, which I retained through all the vicissitudes of scene and climate, and I may add that I met with no serious mishap to mar the pleasure of the journey.

In attempting to describe the "Land of the Arabian Nights," as it appears to-day, I have confined myself, in a great measure, to what passed under my own observation, and have endeavored to give a faithful picture of such adventures as would naturally befall a traveler; making no attempt at fine writing or high-flown description.

As a book of scientific exploration this volume makes no pretentions. The works of Rawlinson, Layard, and more recently of George Smith, have opened a new page to the student of history, by bringing to light the long-buried treasures of Nineveh and Babylon. The space I have devoted to these discoveries is of course quite inadequate to do justice to a subject so full of interest from a scientific point of view; but, at the same time, I think that the reader will find something to interest him in the sketches which I have given of my own visit to the Plains of Shinar, and what befell me near the ruins of Babylon, and among the Arabs of the surrounding country.

The full-page illustrations are from original photographs, of which I believe no other copies have been taken. They are therefore unique. It was my good fortune to meet at Bagdad a young English gentleman, to whom photography was a pastime. The views of street life in Oriental cities, and other interesting scenery here reproduced, are strictly true to nature, and were certainly the first ever taken in the various localities which they represent.

The small illustrations are all from original drawings, from the pencil of a well-known American artist, and the author can certify to their correctness and excellence, both in design and execution.

The unexpected courtesy and kindness everywhere met with during my travels, from both foreign residents and natives, and the many chance acquaintances then formed, and which have since ripened into friendships that will endure for a lifetime, are among the pleasantest *souvenirs* of my journey

W. P. F.

CLEVELAND, August, 1875.

# Contents.

## CHAPTER I.

### LONDON TO ALEXANDRIA.

## CHAPTER II.

### ALEXANDRIA TO CAIRO.

## CHAPTER III.

### SCENES IN CAIRO.

## CHAPTER IV.

### MEMPHIS AND THE PYRAMIDS.

## CHAPTER V.

### CAIRO TO PORT SAID.

## CHAPTER VI.

### PORT SAID TO JERUSALEM.

## CHAPTER VII.

### THE HOLY CITY.

## CHAPTER VIII.

### JERUSALEM, AND OUR RETURN TO JAFFA.

## CHAPTER IX.

### THE SUEZ CANAL.

# CHAPTER X.

## ON THE RED SEA.

# CHAPTER XI.

## MAHOMET AND HIS RELIGION.

# CHAPTER XII.

## ADEN.

# CHAPTER XIX.

## THE PASHA OF BAGDAD.

# CHAPTER XX.

## HABITS AND CUSTOMS OF THE ARABS.

# CHAPTER XXI.

## EXCURSION TO BABYLON.

## CHAPTER XXII.

### HOSPITALITIES IN KERBELLA.

## CHAPTER XXIII.

### THE RETURN FROM BABYLON.

## CHAPTER XXIV.

### NINEVEH AND ITS REMAINS.

## CHAPTER XXV.

### VISIT TO THE PUBLIC INSTITUTIONS.

## CHAPTER XXVI.

### SOCIAL LIFE OF NATIVES AND FOREIGNERS.

# Illustrations.

# CHAPTER I.

## LONDON TO ALEXANDRIA.

Gerard Rohlf's Expedition—Exploring the Great Sahara Desert—The Writer's Plans—By Express Trains through France—Steamer Missed at Marseilles and still Missing—The Entrepot of France—Toulon—"Horse Marines"—Nice to Genoa—A Grand Panorama—"Parlez-vous Anglais?"—Doctor Antonio and the Corniche Road—Genoa—"Is he Dead"—Leghorn—Pisa—Naples—False Pretenses—Messina and Sicily—A Wonderful Relic—Oranges by the Basket full—The Sicilia and her Passengers—Young England—The Hurricane and a Lee Shore—We almost touch at Crete—Arrival at Alexandria.

HEN I bade adieu to America in January, 1874, I had no intention of extending my journey to Bagdad and Persia. My plans were to proceed directly to Egypt, and there, if possible, to join an expedition to explore the great Sahara desert, which was then being fitted out by the Khedive, under Gerard Rohlfs, a distinguished German traveler in Northern Africa. The objects and aim of this enterprise were to re-discover those great oases of the Libyan desert which are known to exist, and supposed to contain large tracts of fertile territory and a population of many thousands, but which have never been visited by Europeans. I relied upon my acquaintance with American officers in the service of the Khedive, and our Consul General in Cairo, whom I had met during my former travels in the East, to obtain permission to join this expedition. That it would be full of danger as well as of exciting adventure I was well aware, and I therefore said very little to my friends at home, as to my proposed plans.

Reaching London about the middle of January, I crossed France on the fastest trains, stopping but a few hours in Paris, and reached Marseilles just twelve hours too late for the steamer to Alexandria. Making the best of the situation, I changed my plans, leisurely taking Nice, Genoa, Leghorn, Naples, and Messina *en route*. When I reached Alexandria I learned that the French steamer I had missed at Marseilles, had not arrived, and was supposed to be lost with all on board.

The old French city of Marseilles, founded by the Phœnicians 600 years B. C., well repaid the day spent there, and, through the kindness of the American Consul, F. W. Potter, Esq., I was enabled to see many things of interest to a traveler. The French colony of Algeria is directly opposite, and its trade, monopolized by this city, has added immensely to its population and commercial prosperity. The silks of Lyons, the wines, olives, and other products of Southern France, here find their outlet to all parts of the world. Its commerce is far more extensive than that of any other port of France, and its trade with America double that of Havre. A line of first-class steamships direct to the United States, would command not only an immense freight, but also a large passenger traffic. By them we could reach in winter the sunny, genial climate of the Mediterranean, avoiding the stormy Northern Atlantic, and one thousand miles additional travel.

Marseilles is the birth-place of Thiers—historian, ex-premier and ex-president—the son of a blacksmith—and to-day, though out of office, the foremost man in France. At the time of the first revolution, it gave its name to a hymn that has become the tocsin of liberty throughout the world.

I made a few hours' stop at Toulon, forty miles west of Marseilles, one of the greatest naval arsenals in the world. Its batteries, reaching from the shore to the summits of the hills commanding the town, make the place seem impregnable. Here at Toulon, in 1794, young Bonaparte, then a lieutenant of artillery, had the first opportunity to display his great military genius, in planning the batteries that in a few days compelled the British to evacuate the town and put out to sea.

Strolling along the streets crowded with officers and soldiers in bright uniforms, I met two fine looking officers whose elegant dress especially attracted my attention. I supposed that they must belong to the naval service, as the " foul anchor " was embroidered in gold upon collars and cuffs. As they passed me I turned to admire their rich uniform, and noticed, to my great surprise, that both wore spurs attached to their boots. A *gens d'arme* standing near, I touched my hat and asked him to what service they belonged. He courteously returned the salute, and told me that they were officers of marine. I wanted to ask the cocked-hat official, " Why, then, the spurs ? "— but for the life of me I could not at that moment remember the French word for spurs. So the mystery remains unsolved, unless we may suppose they are attached to that corps which is generally regarded as a myth, the " Horse Marines."

The railway to Nice winds along the shore, through a country cultivated like a garden. On our right is the blue Mediterranean sparkling in the sun, and on our left the horizon, bounded by the snow-capped summits of the Maritime Alps. The vineyards cover every hillside, and there is a constant succession of olive groves,—old gnarled trees, —among the dark green foliage of which, the blossoms of

" THE HORSE MARINES."

early plum trees are brought out in bright relief. Now we pass a pretty villa in a grove of orange trees, roses blossoming in the garden. To one coming from the cold north in "search for winter sunbeams," it is a picture full of beauty and enjoyment.

Nice detained me but one day. This great sanitarium of Europe, seems made up entirely of hotels and boarding houses. All great watering-places in the height of the season have a similar appearance. The shop windows are full of fancy goods and knick-knacks, tempting the idler, articles which no one buys at home, and are called by ill-natured people, " rubbish."

The next morning, as I was stepping into the carriage for the railway station to Genoa, 120 miles distant, I asked the *portier* at what hour we should arrive. He replied that near San Remo, one of the hundred tunnels between here and Genoa, had caved in, and we should have to take a carriage to cross the break, but a steamer leaving that morning would reach Genoa the same evening; so I changed my order to the driver from the *Chemin de fer* to the *Bateau-a-Vapeur.* A most fortunate change it proved. I turn to my note-book and find that the record of that day's experience is almost blank. It was one of those days so impressed upon the memory, that no written reminders are necessary, and it seems at the time that no after-experience can ever dim the brightness of the picture. The sky, the air, and the sea were in perfect accord. So pure was the atmosphere, that the island of Corsica was seen that day from the French coast, an event that occurs but few times during the season. The island itself is distant about one hundred miles, but the peaks of its central mountain range loom up eight thousand feet above the sea, and are fully one hundred and twenty miles from the shore of France.

Our little steamer, named after the Prince of Monaco, carried about thirty passengers, nearly all French or Italian; but a gentleman who had a slightly English look, and seemed as hungry as myself for some one to talk to, attracted my attention. We accosted each other simultaneously and in the same words, " Monsieur, parlez vous Anglais ? " He proved a most agreeable companion, had traveled all over America, sketching its scenery from the Thousand Isles to the Rocky mountains. His pencil was busy to-day, and I envied him the wonderful facility of transferring to paper by a few rapid touches, the charming views spread out before us.

We coasted along from one headland to another, where the spurs of the Alpine range push their bold rocky promontories far out to sea, enclosing within their protecting arms many beautiful towns and villages, some close to the shore, bathing their feet in the silvery waves, some stretching up the mountain side like flocks of sheep; here the ruins of some old church or castle crowning the summit of a sea-washed cliff, there a series of marble palaces or painted villas, surrounded by vineyards and groves of orange and lemon trees. We passed the towns of Mentone, San-Remo, and Ventimille, then the little village of Bordighera, its church surrounded by palm trees. For many centuries, this village had the monopoly of furnishing palm branches to Rome for the holy week, but to me it was far more interesting as the opening scene of that charming novel, "Dr. Antonio." The famous Corniche Road winds along the shore, following all the indentations of the coast, sometimes on a level with the sea, then climbing up the mountain side, a narrow shelf, cut from the solid rock. The railway, a modern institution, runs close to the shore, and we see a train of cars, but the next moment it disappears in the base of a cliff, then emerging from the tunnel, it leaps across the valley on a stone arched bridge.

Such was the grand panorama which nature and art united to unfold—the sea in front, the Alps behind, and overhead the splendors of an Italian sky.

We reached Genoa after dark, and were lodged in the palace of one of her old merchant princes, now transformed into a modern hotel. The next day we visited two or three "Palazzios," as many old churches, and the

Campo Santo; the latter, tenanted only by the dead, was by far the most interesting. Of course our cicerone must show us the statue and the old manuscripts of Christopher Columbus. I could only think of Mark Twain's oft re-peated question, " Is he dead ?"

From Genoa down the Italian coast to Leghorn, famous for its straw braids, and to Pisa, where every tourist must climb the winding stone steps to *lean* over the parapet of the Leaning Tower, thence to Naples to do Vesuvius, Pompeii, Sorrento, and the blue caves of Capri. The bay of Naples is very charming; the lazaroni, eating long strings of maccaroni, are picturesque in red caps and rags, but the Neapolitans are proverbially great liars. Every year about this time, they spread abroad the report that old Vesuvius is groaning and smoking frightfully—sure premonitions of a grand " blow out." I had heard as far away as London, that a great eruption was daily looked for, and that already the sky at night was red with flames from the crater, and I expected, of course, to see the molten lava pouring down the sides of the mountain. But there was nothing of the kind on exhibition. Arriving at night, the only lights were the city lamps and the stars overhead. Not a groan could be heard from the old vol-cano, and the next day one could see only a light whiff of smoke, puffed from his old pipe-bowl. The performance was well advertised, but the principal actor did not put in an appearance. Hundreds of strangers are attracted here watching and waiting. They crowd the hotels, liber ally fee the beggars, buy corals and relics of Pompeii, make business lively, and the Neapolitans are gay and happy.

The steamers leaving Naples for Alexandria, pass the second day through the narrow strait that separates the island of Sicily from the main land, and stop for a few hours at the quaint old Sicilian city of Messina. We go on shore to mail our last letter for Europe. The city presents a very imposing appearance from the harbor. It is crescent-shaped, and the hills in the background rise in the form of an amphitheatre, covered with vineyards and orange groves. The houses are built of white limestone, and the principal streets paved with square blocks of lava.

The postal arrangements of this city of one hundred and fifty thousand inhabitants, are not very extensive. They consist of a window opening into the street, where the people stand to enquire for letters or buy stamps, and a hole in the wall to drop letters in. We go from the post-office to the old Cathedral, dating back to the twelfth century, to get a sight, if possible, of a wonderful relic which all Messinians are supposed to believe authentic. It is no less than an *autograph letter* written by the Virgin Mary, in which she promises her special care and protection to the inhabitants, and to make the matter doubly sure, she sends a lock of her own hair by the person entrusted with this letter. You may be certain we did not see these remarkable relics; either the priests could not understand our imperfect Italian, or suspected from our dress and language that we were *Anglese*, infidel heretics. The market, however, did not disappoint us. Such splendid oranges, four for a penny! Two shillings bought a basketful, and the boat that took us back to the steamer was loaded down with the golden fruit. Passing out of the Straits of Messina, we saw on the Italian shore a small white monument, erected on the spot where Garibaldi landed with a handful of men and inaugurated a revolution that drove the tyrannical Bourbon from the throne of Naples. Far away to the right, near the center of the island, we could just discern the peak of Ætna, nearly eleven thousand feet above the level of the sea.

The distance from Messina to Alexandria is eight hundred and fifty miles, usually taking the steamer four days. The direct course would be fifty miles westward of Crete, or Candia, whose unwelcome acquaintance we were destined to make. Our steamer, the "Sicilia," was a staunch, Clyde-built iron vessel of about eight hundred tons, belonging to the Italian "Rubatinno" line, and its officers had the reputation of being skillful seamen, as well as courteous gentlemen. My experience on a steamer of this line three years ago, from Bombay to Suez, had been very favorable. When we left the straits on Monday afternoon, the weather was rough and the wind blew hard from the south-west. We had a pleasant lot of passengers, only eight in number, all English but myself. They comprised an artist and his wife (the only lady on board) for Egypt, four Englishmen bound for India, one of them, a clergyman, having in charge a young man of eighteen, a kind, good-hearted fellow, full of fun, but as irrepressible as a young bear. The butt of many a joke, he soon became a general favorite, and within two days was familiarly called "Tom" by us all. A young English merchant bound for Bagdad, and myself, completed the list.

On Tuesday the gale increased, but as yet causing no anxiety. Tom's appetite was ravenous, and he would smoke his meershaum on deck, when it was blowing a gale. His call to the waiters, *anchore du figaro*, meaning more figs, made our good natured captain roar with laughter. The first two days he was popping away with his revolver at the sea-gulls and Mother Carey's chickens, until stopped by a protest from the superstitious Italian sailors. On Wednesday night the gale was at its height, and for a few hours it blew a hurricane. We were then off Crete, and the wind was blowing us directly upon a lee shore. For twenty-four hours it had been too rough to do much cooking on board, or to set the table for a regular meal. The little steamer pitched and rolled awfully, and all that night we sat propped up by cushions and pillows on the cabin floor; chairs, satchels, and personal luggage scattered about in the wildest confusion. The engineer was instructed to put on full head of steam, and the vessel shook and quivered as if she were a living creature straining every nerve to save herself from destruction. A slight break in the machinery, and no human power could have prevented our being dashed to pieces on that rocky coast, which St. Paul found so inhospitable eighteen centuries ago. A hundred life-preservers would have been useless, and no boat could have lived for a moment in such a sea. Once in a while, some one of us would crawl up the companion-way, and try to peep outside, but none of us could stand on deck. The artist, cheerful and sanguine of temperament, would always come back with some encouraging word. But once, when the gale was at its height, he came silently back, and, sitting down beside his wife (a brave lady she was), took her hands in his, while she rested her head upon his shoulder. Then I knew the crisis had come. That last half hour of the unfortunates on the " Ville du Havre " came vividly to my mind, and I wished Egypt, the Nile, and the Khedive, all at the bottom of the Red Sea with Pharaoh and his hosts.

We were then trying to bear up against the gale, and get around the north point of Crete, so as to gain a shelter behind the island. If we could only hold on an hour or two longer it could be done. The captain afterwards said that for two hours his hair stood on end. Just at this time, the irrepressible Tom said he was awful hungry, and called out to the steward to bring him some bread and cheese. The idea seemed so ludicrous that it acted as a relief to our intense mental anxiety. The good ship did hold on, and before daylight we had weathered the point of land, and reached smoother water. Our captain came down, all dripping in his oil cloth suit, and fairly danced as he said in Italian (his English failing him at the moment,) that we were safe. No interpreter was needed, but we all crowded around him and gave him *bravos* more hearty than ever greeted his countryman, Mario, on the stage.

On Thursday we ran down along the east coast of Crete, its high rocky cliffs protecting us from the fury of the gale. The next two days were exceedingly rough, but nothing in comparison to what we had passed through, and on Saturday we reached Alexandria, where we heard of many disasters from the storm.

As we left the steamer for the wharf in a boat rowed by half-naked Arabs, we gave three hearty English cheers for the "Sicilia" and her officers, who were waving their caps to us from her deck, and shouting their *addios*.

3

# CHAPTER II.

## ALEXANDRIA TO CAIRO.

Scenes in Alexandria—Pompey's Pillar and Cleopatra's Needles—An Apology—Up the Nile—Ships of the Desert—Well Sweeps and Water Wheels—Civilization in Egypt—Cairo Unchanged—A Princess' Marriage and Splendid Fêtes—The Story of the Bride—How a Slave Girl became a Princess—Our Consul General in Egypt—The Sahara Exploration Party already Started—A Disappointment—Sir Samuel Baker's Expedition not a Success—Dissatisfaction of the Egyptian Government—Colonel Gordon—Change of Programme—To Bagdad and Persia instead of Central Africa.

LEXANDRIA, founded more than two thousand years ago by the great Conqueror, is a mixture of the Oriental and the European, where Parisian hats struggle with Moslem turbans for predominance. Nowhere else upon the globe can such a medley of costumes and nationalities be seen as in these streets. To one landing here from the North, the sights are much more novel and exciting than to the traveler who has seen the real Orient. The population of all the large cities on the south shore of the Mediterranean may be described as mixed, but here it is especially so. You meet an Englishman just landed from the steamer, who with great effort tries to maintain his natural air of disdain and *nonchalance;* then a full-rigged

Turk, whose *sang froid* is seemingly unruffled by the saucy glances of the wearer of that stunning Parisian bonnet; all surrounded by crowds of Arabs, Nubians, Greeks, Maltese, Jews, and Europeans.

After a struggle with the donkey boys, amid a din compared with which a crowd of New York hackmen is a heaven of repose, our Sicilian party are mounted on full-grown donkeys, perhaps three and a half feet high, and I act as *cicerone* to show them the sights. Leaving the European quarter, we thread the narrow, unpaved, filthy streets outside the wall, through a gate guarded by Egyptian soldiers, fat, lazy-looking fellows, in zouave uniform and carrying the improved breech-loading Remington rifle, then past a neglected, unenclosed cemetery, where the crowded headstones are each surmounted by a marble turban or fez, to the top of a plateau perhaps one hundred feet above the sea, upon which stands a solitary pillar of red polished granite. Its height, including the pedestal, shaft, and capital, is ninety-eight feet. Its diameter at the base is ten feet, tapering slightly towards the top, and is surmounted by an elaborate capital, upon which it is supposed there was once a statue. Savans do not agree as to its age and origin, some maintaining that it was erected by a Roman prefect of Egypt in the second century, others that it is the only one left of a long colonnade that formed the front of a temple, dating back thousands of years before the Christian era. We were at once surrounded by begging children in scanty raiment, crying, *Howadji, Baksheesh!* The copper coinage of Egypt runs fortunately into very small denominations, and a half-franc's worth of copper was dealt out sparingly among the crowd, but the more we gave, the more the crowd increased, and they came pouring from the adjacent hovels in such numbers, that we whipped up our donkeys and beat a retreat.

Then to Cleopatra's Needles in the suburbs near the shore, two obelisks of red granite, about seventy feet high and covered with hieroglyphics, one still erect, the other lying ignobly on the ground and half covered with rubbish. They go back one thousand four hundred and ninety-five years before Christ, and are genuine antiques. I am sorry to say that it was quite impossible for me to keep my promise about carrying home a package of these needles for distribution as *souvenirs* among my lady friends. My trunk was rather small, and besides at the rate one had to pay for all luggage above sixty pounds weight, my funds would have run short.

Having done the sights of Alexandria, we prepared to leave the city which Napoleon once said would yet be the capital of the world. But the first Napoleon, though a great military genius, was no prophet, and his " Republican or Cossack" prediction about Europe is in a very slow way towards fulfilment. As the seat of learning, and home of literature and philosophy, its greatness passed away with the smoke of its seven hundred thousand volumes burned by the Caliph Omar. It now depends upon the northern barbarians, whether it shall again become a great city as the stepping-stone between Europe and India.

Our way up the Nile to Cairo, one hundred and thirty miles, was by rail. How incongruous a railway seems to all one's surroundings in the East! The camel, that " noble ship of the desert," is the only means of convey-ance which seems in perfect harmony with the scenes about us. Slow, patient, plodding, swaying to and fro under his heavy load, carrying within his water supply for days together, his large, flat, spongy feet adapted for travel over the yielding sand—if not originally created in his present type, how many ages upon ages it must have required to perfect these qualities by " natural selection."

We speed across the Delta, through the fruitful fields along the Nile, where the half-naked *fellaheen*, or peasants, are at work, some plowing with sharp-pointed sticks

EGYPTIAN PEASANT PLOWING.

drawn by bullocks, others raising water from the river for irrigation by the most primitive machinery—sometimes a straw bucket swung between two men dipping the water from one level to the next, then a series of old-fashioned well-sweeps. A little further on we see the oxen plodding round and round, turning the rude Egyptian water-wheel, to the rim of which earthen jars are tied,—the germ which western brains have elaborated into magnificent grain elevators,—past mud villages built upon the ruins of towns that have occupied the same sites for thousands of years. Such is modern Egypt, the same cloudless sky and ever flowing river, the same coffee-colored, slender-limbed people, as patient under the yoke of the Moslem as of the Pharaohs.

From our western stand-point, the Egyptians seem miser-

ably ground down and unhappy.  But I question whether
that idea is correct.  They are better off than were their
ancestors, slaves of the Pharaohs ; better fed to-day than
the people of British India, where starvation and famine
will this year destroy thousands, and as for clothing, that
is a matter entirely conventional.  In this climate very
little is required.  They gather around us at the stations,
chattering like magpies, and seemingly more happy and
contented than the peasantry of Europe.  It is that sort of
careless happiness, enjoying only to-day, without ambition,
and regardless of to-morrow, once a characteristic of the
negro population of the South, but now said to be fast
fading out under the stimulus of a personal responsibility
and a higher standard of life.  But it is happiness, never-
theless, which will probably disappear when Egypt shall
have a republican government and universal suffrage.

I notice that the engineer of our train is a European, and
we are whirled along fully twenty-five miles an hour, past
more collections of mud huts, through long stretches of
meadows made amazingly fertile by the sun-quickening
slime which the river leaves behind after its annual rise,
richer by far than bone-dust or guano ; past fat cattle
browsing in rich pastures, like Pharaoh's fat kine, in
striking contrast to the lean, ragged peasants at work
in the fields ; past rows of graceful palms, shooting up
like so many obelisks, behind which we catch a glimpse of
one of the Viceroy's many palaces.  Ten miles away across
the sandy plains on our right, we discern the three great
pyramids of Ghizah, and now the tall minarets of the
capital of Egypt are before us.

We arrive at Cairo promptly on time, and I find myself
in my old quarters at Shepherd's Hotel.  The door of my
room opens on a garden where a fountain is playing amid
tropical palms and banyan trees.  In front of the hotel are

the same sharp *gamins* of donkey boys, the same curious and fascinating sights in streets and bazars. Why should I expect any change ? Three years or three thousand are all the same to Egypt.

I am very fortunate to reach Cairo just in time for the closing scenes of the great fêtes given by the Viceroy on occasion of the marriage of his daughter. The illuminations and fireworks for the past two nights have been very grand. The flags of the Khedive, a crescent and star on a red ground, are flying everywhere. Miles of streets and bazars are made brilliant at night, by all that European ingenuity can contrive in the way of pyrotechnic display. Last night, upon the grand square in front of the palace, there were six immense tents, gorgeously decorated with flags and lit with hundreds of gas jets from crystal chandeliers. In each tent was a band of music, and a high officer of the Khedive stood near the entrance to welcome every comer, high or low, in the name of his master. Coffee, cigars, and cigarettes were freely distributed to all, by servants wearing the royal livery. It was a display of " Oriental magnificence" and hospitality quite regardless of expense. An immense crowd of people were there from all ranks of society, but everything was quiet and orderly. No wines or liquors formed a part of the entertainment. These are never used by a true Mussulman, unless he has become demoralized by contact with Christian nations of the west. When I returned to my hotel it was nearly midnight, but the streets were as quiet and perhaps more safe than those of New York.

The story of the bride, who is said to be very beautiful, reads like one from the " Thousand and One Nights." She was born a slave of Circassian parentage, and when but three years old, was adopted as a daughter by the third wife of the Viceroy. General Loring told me that he had often seen her before she was twelve years old, with the other children of the Khedive in an open box at the opera. At that age, in accordance with the Turkish custom, she was veiled and entered the harem, her face no more to be seen of men, except members of her own family, and by her husband after the marriage ceremony. The groom is a young prince of the Mohamet Ali family, and so the little slave girl has become a princess. To "point the moral and adorn the tale," I ought to add that the princess is as good as she is beautiful.

THE WIFE OF A PASHA.

Upon reaching Cairo, my first inquiry of Mr. Beardsley, American Consul General to Egypt, who fills that position with credit both to himself and the country he represents, was in regard to the Rohlfs expedition. I found to my great disappointment that it had started some weeks before, and was already far away on the desert. It had been fitted out with great liberality by the Egyptian government. One hundred camels, ninety guards and servants, provisions, tents, galvanized iron tanks containing sixteen gallons of water each, and every practical requisite for scientific exploration as well as for comfort and safety, had been provided. The objective point of the expedition was a large oasis called Kufrah, supposed to lie in the very heart of the great Libyan desert, which the adventurous explorers are confident is no myth, but is large, fertile, and well watered, and contains a numerous population, who have had no connection with the outside world for many generations.

It is no secret among the Americans in Egypt, that the Khedive was very much dissatisfied with the results of Sir Samuel Baker's expedition into Central Africa, from which he returned last year, with such a flourish of trumpets, announcing that he had suppressed the slave trade and added immense territories to the dominion of the enterprising ruler of Egypt. His instructions were to conciliate by kind treatment and liberal presents, the warlike tribes, and open up a country supposed to abound in ivory, to civilization and commerce, with a view, by controlling the chiefs, to stop their constant internecine warfare, and thereby dry up the source of the inhuman traffic in slaves. But that famous traveler, instead of pursuing a conciliatory course, defeated the interior Africans in several hard fights, where, of course, the repeating rifle was more than a match for clubs and spears. At last when he could penetrate no farther on account of the overwhelming numbers that opposed him, he returned down the Nile, having accomplished nothing of importance in the way of geographical discovery, and leaving the tribes behind him greatly exasperated against the Egyptian government.

A new expedition into the upper Nile region is now being organized by the Khedive, which will be under the command of Col. Gordon, an Englishman who won a reputation for gallantry and nerve while serving under the American General Ward, in suppressing the great Tai-Ping rebellion in China. Through the influence of my friends in Egypt I could have joined this expedition under Col. Gordon, and it was no small temptation, to be connected, perhaps, with the solution of that great geographical problem, the sources of the Nile. But the certainty of having to spend at least two years among the pestilential swamps in the heart of Africa, was too much for one who has no ambition to meet the fate of Dr. Livingstone.

Among the passengers on board the " Sicilia " from Naples to Alexandria was an English merchant, a member of the firm of Lynch, Bros. & Co., who was on his way to visit their branch houses in Turkish Arabia. Our acquaintance was cemented into a warm friendship by the events of that memorable night on the Mediterranean, when we momentarily expected to be driven on to the island of Candia. An urgent invitation to accompany him to Bagdad was at that time declined, but now it was renewed so earnestly, that after some hesitation I assented to this change of programme. The vista of ancient Babylon, Nineveh and the " Land of the Arabian Nights " opened before me more attractive by far, than the sandy desert of Sahara, or the wilds of Central Africa. The English steamer, bound for the Persian Gulf, has already sailed from London for Port Said, the entrance to the canal on the Mediterranean, and we shall join her at Suez for our long voyage down the Red Sea, up the Indian ocean and the Persian Gulf, to the mouth of the Euphrates.

# CHAPTER III.

## SCENES IN CAIRO.

HE sound of a sweet toned bell woke me early this morning, and for a moment it seemed that I must be once more in a Christian land ; but a glance from my window across the little garden by the side of the hotel, showed the sun rising over the domes and minarets of the capital of Egypt, and in the streets below were long lines of camels, crowds of swarthy Egyptians all wearing the universal red fez cap, and innumerable donkeys half buried under enormous burdens of fresh cut grass. A sonorous bray from one of these would for the moment drown all other sounds, even the chatter and clamor of their masters, which is incessant except during the hours of darkness. I now fully realize that I am not in America, nor in any other civilized land, and that the sound of the bell does not bring with it the Christian Sabbath. Opening the door I clap my hands, and a native servant appears with a tray on which are *cafe-au-lait*, eggs and bread. The regular breakfast is not served until twelve o'clock. Around the porch of the hotel, which faces a large and handsome square, is a scene full of amusement and novelty to the stranger. But before I can reach the door, I am assailed by a crowd of gaily-dressed dragomen and guides, all most anxious to serve me, each provided with a handful of testimonials in various European languages. But I have learned by experience that this class are almost universally a set of thieves and swindlers, preying upon strangers, and their exactions are only limited by the ignorance or weakness of those who may fall into their hands. It is a Levantine proverb that the three nuisances of the East, are plague, fire, and dragomen. So for the present I decline their urgent offers of service, and stand at the door watching the curious scene. Here are a dozen peddlers of antique relics from the pyramids (probably bogus), canes, bright silk scarfs and turbans; another enterprising dealer has a basket full of young alligators or crocodiles, about a foot long, and holding up one of these charming productions of the Nile urges me to buy it—" only one franc, sar." On the opposite side of the street a mountebank is swallowing swords and snakes, surrounded by an admiring crowd of donkey boys, cab-drivers, and " hangers-on." As a European passes by, he airs perhaps his whole stock of English —" Me very good Juggler—look, see ! " Dogs without number fill every vacant space, their snarling and barking now and then varied, when a vigorous kick sends them yelping away. A private carriage drawn by a pair of handsome Arabian horses drives rapidly by, and in front of the horses run two Nubians with long white rods, screaming to the people to get out of the way.

But a new face is descried by the donkey boys and they go for me at once. These boys and donkeys together form an institution without which Cairo would lose half its attractions. The latter are generally fat and tough, and endowed with all the laziness and obstinacy of their race. The large soft saddles are covered with red morocco, and the trappings are flashy and ornamented with cowrie shells. The stirrup straps are not fastened to the saddle, but

A CAIRO INSTITUTION.

merely pass over it, and unless the boy holds the opposite one, in mounting or dismounting, you come down with a run. The fall, however, can never be much, although somewhat awkward to the stranger with so large a crowd of lookers-on. The donkey boys, generally about half-grown, are the keenest little *gamins* I ever saw, and for antic drollery have no equals. One steps up to me, pulls his forelock with one hand and gives a corresponding kick behind, *accidentally* hits another boy in the region of the stomach, and with a grin of humor on his dirty face says: " Take ride, sah ? Mine splendid donkey. Name Prince"—then catching an English word I uttered, he quickly adds, "of Wales. Prince of Wales, sah "—if I had uttered a French word the name would have been " Prince Napoleon." Others behind him taking the cue call out, " Mine Billy Button," " Tom Jones," " Waterloo," " Duke Wellington," etc But one bright-eyed little urchin (was he so much brighter than the rest?) calls out " Mine Berry good donkey Yankee Doodle "—" General Grant." That last shot told, and I followed the boy to take my first ride on the " donk " with so illustrious a name.

Before I had been long in Cairo, I discovered that it would be a matter of economy as well as comfort to invest in a fez. My friends at home will understand that to wear a fez in the East, does not necessarily make one a Turk ; but it will save by about one-half what you have to pay in the bazaars, as it implies that you are not a stranger to be taken in. English travelers are everywhere the least inclined to adopt the costume or language of a foreign country, and are made to pay accordingly. The French and Italians have that happy facility of identifying themselves with the people wherever they may be, which in the East has very much increased their popularity and influence. Here the nationality of a stove-pipe hat is recognized on sight. In order to see and understand the peculiar customs and life of a strange people, one should drop that haughty air of disdain and superiority, and so far as is consistent with propriety and comfort, mix with the people in a dress that will not attract the special attention of every one he meets.

The bazaars of Cairo are only surpassed by those of Damascus and Constantinople in the extent, richness, and variety of the thousand-and-one articles of Oriental manufacture ; and can best be seen on foot and donkey. The streets are so narrow and crooked that the older part of the city resembles a huge honey-comb. The upper stories project over the one next below, and the front is usually of lattice-work, which enables the bright-eyed damsels to watch all that passes in the street without being seen themselves. There are no sidewalks or pavement, but the streets are cool and moist, the high, projecting buildings shutting out the heat of the sun, and in many places, canvas or boards completely roof in the narrow space at the top, and form an arcade. Troops of hungry dogs do duty as scavengers and keep the streets in tolerable sanitary condition. The only sprinkling machine known here is the same generally used in the East—a water-carrier with a goat-skin slung across his shoulders.

My donkey-boy followed up the " General," making his presence known by frequent whacks over the flanks of the poor beast, and emphasizing them with epithets rather rough and emphatic, than complimentary to his pedigree. The " donk " from instinct or long experience seemed to know when the blow was coming, and would make a sudden spurt to avoid it, which threatened the rider with being dropped off behind. The bazaars swarm with people. Men and women, donkeys, camels, and oxen, bearing heavy loads, are inextricably mingled, every one in the way of others, with no rule of turning out to the right or the left, all shouting, screaming, pulling and whacking the beasts, with most ludicrous appeals to the Prophet. It now requires a sharp lookout, not so much for fear of running

over some one—for the foot passengers have a miraculous
way of escaping danger—as to avoid coming to grief by
being wedged in between a camel laden with stone or
wood, and the projecting panniers of a mule filled with
vegetables or boxes of merchandise.  Regardless of the
hubbub and confusion of the street, you can see the tur-
baned merchant sitting cross-legged on a mat in front of
his little seven by nine shop, smoking his *chibouk* and sip-
ping his coffee with true Mussulman coolness and gravity.
Turning into a by-street, I slipped off the " General," and
leaving him in charge of the boy, I found a standing place
on the corner to watch the passers by.   As I wore the fez
I attracted no special notice, and a grim old Turk made
room for me on the board in front of his shop.   Here

OLD ABRAHAM COMES TO GRIEF.

comes a woman out shopping, an occupation of which the
fair sex are as fond in Cairo as in New York, followed by
a eunuch, black as Erebus, with an armful of parcels.

She may be the "light of the harem," or her grand-
mother, for aught I can tell, as she is wrapped in the
universal white cotton winding sheet, and her face is hidden behind a brown figured gauze veil. She does not
vouchsafe to shoot "an eyelash arrow from an eyebrow
bow" in this direction, so I presume she is old and ugly.
Next comes the very personification of the "Father of
the Faithful," with long, white beard, a massive, wrinkled
face, and Oriental dress, identical with that worn by the
old patriarch. He rides an easy going mule, and seems
absorbed in holy meditation. But at the intersection of
a narrow side street, he comes in contact with a mettled
Arab, ridden by a young fellow at a sharp canter, and over
goes old Abraham sprawling in the dust. This occurrence
is not so unusual as to cause any excitement, and it is
only the stranger who laughs at the catastrophe. He
picks himself up, remounts, his mule more astonished,
perhaps, than his rider, and jogs on again, as if nothing
had happened. Near by is a barber shop, where, if I
understood Arabic, I could hear the latest Caireen scandal,
and in the café over the way, a story-teller is surrounded by a crowd of eager listeners, as in the times
of the Caliphs and the "Arabian nights." For half an hour
I watched the passing throng, and longed for the pencil of
a Hogarth or a Nast to fix on paper the comical scenes.

Then with the donkey boy and the "General," I take a
quieter route toward the Citadel, which is located on a
high bluff overlooking the whole city and its environs.
The glistening domes and minarets of the four hundred
mosques of which Cairo boasts, are at our feet; to the east
are seen the obelisk of Heliopolis and the tombs of the
Mamelukes; on the west and south, are the ruins of old
Cairo, the grand aqueduct, the island and groves of Rhoda;
while further on across the Nile are the pyramids of Ghi-

4

zah and Sakharra, and beyond these lies the great Libyan desert. Close by is the famous " Mameluke's leap," where fifty years ago that bloody old tyrant, Mohamet Ali, having enticed these unruly chiefs into the Citadel, shut the gates and slaughtered them all but one, Emil Bey, who dashed his horse over the low parapet, and down the face of the wall, forty feet, escaping with his life, although his horse was killed. As I looked over the wall down the steep precipice, this feat seemed a most daring one, and the escape almost miraculous. The tombs of the Mamelukes are magnificent monuments of these descendants of Circassian girls, torn from their mountain homes by ruthless slave-dealers. But their sons lived to rule with iron hand, the offspring of those who wrought their mothers' shame, and, as bold warriors, twice to hurl back the Tartars from Europe, under the fierce Tamerlane.

In the center of the citadel is the mosque of Mohamet Ali, the finest in Egypt, and second only to that of St. Sophia at Constantinople. At the entrance, an old priest takes me in charge and points to my boots, which I understand to mean, " Put off thy shoes from off thy feet, for the place whereon thou standest is holy ground." I give him a franc, and he brings a pair of large, loose slippers which he ties on over my boots. Shade of the prophet! how degenerate have we become in these latter days! An unbelieving dog of a Frank enters the holy precincts with his boots on! A circular marble colonnade encloses the large courtyard into which we first come. In the center is a fountain of marble, elegantly carved, where the faithful, having left their slippers outside, wash their feet before entering the sacred mosque to perform their devotions.

Standing beneath the grand dome, which is of beautifully-stained glass, the walls and pillars of variegated

MOSQUE OF MOHAMET ALI.

*From a photograph in possession of the Author.*

marble, and hundreds of lamps and chandeliers of fine
crystal overhead, the effect was most impressive. A "dim
religious light," in strong contrast with the noonday glare
without, pervaded the interior. The marble floor was
covered with Persian carpets, on which a crowd of worshipers were kneeling, all facing toward Mecca, and mut-
tering prayers, while at regular intervals they reverently
bumped their foreheads on the ground. Some of them
glanced scowlingly at me, but I knew the old priest, in
view of the expected *baksheesh*, would not let me come to
grief. In one corner, protected by a screen of gilt lattice-
work, is the tomb of the builder of the mosque, Mohamet
Ali. In the midst of all this magnificence, where marble
and gold, crystal and precious stones have been lavished
without stint, I was surprised at hearing the twittering of
hundreds of sparrows, who seemed quite at home in the
cool and quiet interior of the mosque. They were flying
all around under the dome, and their chirping could be
heard above the murmuring of the faithful, kneeling on
the floor below. How much more acceptable to the Almighty were their voices of praise, than the mummery of
the ignorant and superstitious crowd beneath!

This mosque, upon which immense sums of money have
been spent, with its stained glass and somewhat gaudy
decorations, bears little resemblance to those beautiful
temples erected by the Moslem conquerors of India. There
the lightness and elegance of Saracenic architecture, have
united with most wonderful skill in carving the pure white
marble; and the "Pearl Mosques" of Agra and Delhi
seem infinitely superior in beauty and simplicity, to this
tawdry specimen of the Mahometan architecture of the
present age.

During our ten day's stay in Cairo we visited many
places and objects of interest. One fine cool morning we

crossed in a boat to the island of Rhoda, where the Khedive
has a palace in the midst of a beautiful garden fragrant
with orange blossoms.  Here, according to tradition, the
infant Moses was launched among the bulrushes and found
by Pharaoh's daughter.  While musing on the strange
scenes which this old river had witnessed, the lines of Dr.
Holmes occurred to me, in which he comically inquires
the whereabouts of the good, far-gone days of childhood,
with their brightness and freshness :

> " Where, oh, where are life's lilies and roses,
>   Bathed in the golden dawn's smile ?
> Dead as the bulrushes 'round little Moses,
>   On the old banks of the Nile."

Here on the Island of Rhoda is the famed Nilometer, a
slender stone pillar in the centre of a well, graduated with
cubits—one of the most ancient relics of a remote age.
Herodotus mentions that the measurement of the river's
rise and fall, thereby to calculate the probable extent of
the harvest, constituted a part of the priestcraft of the
Pharaohs.

Returning to the main shore, we visited Boulac, a portion
of the city which contains an immense government foundry and a museum of Egyptian antiquities.  In this
neighborhood, we had been told, were the granaries of
Joseph—the first great speculator in wheat of whom we
have any record—but we were unable to find them, and I
am inclined to think them a myth.

We also visited the Shoobra gardens and palace, having
first obtained a government order through our Consul.
The drive to this famous place is through a splendid avenue four miles long, shaded by very large and old sycamore trees.  Here in the center of a beautiful garden was
the favorite palace of old Mohamet Ali.  Sparkling foun-

tains, marble kiosks, elegant furniture, divans embroidered
with gold and covered with the richest brocade, decorations of finest alabaster—nothing had been spared to make
this an earthly paradise.    The present Viceroy rarely
comes here, but keeps up the place in honor of his grandfather, whose memory is held in great respect.    Mohamet
Ali, whose portraits hang on the walls and appear in
several places among the frescoes, is represented as a
grizzly old Turk, with an immense white beard, in Oriental turban and costume, surrounded by the ladies of his
harem as beautiful as the houris of a Mahometan's paradise.    He was crafty and ambitious, but a daring and
energetic ruler.    He massacred the Mamelukes in cold
blood because they stood in the way of his ambitious
schemes.    Having made himself master of Egypt and
Syria, he would have won Constantinople and perhaps
have established there a strong government, had not the
English interfered to save the present effete dynasty.

It is a pleasant drive of six miles from Cairo to Heliopolis, the "City of the Sun."    In old times, when Joseph
ruled in Egypt, this was a place of much importance.    It
was called "On," and here Joseph lived and took the
priest's daughter for a wife.    All that now remains of the
ancient city is a single red granite obelisk seventy feet
high, covered with hieroglyphics.    It was erected four
thousand years ago, and successive inundations of the
Nile have raised the surface of the ground twenty-five feet
above its base—perhaps even much more, as it was usual
to place these structures on high mounds.    Near the site
of this ancient city is the old sycamore tree, under whose
branches, many centuries afterward, Joseph and Mary, as
they journeyed to Egypt with their little boy, sat down and
drank from a cool spring, the water of which instantly
changed from salt and bitter, to the pure sweet fountain

which it remains to this day. Of course this is perfectly *authentic.* To doubt or question the genuineness of the old world's traditions and relics, would not only deprive these

OBELISK OF HELIOPOLIS.

places of half their interest, but dispel those pleasant illusions so attractive to the visitor.

In the center of Old Cairo is a mosque and college of dancing dervishes or fakeers, and every Friday, they hold a *séance.* We reached the place after threading a labyrinth of crooked streets, and were ushered into a room in a building adjoining the mosque, where several other parties of foreigners were assembled. We were offered seats on the divan extending round the room, and a servant brought tiny cups of coffee of fine flavor, but thick and sweet as syrup. Then came *chibouks,* and cigarrettes for the ladies. After a half-hour's delay we were shown into the mosque, where the performance came off. A circular space about forty feet in diameter and smoothly floored, was enclosed in a low railing, outside of which were the spectators, and in a small gallery seats were provided for us as specially invited guests. In the gallery opposite was the orchestra, consisting of eight instruments like clarionets, and four small drums. Twelve dervishes then marched into the arena and ranged themselves around the inner space, after bowing to each other and to their superior or head priest, who wore a green robe and turban, indicating that he had made the pilgrimage to Mecca. All but the head fakeer wore tall, steeple-shaped felt hats, without any brim, short jackets and long white robes tied about the waist. Their faces looked pale and emaciated with fasting. One of them went into the musicians' gallery, and read from the Koran for about twenty minutes in a drawling, sing-song tone, while his bretheren knelt on the floor below, frequently bowing their heads to the ground. The music then struck up and the performers rose from their knees and marched several times round the arena. The head dervish, who seemed to be held in special reverence, stood on a mat by himself, and each one in passing him stopped to make a low salaam, and then turned round and salaamed the one next behind. Then the music became gradually more lively, and one after another threw up their hands and began to whirl. Faster and faster they whirled, their arms now extended at right angles, and with eyes closed in a sort of dreamy ecstasy, then spun round like tops, their gowns spreading out with the rotary motion to the size of most extravagant crinoline. I timed them with my watch and found that seventy times a minute was the maximum speed. They kept up this performance for about an hour with occasional intervals of rest, when they would suddenly stop, fold their arms over their breasts, and march slowly around the arena, apparently made no more dizzy by their gyrations than the ball-room belle who has been " taking a turn " to the music of Strauss.   At last the orchestra ceased playing and the *séance* was ended. When the performers, having put on their outside robes, quietly left the building, the true believers bowed very low as they made room for them to pass.   They evidently considered them very holy men who would whirl themselves into the highest seats in paradise.

This performance comes off every week, and crowds of Mahometans, as well as nearly all the foreign visitors in Cairo, go to see it.   It is a free exhibition—no tickets being taken at the door—nor is any contribution box passed round.   The dervishes are all Turks, and their complexion, pale from fasting and abstinence, is so much lighter than that of the native Egyptians, that they seem to us as white as Europeans.   This curious sect is of modern origin, and Mohamet Ali brought them from Constantinople to Cairo, more than fifty years ago.   Nothing in civilized lands resembles their performances so much as the whirling of the Shakers.

# CHAPTER IV.

## MEMPHIS AND THE PYRAMIDS.

El Kaherah—The Nile—Ancient Knowledge of the Egyptians—Lost Arts—
Visit to Memphis and Sakharra—An Early Start—Rival Boatmen—Sand
Storm in the Desert—The City of the Pharaohs—Temple of Apis—Ma-
riette Bey—Cemetery of the Sacred Bulls—Lunch among the "Old Mas-
ters"—An "Antique" Factory—Typhoons at Sea and Siroccos on Land
—Pyramids of Ghizah—A Left-handed Regiment—Fertility of the Soil—
Old Cheops—Up we go—Sunrise from the Summit—The Heart of the
Great Pyramid—The King's Chamber—The Sphynx—A Nubian Type
of Beauty—No Immortality from Piles of Stone.

IT is written that " El Kaherah," which the Europeans
have metamorphosed into
Cairo, was founded by a
general appointed by Ali,
the husband of Mahomet's
fair daughter Fatima ; but
the present city was not built
until some centuries later,
for Egypt is quite a mush-
room of a town, only some
nine hundred years old.
But it was built on the
ruins of much older cities,
near the site of the earliest temple-palaces of the Pharaohs ;
and, after Constantinople, is the oldest Mahometan city
in the world.

The Nile, the most mysterious of all rivers, flows on the
same from age to age, its greasy, muddy, turbid waters

the source of fruitfulness in a land that without them would speedily become a desert. Unchanged they have rolled on since the touching story of Joseph and his brethren was enacted on their banks, since Pharaoh's daughter bathed in the turbid stream, since the Israelites slaved along the shores, and many centuries later they bore the gorgeous galleys of the voluptuous Cleopatra.

Egypt was for ages the storehouse of knowledge, and the art of magic is still studied in the land, where of old the potentates, who united the kingship and priesthood in one person, called in its aid in humbugging the masses of the people. We are taught that the early race of men was originally endowed with miraculous powers, the knowledge of which lingered for centuries among the Chaldeans. They were skilled, perhaps, in those wondrous sciences, such as mesmerism and clairvoyance, of which the world is just now beginning to regain the knowledge. If these are among the "lost arts," it is not surprising that they represented magic to the people in that early age; for even now, with all the science and skill of modern civilization, they are almost a sealed book. We read in the Bible that Moses was skilled in all the knowledge of the Egyptians. What was this knowledge, known only to the wily priest-hood to which all the Pharaohs belonged, and into which the adopted son of Pharaoh's daughter was doubtless initiated? The story of Moses leading God's chosen people through the desert toward the promised land, discloses some of his skill in controlling the masses, who were probably quite as ignorant as the Egyptians among whom they had delved as slaves.

Having exhausted the sights of Cairo, except the bazaars, which one never tires of visiting, we arranged for a trip to Memphis and the pyramids of Sakharra. To accomplish this in one day required an early start, and

soon after the sun was up, we found ourselves on the banks
of the Nile, looking for transportation across its rapid
muddy current. The floating bridge had been rendered
impassable by some accident, and we could only cross by
boat. The struggle among the rival boatmen as to who
should take us over was exciting. Being only *passengers*,
my friend and I stepped back out of the crowd of shouting,
screaming, scolding Arabs, and let them settle the matter
in their own way. Any attempt to touch us or our effects,
was instantly resented with a rap from our rattans, for
although we did not understand Arabic, the logic of a stick
is well understood everywhere in the East. The shaking
of fists and gesticulations were numerous, but we knew
they were " mere sound and fury signifying nothing." At
last the din and hubbub ceased, and we stepped quietly
into the boat of the victorious party, and were quickly set
across the river. At the railway station on the west side,
we took the train to Budershain, twelve miles up the river.
There were crowds of filthy Arabs swarming over the
third-class cars, and so much delay in starting on account
of the broken bridge, that we did not arrive there until
ten o'clock. We hired donkeys at the station to go to the
site of Memphis, five miles distant. Before starting, we
noticed that the sun was clouded in, and to me it seemed
that a rain storm was coming up. But it very rarely rains
in Egypt, and to one familiar with the climate the signs
indicated something infinitely worse—a sand storm. We
had not reached a mile from the station when it came
down upon us with great fury. The force of the wind was
terrific, and the flying sand seemed to cut the skin like a
knife. In a minute we were blinded in spite of the green
goggles we wore, and the sand penetrated eyes, nose, ears,
and mouth. We were in a desert of sand, and the air was
so full of the fine cloud that we could not see ten feet be-

fore us. We turned our backs to the gale, and the howling of the wind and the braying of the donkeys, made such music as I never heard before, and hope never to hear again. I had read of caravans being overwhelmed and buried in the sands, but could never before realize the horrors of such a catastrophe. I took the *puggree* off my hat and tied it over my face for a veil, and holding on to our " donks " for dear life, we took refuge under the lee of of a sand hill until a gust had passed. It lasted about twenty minutes, and left the sand drifted in places like snow. As soon as the storm lulled, we pushed forward to a collection of mud huts where once stood the great city of Memphis, the proud capital of ancient Egypt—the city from which Pharaoh is supposed to have led forth the chivalry of the land, in pursuit of the hosts of Israel on their march for freedom. A beautiful forest of palms covers a portion of the site, a noble burial place even for such a city. Its circumference, according to ancient writers, was over seventeen miles, and the ruins of its famous temples are now covered by the sand of the desert and the alluvial deposits of the river. Excavations have been made in various places, and the ground is littered with broken statues of granite and marble. One colossal figure lies prone upon the ground, supposed to be the statue of Sesostris. The expression upon the upturned face is of quiet, benignant repose, or of pensive sorrow; in harmony with the desolate aspect of the whole place. It represents a once powerful king and ruler, prostrate amid the ruins of his capital. A crowd of Arabs surrounded us, screaming for *baksheesh*, and they scrambled and quarreled for the few copper coins we threw them, like a pack of half-starved dogs.

After a short rest we again started over the plain for the pyramids of Sakharra, four miles distant, but before reaching them we were overtaken by another sand-storm, fiercer, if possible, than the first. Luckily, it came from behind, and we fled before the blast which nearly took our poor donkeys off their feet. These pyramids are older and much more dilapidated than those of Ghizah, near Cairo. Before these crumbling mounds are the Sarapeum, or Temple of Apis, and the tombs in which the sacred bulls are buried. These have lately been discovered, and are among the most interesting monuments of Egypt. An enterprising Frenchman, Mariette Bey, has spent several years and a large sum of money, in bringing to light these wonderful relics of antiquity. We took refuge from the storm, in a small building erected for his residence while superintending these excavations, where we found an old Sheik, who claimed authority over this part of the desert — which simply means the privilege of levying blackmail on all visitors. We paid the fee, and with a young Arab for a guide, commenced our explorations. The surface of the country for miles in every direction is a desert, and the sand-drift has covered many feet deep these ancient remains. It is probable that once this barren waste was as fertile as any part of the Nile valley, but a change in the bed of the river, and the gradual encroachment of the desert has made it what it now is.

We descend by a sloping path to the entrance, and lighting our candles, find ourselves in a long rock-hewn gallery, which formed the cemetery for the bulls that were worshiped in the adjoining temple of Apis. Opening from this gallery like side chapels, are twenty-four recesses cut out of the limestone rock, and in each of these is an immense sarcophagus, formed from a single piece of black porphyry. They are of uniform shape and size, about sixteen feet long, eight feet wide, and about nine feet in height. The outside is covered with hieroglyphics, with edges as clean-cut and fresh as if just finished. On two or three the figures are only traced, as if the work had been abruptly stopped. They are polished outside and in, smooth as glass, and the heavy lids of most of them have been pushed off a few feet, so that we can see the interior. They are now all empty, the sacred bulls they once contained having long ago crumbled to dust. With the assistance of my companions, I let myself down into one and examined the interior. The space inside was large enough to contain a mammoth ox, the surface was beautifully polished, and the side, when struck by the hand, gave out a clear, bell-like sound. It seemed strange and almost ludicrous thus to stand, candle in hand, within the stone coffin of a sacred bull! "These be thy gods, O Egypt!" Strange that a people so advanced in the arts and sciences, so distinguished for wisdom, who have left behind ruins that are still the admiration of the world, should have religious ideas so low as to worship four-footed beasts, birds, and creeping reptiles! What an immense amount of money, time, and labor have been expended to excavate these long galleries, to bring these huge blocks of porphyry many hundred miles, to carve and polish them with almost miraculous skill, and then to fit each one in a niche to become the coffin of a—bull. And this was done, too, by a people without labor-saving machinery, who knew nothing of the use of iron tools—for I believe no iron instrument of any kind has been found in Egypt. The tools they used were of an alloy of copper and tin, but hard and pliant as steel. How to make it so, is one of the "lost arts," which all the machinery and boasted knowledge of Birmingham or Sheffield, cannot now accomplish.

We afterwards visited the temple near by, and wandered through several rooms which have but lately been recovered from the sand. They are lined with white marble or cement, and upon the walls and ceilings are paintings as bright in colors and fresh-looking as if executed only yesterday.

In one of these rooms, seated on the sand, and surrounded by the works of the " old masters " (probably 4,000 years old), we took our frugal lunch, and drank English ale to the memory of the quaint old fellows whose pictures stared at us from the walls—then tossed the bones to their descendants, a crowd of hungry Bedouins, who eagerly picked up every scrap.

Outside we found a lot of Arabs employed in unrolling mummies, thousands of which are buried in a pit near the temple. Great piles of skulls, crumbling bones, and scraps of mummy cloth were scattered around. We secured here some genuine relics and antiques, old as the Pharaohs. Most of the so-called antiques sold in Cairo, especially the *scarabei*, or sacred beetles, are made, as I am told, at the factory of an enterprising Yankee or Englishman named Smith, in Assouan, at the foot of the first cataract of the Nile.

Having spent three hours at Sakharra, we started on our return. Our intention had been to cross the desert from here to Ghizah, but the weather made such an expedition dangerous, if not impossible. At intervals all day, the fierce sirocco would break on us, and we caught two more before we could reach the station at Budershain. I have had a little experience of typhoons at sea, and I would much rather face the cyclone of the Pacific, with a good ship under me, than the sirocco of the Sahara desert, where sand instead of water is the moving element, mounted on a miserable little half-starved donkey.

The great pyramids of Ghizah are situated at the edge of the desert on the opposite side of the river, and about six miles distant from Cairo. To see the sun rise from the summit of Cheops, is well worth the effort required to ensure an early start.    There is a fine smooth carriage road all the way.    Having crossed the Nile by the new iron bridge, we drive for three miles through a beautiful avenue of acacia trees, past a large palace of the Viceroy, and long barracks around which soldiers are lounging— fat, saucy-looking fellows, who look better fed and clothed, and more happy than the miserable laborers from whom they are conscripted.    In former times, to save a son from being forced into the Pasha's army, it was not an unusual thing for a parent to put out the right eye of his child, or cut off the first joint of the forefinger of his right hand. But this mutilation was stopped when the Pasha formed a regiment of left-handed men, which proved quite as efficient as the rest of the army—which is not saying much.    The last three miles of the road, is on a dyke or embankment which saves it from overflow by the river.    The date-palms which we see scattered over the plain are now in blossom, and produce the finest dates in the world.    We meet hundreds of donkeys and camels plodding slowly along towards the city, bearing immense loads of vegetables and fresh cut grass.    On either side of the road are fields of grain, maize, clover and lentils, growing most luxuriantly from a soil so rich that it actually looks greasy.    It is entirely an alluvial deposit from the Nile, and on it the crops spring up very swiftly, having a peculiarly bright green appearance, and are very tender to the touch from their rapid growth. Two crops of grain, sometimes three, and of grass and vegetables usually four crops, are taken from the same soil every year.

For a long time the pyramids were right before us, and so deceptive is their appearance under the cloudless sky, with no other object upon the vast plain with which to compare them, that they seemed actually to grow smaller as we approached. We drove to the very foot of the great pyramid of Cheops, and our carriage was at once surrounded by a crowd of Arabs. We drove them all away and demanded to see the Sheik, who lives here and professes to control these wild children of the desert. We told him to select for each of us, two good men from the expectant crowd, and commenced at once the ascent. Figures can convey but an inadequate idea of the immensity of this vast pile. It is four hundred and eighty feet high; higher than the tallest spire in Europe; two hundred feet taller than Trinity Church steeple. The base is seven hundred and sixty-four feet on each side, and it covers an area of twelve acres. To build a causeway to carry the stone from the Nile, would require one hundred thousand men for ten years, and to build the monument, three hundred and sixty thousand men for twenty years. The difficulty of climbing the pyramid is not so much from the steepness of the ascent, as the great size of the blocks of stone composing each layer. An Arab taking hold of each hand, lifts us up from one layer to the next, and it is a succession of steps about three feet high, with a space of one or two feet to stand upon. When about a third of the way up we stopped to rest, and another Arab popped out from behind a stone and urged us to engage his services. He explained by pantomime how useful he could be in pushing us up behind. Boys carrying small earthern bottles of water followed us up, knowing that we should be thirsty enough to give them a few piasters for a drink, before we reached the top. Our Arabs wore no clothing but a white cotton shirt, and kept up a constant chattering like so many black-birds. To spring from block to block and pull us up after them, did not seem to tire them in the least. On the summit is a space about twenty-five feet square, the apex as well as the casing of the pyramids, having been

5

removed by the Caliphs, for constructing mosques and palaces at Cairo.   We reached the top just in time to see the
sun rise above the horizon of the great ocean desert, and
spread out before us, was one of the finest panoramas in

CLIMBING THE GREAT PYRAMID.

the world.   The dryness and purity of the air in Egypt
enables one to discern objects at a great distance.

We could see the Nile winding its way through a carpet
of verdure, on which are many scattered villages—the city
of Cairo with its domes, minarets, and palaces glittering
in the morning sun—and beyond all, the white shining
sands of the desert.

The Arabs pointed out the autograph on stone of the
Prince of Wales (very badly cut), and offered us hammer
and chisel, but we declined the cheap immortality of
enrolling our names so high up on tablets of stone, along
with those of Jones, Smith, and Robinson, which cover

nearly every inch of the space. To descend was more difficult and dangerous than to climb up, for it requires steady nerves to look off from such a dizzy height, standing upon a shelf scarcely a foot in width. But our faithful Arabs never let go of our hands for a moment, until we reached *terra firma*, where a liberal *baksheesh* made them dance around us like so many wild Indians. " Yankee Doodle, good, good," was the style of their returning thanks. This title seems to denote high rank in Egypt, and is used as an especial compliment to all Americans.

Resting on the huge blocks of stone on the shady side, we took our lunch and indulged in a fragrant *chibouk*, before entering the long, narrow, dark passages that lead to the heart of the great pyramid. After climbing several inclines and sliding down others, with barely room to stand upright, we reached the king's chamber, where our tapers made little impression on darkness so intense that it could almost be felt. This apartment is lined with polished granite, and is thirty-four feet long, eighteen broad, and about twenty in length. In the center stands a red granite sarcophagus, in which King Cheops was buried, ages before the time of Moses. The air here was so stifling that we did not tarry long, and were glad to escape into the open air once more. The second and third pyramids are somewhat less in size than that of Cheops ; and the six others comparatively small. In front of the great pyramid and facing the river is the Sphinx. This most fantastic animal, has ever been looked upon as one of the greatest wonders of Egypt. A colossal female head rises above the sand, attached to the body of a lioness, about which excavations have been made so as to show its form hewn from the solid rock. The features have the thick lips and high cheek bones of the Nubian, which was the type of beauty to the ancient Egyptians.

The circumference of the head measures over one hundred feet. Time and ill-usage have made sad havoc with the monstrous face, but there is a placid beauty about its features, an abstracted expression, resembling that of the large Buddhist idols of Japan and India. The conception is a grand one, and well calculated to inspire with terror the weak minds of its worshipers.

As we ride back to Cairo we turn around to gaze upon these marvelous structures, and are lost in amazement at the immense amount of labor expended for no practical utility. If their sole object was to perpetuate the names of the builders—Pharaohs, kings, and priests—whatever their titles may have been, how futile the attempt at immortality, for the names of the builders have in most cases passed away.

> "Proud monuments of kings, whose very names
> Have perished from the records of the past."

# CHAPTER V.

## CAIRO TO PORT SAID.

'BAKSHEESH!!!"

THE steamer upon which we were to embark at Suez having been unexpectedly delayed in London, and being advised that we should have two weeks time on our hands, we at once determined to make a short trip to Jerusalem and back, via Port Said and Jaffa.

Our route was from Cairo to Ismailia, one hundred miles, by rail, thence by the Suez Canal to Port Said. At the station, while waiting for our train, I witnessed a scene characteristic of Turkish married life outside the harem. A venerable looking old gentleman, whose rich dress and number of attendants indicated wealth and position, was about to take a journey by rail accompanied by two of his wives. An inner waiting room is provided at

the station for Turkish ladies, and it was not until the
train was nearly ready to start that he made his appearance, and walked across the platform to the compartment
reserved for his party, followed by the two closely veiled
ladies. They were dressed in loose, baggy white gowns,
their faces so completely covered that not even an eye
could be seen. A eunuch, black as Erebus, walked beside
each, and hurried them into the train, then quickly pulled
up the blinds. Perhaps they were young and handsome
as the "light of the harem," or they may have been old
and ugly, which is quite as probable. The servants put into
the compartment several large bundles which seemed to be
silk and satin dresses, tied up in white cloth. Ladies in
the East never use Saratoga trunks when traveling. The
head eunuch was a large, finely proportioned Nubian, over
six feet high, with a bright intelligent face. He was
dressed in European costume, all but the fez. His feet
were encased in patent leather boots, and altogether he
was got up in most nobby
style. He ordered the cop-
per-colored Arab servants
about, with a grand air, and
while he stood by the door
receiving the pasha's last
orders, he glanced rather su-
perciliously at the pale-faced
strangers. As his master's
confidential servant, major-
domo, or head guard of the
harem, I could imagine the
orders given him to look
sharp after the ladies left
behind, and especially to
keep an eye on that black-

THE EUNUCH.

eyed young Circassian girl, " Lulu," who was quite too fond of going shopping in the bazaars, and gadding around while her lord and master was away. The train started, the eunuch strutted off, and I saw him driven away in the elegant carriage that had brought the pasha and his wives to the station.

This railway, like all others in Egypt, is owned by the Khedive and managed by government officials. It is smooth and well equipped, the cars and locomotives being of French manufacture. We left Cairo at nine in the morning, and our course for the first hour was down the Nile valley, then branching off to the east we followed the line of the Sweet-water canal, originally built by the Pharaohs to connect the Nile with the Red Sea at Suez. In the lapse of ages it became filled up by the desert sands, but was re-opened a few years ago as far as Ismailia, to supply water to that new " city of the desert," situated on Lake Timsah, now the central station of the great Suez canal, and half way between the Mediterranean and the Red Sea.

We reached a station called Zag-a-Zig about noon, and were at once assailed by the half naked beggars, who with arms extended, loudly called for " *baksheesh! baksheesh!* " Here we were to change cars, and waited for two hours to take the train from Alexandria to Suez via Ismailia. The station house is large and well built, and includes a hotel kept by a Frenchman, who provided us a very good dinner. The native guards and railway officials are generally very civil and attentive, especially to the first class passengers, who are mostly Europeans. They all speak French as well as Arabic, but few can understand a word of English. As I strolled along the platform, which was crowded with people of almost every nationality and condition of life, I was attracted by the gay costume of an old grey-bearded Turkish officer, with bright turban, loose blue trousers, and cashmere shawl tied around his waist, in which was stuck a pair of handsome silver mounted pistols. He wore an elegant sword, scimiter-shaped, in a silver scabbard, and was what the English would call a " great swell" among the humble *fellahs*, or Egyptian peasants, around him. Nothing daunted by his formidable appearance, I saluted him courteously, and by pantomime expressed my admiration of his armament, which so gratified him that he unbuckled his scimiter for me to examine. Though silver mounted and very handsome, I found it exceedingly dull and even rusty. The pistols were old fashioned flint-locks, without any flints; and upon a close examination I could see that his whole " get up" was more for show than use. With my little " Smith & Wesson" and a good stout club, I should have been more than a match for him in close quarters.

At a station a few miles further on, an amusing scene occurred. Near by is an encampment of perhaps a thousand Egyptian soldiers. They wear a neat, white undress uniform, are of fair size, and look well fed and serviceable. Their arms are breech-loading rifles of modern pattern. The officers are dressed in dark blue frock coats and red trousers, and all—officers and men—wear the red fez cap. As soon as the train stops the soldiers make a rush for the cars, and clamber over them in every direction. The officers, armed with rattans, beat them back with solid whacks, laid on with a will. No one seems to take offense, and they run like a flock of sheep. To submit thus to blows, shows a want of manliness and spirit, characteristic of the modern Egyptian. It would never be submitted to by the soldiers of any civilized nation. Even in India a blow from an officer would fire the blood of the lowest Sepoy, and result either in immediate vengeance, or in the suicide of the poor fellow, whose self-respect would be forever lost by such an insult.

Leaving the " skirmish " in full blast, the signs of vegetation rapidly diminished, until the green trees and narrow strip of fertile soil which line the track of the re-opened canal on our right, were the only relief to the eye. All else is a sandy desert, broken up into ridges by the wind, and in appearance not unlike the alkali plains of the Humboldt Valley. We had now a new experience in railway travel. Our speed diminished and about four o'clock we came to a stand-still. A fierce gale was blowing from the northwest, and the fine sand drifted by the wind had covered the rails, stopped the train, and we were *sanded up*.

I have a vivid recollection of being snowed up many years ago, between Dunkirk and Buffalo, but this was quite a different sensation. Alighting from the train to view the situation, we were soon glad to again take refuge in the cars and tightly close all the windows and blinds, as the sand driven by the fierce sirocco, penetrated our clothing and blinded our eyes, while the howling of the natives engaged in clearing the track, filled our ears with discordant din. Of all the languages I have ever heard among heathens or Christians, I think Arabic deserves the distinction of requiring the most words to express the fewest thoughts. The Arabs are a most voluble race, and whether at work or play I will match their tongues against three times the number of any other people on the earth. A stranger would think a frightful combat was imminent, but they rarely come to blows, their excited jabbering being but empty sound signifying nothing. After a long delay the train started on, but soon again came to a stand-still. We at last reached Ismailia, several hours behind time, with no other damage than could be repaired by a bath and a thorough shaking of our well sanded garments.

Ismailia, named after the Khedive of Egypt, was four years ago a town of great expectations. Its short history is the counterpart of many a promising city along the line of the great railways of America. Its pleasant situation upon the shore of Lake Timsah, and its central position, being midway between Port Said and Suez, seemed to indicate that it would rapidly become a place of importance. When I was here three years ago, it was very flourishing, and boasted a population of over five thousand. Speculation in corner lots was rife, and new buildings, not very substantial, to be sure, but good enough for a climate like Egypt, were pushing back upon the desert sands behind the town. It had a large and elegantly furnished hotel, several handsome residences surrounded by gardens, and a public square, and wide streets planted with shade trees, near which along the gutters, trickled a stream of pure fresh water.

That "water is gold" is as true in Egypt as in India, where the proverb originated. Its magic effect in converting a desert into a garden, is shown by the Mormons in Salt Lake City. Behind the town and between it and the desert, is a wide sweeping double crescent of trees growing newly out of the sand, but fresh and green from a channel of water running near their roots. When fully grown these trees will protect the town from the encroachment of sand swept in before the fierce winds from the desert. This sand, which looks so hopeless and useless as an element of fertility, is not pure silica, but a mixture of calcareous loam and sand, needing only the addition of fresh water to form a rich and fertile soil. The desert of Suez, which stretches for ninety miles from the Nile to the Red Sea, was doubtless once well watered and fertile, and cultivated like a garden. That it has now become a howling wilderness, is accounted for by some depression of the Nile bed, or change in its course, by which its eastern outlets have become closed. As it never rains in this country, cut off the supply of water and it would all turn to a desert. Take away the Nile from Egypt, and the whole land would become a mere counterpart of the desert of Suez.

But the Ismailia of to-day is in sad contrast with its bright promise of three years ago. As we remained here until the next day, we had an opportunity to stroll through the largest deserted village I ever saw. Not one in twenty of the buildings seem occupied, and the few that show signs of habitation are mostly saloons where the occupants are playing cards or billiards. Only about one thousand people are left, who seem too poor to get away. The fine hotel is closed, its elegant furniture having been removed to a much smaller house, where we found no other guest but ourselves.

The grand palace built by the Viceroy of Egypt to entertain the Empress of France, the Prince of Wales, and other royal personages, is dilapidated, the windows broken, and the court-yard half filled with drifted sand.

The administration of the canal has its central offices here, and the elegant residence of Ferdinand de Lesseps, surrounded by a grove of semi-tropical trees, seemed like an oasis in the desert. He is still the head of canal affairs, and though nearly seventy years old, has all the energy and activity of mind and body that enabled him to over-come the most disheartening difficulties, and complete one of the greatest engineering works of the nineteenth century. It will remain a grander monument to his memory than any of marble or bronze.

We saw him ride past in a basket phaeton with his young wife and three children, the largest not over five years old. This is the only wheeled vehicle left in the town, and was the only sign of life in the streets, except a few disconso-

late-looking donkey boys and a boot black, perhaps the
identical young *gamin* who hailed me here three years
before, when Ismailia was in its glory, with the question,
in pantomime, " Have a shine, Sir ?"

This bright little Arab boy, who looked as if he might
have slept the night before in a dry goods box in Ann
street or the Bowery, was in waiting at the hotel door with
" Black your boots?" " have a shine, Sir?" in pantomime

"HAVE A SHINE, SIR?"

as plain as if spoken in English.  Of course I went in for
a " shine."  The whole double-handed performance, con-
cluding with a sharp rap on the box, was so completely *a la*

*New York*, that I am sure it never originated in this out of the way corner of Asia and Africa, but was introduced by some enterprising New York *gamin*, probably at the great celebration when the canal was opened. Perhaps, like the wandering Jew, he is still on his travels, and future explorers may trace this "march of civilization" among the little "pigtails" of Canton and Pekin.

The immense pumping works erected by the canal company to supply water to the town of Port Said, forty-two miles distant, are located in Ismailia, and well repaid our visit. The engines are of French manufacture, very powerful, and as elegantly finished as any machinery I ever saw. While inspecting these works we had the good fortune to meet M. de Lesseps, the "*Fondateur*" of the canal, as he is called, who very kindly showed us around the works and explained many interesting details in the administration of the canal.

Late in the afternoon we embarked on a little steamboat not over thirty feet long, with a high-pressure engine that whizzed like one of our steamers in full play at a fire, suggesting the possibility of our being at any moment scattered in small pieces over the banks of the canal and into the desert beyond. We preferred to spend the five hours required for the trip to Port Said on deck, as far aft as possible, prepared to jump, in case we heard any unusual noise in the boiler-room of our little craft. Once, by invitation of the captain, to whose kind attentions we had been specially commended, we descended into the miniature cabin, but the sound through the thin partition, of the combined engineer and fireman stirring up the coal under the boiler, convinced us that the deck was a more healthy place, and better adapted for viewing the canal.

It was late at night when we reached Port Said, where the runners from the different hotels pounced on our luggage in a style peculiar to seaport towns all over the world. In such cases words are of no account, and the only persuasive argument is a good stout stick. There are several hotels, all French, but neither can be recommended as good.

Port Said is a lively town. The population is made up in great part of adventurers from every nation bordering the Mediterranean. The abounding hotels, restaurants, casinos, and the wide, sandy streets, remind one of a new town in America. French, Italian, Greek, Arabic, and Turkish are heard in the streets quite as often as English. Speculation is rife, and the business of the place increasing rapidly. Every line of coasting steamers between Alexandria and Constantinople touch here, as it has the most accessible harbor on the whole southern coast of the Mediterranean. The sanguine talk of Port Said, as the " Silver Gate between the Orient and the Occident," in fifty years to be a modern Venice, the rival of Alexandria. Its harbor is entirely artificial; formed by two parallel piers running out from the shore into the open sea a mile and a half— the longest piers in the world. They are built of artificial blocks of stone weighing twenty tons each, composed of desert sand and hydraulic cement. Some of these have been exposed for over six years to all the fury of the fiercest gales, without in the least affecting their stability. This harbor is said to be better than that of Alexandria, (one hundred and fifty miles west,) and can be safely entered by day or night, at all seasons of the year.

The next day was Sunday in western lands; but this can hardly be classed among the Christian cities, and in Port Said, Sunday is said to be the liveliest day in the week. The French steamer for Jaffa was to sail at five P. M., so we had ample time to look about us. Moored in the harbor, near the entrance to the canal, were many steamers and ships loading or discharging cargoes. Nearly all steamers bound through the canal to India, here take supplies of coal that last as far as Aden, at the foot of the Red Sea.

On the broad quay a large crowd had collected around an Arab juggler, who, assisted by a little imp of a boy, was performing the well-known egg trick in a manner decidedly amusing and original. As we stood for a few minutes on the outside of the throng, laughing at the novel performance, his quick eye espied us, and the youngster dove head foremost through the crowd to present his cap for *baksheesh*. In this he was not disappointed, and as we turned away we concluded that our liberality would afford a free show to the crowd for the next half hour.

# CHAPTER VI.

## PORT SAID TO JERUSALEM.

A Night on the Mediterranean—The Americans Fraternize—Bishop Harris —Jaffa, the Ancient Joppa—Noah, Andromeda, The King of Tyre and the Queen of Sheba, Simon the Tanner, Jonah, and Napoleon—The American Colony and its German Successor—Rolla Floyd—"Wanted, a Bergh"—Jaffa Oranges—Ramleh, the Ancient Arimathea—Our Land-lord an Office-seeker—An Early Start—The Bishop Leads the Van—Gateway to the Plain—The Inn-keeper, with a "smile so child-like and bland"—Weary Pilgrims—A Good Old Methodist Hymn—Godfrey de Bouillon—We Pass the Jaffa Gate.

O**N** Sunday evening, we steamed out from the harbor of Port Said, and turning eastward, directed our course towards Jaffa, 150 miles distant. More than half the passengers were Americans, among whom were several ladies, all bound for the "Holy Land." The night was bright and clear, the sea smooth as glass, and we sat late on deck relating our several experiences in Egypt, and weaving bright fancies of the land of sacred memories to which we were bound. Americans readily fraternize when they meet in a foreign land, and the *personel* of our party was unusually intelligent and interesting. It included Bishop Harris, of Chicago, whose genial

face seemed the mirror of a thoroughly good heart ; Mrs.
B., of California, and two young gentlemen from Mead-
ville, Pa., who had just returned from a trip up the Nile.

At nine o'clock the next morning we were off Jaffa, and
as the sea was quite rough, there was considerable doubt
expressed as to whether we could be landed. Jaffa harbor
has gone to ruin, and steamers are obliged to anchor in
the open roadstead, and in very rough weather it is impossible to land passengers.

Large boats, each manned by eight or ten Arabs, came
alongside, and our thirty passengers—ten of whom were
ladies—had to be dropped singly, as the boat rose on the
waves, into the arms of the native boatmen. The performance was more amusing to the lookers on than to the
actors. Much laughter and some screaming on the part
of our lady friends greeted each successful feat.

Jaffa, the ancient Joppa, rises in the form of an amphitheatre, and makes a fine appearance from the sea ; but
the steep, narrow, and crooked streets, reeking with filth,
destroy the pleasing illusion as soon as one lands and attempts to make his way through the town. There are
many interesting traditions associated with this place. At
this port it is said that Noah built his ark. Here Andromeda was chained to the rock, and in Pliny's time the
marks of the chain were still visible—mythology gets
strangely mixed with Bible history in this country. The
King of Tyre brought to this port the cedars of Lebanon
for Solomon's temple. I think the Queen of Sheba came
this way, but am not quite sure. The house of " Simon
the Tanner " is shown, where Peter had his vision, and
here Jonah embarked, but as the prophet had a " return
ticket," the superstition of the sailors about having a par-
son on board did him no harm. Coming down to modern
times, Jaffa was the scene in 1799 of one of Napoleon's

6

blackest crimes—the murdering of 4,000 Turkish prisoners and the poisoning of 500 of his own soldiers, sick of the plague, who could not be removed. This last story, though a part of English history, must be taken, like the former traditions, with a grain of allowance.

Outside the town, which contains about 5,000 inhabitants, upon high ground commanding a beautiful view of the sea and the surrounding country, we found an excellent hotel, and a cluster of neat white dwellings occupying the site of the unfortunate American colony which came here several years ago from Maine, with the delusive idea of restoring the prosperity of the Holy Land and rebuilding the temple of Solomon, under the leadership of a religious enthusiast, who proved to be a bad manager and quite incompetent to play the *rôle* of a Moses. They speedily came to grief, and after suffering many hardships and losses from sickness and famine, the miserable remnant was sent home at the expense of our government. Their property was sold to a company of Germans from Wurtemburg, who have somewhat similar religious ideas, based, as their pamphlet declares, " upon the sure word of prophecy." They have been here now six years, and are very prosperous, numbering sixty families, and with characteristic industry and frugality, they have converted the waste land into a garden, with hundreds of acres of orange and lemon trees. All their property is held in common, and their spiritual and temporal manager, Pastor Hoffmann, is a man of no mean ability. Their proposed " restoration of the temple " is understood to be spiritual, not literal, which makes their prospects of success far more feasible. Mr. Rolla Floyd, the only one left of the unfortunate American colony, is favorably known to many tourists as the most reliable and accomplished dragoman in Syria, and any party who can secure his services may consider themselves very fortunate.

After a capital lunch, our party of seven mounted their horses for the first stage of the forty miles' journey to Jerusalem. In this country the hour is a measure of distance as well as of time, and signifies about three and a half miles. The Holy City is twelve hours from Jaffa, usually occupying two days; the first stage being to Ramleh, the ancient Arimathea, four hours distant. We had no difficulty in selecting good horses from the great number offered us, and as the season was yet early, they were all in good condition. But woe to the poor beasts when the rush of pilgrims comes a few weeks later. The Arab, unlike his Hindoo brother, has no idea of mercy to animals. A " Society for the prevention of cruelty to animals," with a few efficient agents, would find here a splendid field for philanthropic effort.

For more than a mile our road was through orange groves loaded with their golden fruit—the largest and finest that I ever saw. Their branches reached over the cactus hedges that lined the way, and we could see great quantities rotting upon the ground, as one sees apples at home far in the country, where windfalls have no market value. Jaffa oranges are famous along the Mediterranean coast, and are the principal article of export. We pass hundreds of donkeys and camels laden with panniers of fruit, and boxes and bales of merchandise bound to Jerusalem. This road was built six years ago by the government, and is wide, smooth, and well graded. We see many gangs of men and women carrying baskets of dirt upon their heads, employed in repairing the damages to roadway and culverts caused by the late heavy rains. The road was constructed to facilitate the traffic between Jaffa and the interior, but Eastern prejudice prevents its being used

by vehicles.  It is said that in all Palestine there is not a
wheeled vehicle.  Our four hours' ride was very pleasant,
through fertile fields of young grain, and meadows upon
which were grazing thousands of cattle and sheep, attended

CARAVAN FROM JAFFA TO JERUSALEM.

by Arabs in white turbans and long striped garments
of camels hair.  They are squatted on the ground smoking
the inevitable *chibouk*, while their dogs are watching the
flocks.  They *salaam* to us respectfully as we ride by, and
I can but wonder what ideas they have of the *Howadji*,
masked behind their long-bearded, solemn faces.

Before dark we reach Ramleh, and finding both the
Russian and the Latin convents nearly full, a portion of
our party take possession of the so-called " hotel," a new
institution now in its second year.  Our landlord is a
Dane, and has lost one eye, which defect he conceals with
a pair of green spectacles.  He welcomes us in fair
English, and with his wife does all his limited accom-

modations will permit, to make us comfortable. We order dinner, and the cackling of chickens at once indicates what our bill of fare is to be. We sat late over the remains of our dinner (principally chicken bones) making merry with many a song, and story, and jest, until suddenly the landlord broke in upon our hilarity with the words: " I 'spose you don't know that I have served eight years in the American navy, and held the rank of Quartermaster?" Of course we didn't know it, and he went on to detail the ships he had served in. We at once warmed up towards a fellow-countryman, striving to make an honest living in such an out of the way place. I suggested that he ought to be appointed " Consul to Ramleh " so as to put his " hotel " under the protection of the stars and stripes; and promised to use all my political influence in his behalf. If pen and ink had been convenient I would at once have indited a letter setting forth his claims, to the President of the United States. He seemed immensely pleased with the idea, but like a good many other political aspirants he talked too much, and his next unfortunate remark, that he left the service in 1861, because he " would not fight against the South," was a damper, alike on his prospects of office and our sympathy. I was obliged to withdraw my promise of aid, and told him he had made the great mistake of his lifetime. Once started, however, his loquacity was hard to stop, and we were forced to break in upon his stories and say good night, to catch what little sleep the wicked fleas would allow us, in preparation for the hard journey in prospect on the morrow.

An early start the next morning, while the dew was yet glistening in the sun, was exhilarating to us all. As we filed out from Ramleh, we were joined by our fellow pilgrims, who had been hospitably entertained at the con-

vents.  Our Syrian horses were sure footed, intelligent
animals, and their natural pace is either a walk or a gallop.
The impulse to try the latter was irresistible.  Our California lady's experience in horseback riding on the Pacific
coast, is now greatly to her advantage in this rough campaign.  The portly Bishop soon led the van, and the white
streamers on the ladies' hats were not far behind.  Altogether it was a gay cavalcade, with no suggestion of the
hardships or perils of an oriental pilgrimage.

Less than four hours brought us to Bab-el-Waud, the
"gateway to the plain," where we stopped to lunch.  Here
I must record the only rascally imposition on our whole
trip.  The keeper of the wayside inn could only give us
the plainest meal of bread, eggs, a can of sardines, and
coffee, for which he demanded an outrageous price.  It is
one of the lessons I have learned, as a traveler, never to
get angry at such trifles as exorbitant hotel bills or
swindling hack drivers.  It is far better to put aside, say,
ten per cent. of one's estimate for traveling expenses, as an
"overcharge fund," than to dispute a bill, lose one's temper, and thereby spoil a whole day's enjoyment.  So we
paid the bill and quietly told him he was an arrant knave,
swindler, and rascal, adding other epithets equally deroga-
tory to his self-respect.  But he only bowed and grinned,
as if we were paying him compliments, and all attempts
to disturb his equanimity signally failed.  He understood
our little game, but was more than a match for us.  As we
were mounting our horses he brought out a box of cigars,
and with a bow offered one to me as *baksheesh*.  This
was adding insult to injury.  I took the cigar and flinging
it over the wall I told the fellow with well-dissembled rage,
that I would accept no *baksheesh* from such an unmiti-
gated scoundrel.  He bowed again and with a serene smile,
sent a boy to pick up the cigar, and bade us " *au revoir*."

I felt myself vanquished, and rode away meditating how I could be even with him when on my return I should again pass through the " gateway to the plain."

From this place to Jerusalem was the hardest part of our journey. We now begin to ascend the " hills of Judea" and the road winds around the mountain sides with few signs of life or cultivation. The grade is nowhere very heavy, and much engineering skill is displayed in its construction. In some places high walls of rock protect the roadway alongside of deep ravines. Twice we climbed to the summits of mountain ranges from which we could see the Mediterranean, far away to the north. Descending to a deep valley we cross the brook Kedron, where David picked up the stone that killed Goliah. A few miles further, on a high hill, is the tomb of Samuel. Then we pass a desolate looking village where St. John was born. Not far distant is the place where, according to tradition, the Ark of God remained until taken to Jerusalem by David. This village was, many years ago, the residence of a renowned bandit, who spread terror through the surrounding country, until he was captured and executed by the Turkish soldiers.

The sun was uncomfortably warm, and the unwonted exercise began to tell upon the weaker members of our party. Silently in single file we climbed one hill after another, for Jerusalem is two thousand eight hundred feet above the sea, and some one struck up that old Methodist hymn,

> " Jerusalem my happy home,
> Oh, how I long for thee,"

which was sung with a fervor that expressed our true feelings at the moment. As the last notes died away among the rocky hills, we reached a summit, when a curve in the road brought to sight our longed for goal, about two miles distant.

That splendid painting by Kaulbach, on the walls of the new museum at Berlin, represents the brave old crusader, Godfrey de Bouillon, standing on this spot seven hundred years ago, surrounded by his army:

> "Each throws his martial ornaments aside,
> The crested helmets with their plumy pride;
> To humble thoughts their lofty hearts they bend,
> And down their cheeks the pious tears descend."

But our pilgrims are not sturdy knights, and are too weary for sentiment, so after a brief halt we turn our horses' heads toward the city, and in another half hour pass through the Jaffa Gate, guarded by Turkish soldiers, and find comfortable quarters at the Mediterranean Hotel.

# CHAPTER VII.

## THE HOLY CITY.

UR good Bishop said at dinner to-day, when I proposed to refer to him as authority on some question of Biblical history: "Ah, sir, you ought to be as well posted on the subject as myself." I could only say in reply that scriptural lore was not my *specialite*—and I feel my utter incompetence to describe, from the religiously sentimental point of view, places and localities which reason and plain common sense teach me are only "pious frauds," invented to excite the religious enthusiasm of ignorant people. So I trust I shall not be thought irreverent when I attempt to describe, in a matter-of-fact way, what I saw in Jerusalem, as I would the strange scenes in any less holy city.

If " cleanliness is next to godliness," surely this place is far away from either. In fact, holiness must, according to my experience, when applied to sacred cities, be in inverse ratio to cleanliness. Rome is bad ; Benares, the holy city of the Hindoos, is a degree worse ; Jerusalem a little more so ; and Mecca, by many millions considered so holy that no " dog of a Christian " can obtain admittance, must be a paradise of squalor and filth. The theory of the " rose by any other name," etc., does not hold good, for odors, not always of " Araby, the blest," are wonderfully sweetened by the name and sentimental associations of pious pilgrims. There is the less excuse for Jerusalem, as it is built on uneven ground, and being surrounded on three sides by deep ravines, there is every facility for drainage. One would suppose that the heavy rains, which are frequent here during the spring, would carry off a portion of the " unpleasantness," but my experience in rainy weather shows that then the deep mud only becomes the more sticky, the rough and uneven pavements more dangerously slippery, and the stench almost intolerable.

Literature is very prolific in descriptions of the Holy Land. It is said that more than two hundred books have already been written, and the number is increasing every year. The original city, as it existed in the time of our Saviour, is admitted by all authorities to be from forty to sixty feet beneath the present streets and buildings, so that we may say of Jerusalem, as we are wont to do of Virginia, that " the best part of it is under ground." A glance at history will show the reason for this. The same generation that witnessed the crucifixion saw Jerusalem utterly destroyed by Titus, after a siege, when, according to Josephus, over a million were killed, and one hundred

EAST END OF SOUTH WALL.

*From a photograph by F. Graham.*

thousand taken prisoners. Of the magnificent temple "not one stone was left above another," the walls were razed to the ground, and for many years desolation reigned supreme. Six centuries later it was besieged and captured by the Saracens; four hundred years after, at the breaking up of the empire of the brave and chivalric Saladin, it became the prey of the fierce Turks. For nearly a century it was the scene of a most obstinate and bloody struggle between the warriors of the Crescent and the Cross. During these many wars and sieges, its walls and buildings were repeatedly turned to heaps of rubbish. Upon this accumulated debris, modern Jerusalem is built. Unlike Cairo, Delhi, and many other Eastern cities, its original site is unchanged through all these vicissitudes, for the walls now, as two thousand years ago, are built along the brink of the deep valleys that bound the city on the east, south, and west. Outside the walls, nature has left clear and distinct landmarks that can never be effaced. The valley of Jehoshaphat, the brook Kedron, the Hill of Evil Counsel, and above all the Mount of Olives, are essentially the same to-day as when described in Holy Writ. Within the walls, which are from thirty to forty feet in height, built mostly by the Crusaders, and fortified after the style of the Middle Ages by towers and turrets, there are but two localities in which one can put faith— Mount Zion, and Mount Moriah where the mosque of Omar now stands upon the site of the temple of Solomon.

The area enclosed by the walls seems to the visitor but very small, it being but one mile long by about three-fourths of a mile in width. Nor could it have been much larger at the time of its greatest prosperity. It is hard to understand how it could possibly have contained so large a population as given by Josephus and other historians. Perhaps oriental hyperbole has magnified these estimates.

The experience of King David in taking a census, was not encouraging to his successors. The present population is not far from 20,000, of whom about one-third are Mahometans, and the balance nearly equally divided between Jews and Christians of the various sects, the Greek Church predominating. The Turkish Governor, or " Pasha of Jerusalem," is appointed by the Sultan, but must be confirmed, under a recent arrangement, by the representatives at Constantinople, of the great Christian powers of Europe.

In visiting a strange city it is always a good plan, first to climb to some high point from which a general view of the locality can be had. The " house top " of the Mediterranean hotel, situated upon Mt. Zion, is a capital standpoint, and commands a beautiful view of the whole city and the surrounding hills. At your feet is the " Pool of Hezekiah," a reservoir perhaps 200 feet square, half full of muddy water. The Tower of David overlooks this pool, as in olden time. Before you, but a little to the left, is the Church of the Holy Sepulcher, which is supposed to cover the site of Calvary. It is difficult to believe that this location was the scene of the crucifixion and burial of our Lord. For if this spot was formerly outside the walls, it would diminish the area of the ancient city by at least one-third. Adjoining it is an open space, where once stood the splendid hospital of the Knights of St. John. Directly in front, looking towards the east, is a large square enclosure, in the center of which is the beautiful Mosque of Omar, on Mt. Moriah. Beyond, and across the valley of Jehoshaphat, rises the Mount of Olives, the summit crowned by a Turkish mosque, and the Greek " Church of the Ascension," the sides dotted with olive trees and Moslem tombs. Around the side of Olivet, to the right, you can trace the road to Bethany, so often trod by Jesus and his disciples. Scattered about within the walls are

twenty convents and churches of the various Christian
sects, while to the left, on the Jaffa road, is the immense
Greek Hospice, with accommodations for several thousand
pilgrims within its enclosure.

Our first visit is to the Church of the Holy Sepulcher,
the central point of attraction to all devout pilgrims. We
enter from the street a long crooked and steep passage,
pass under a low archway, designed, it is said, to prevent
its desecration by Turks riding in on horseback, to a
square, open court, thronged by sellers of relics consisting of beads, olive wood, and mother-of-pearl crucifixes,
to be carried away by pilgrims to all parts of the world.
The front of the church is not very impressive, though
its doorways and windows are most elaborately carved; it
shows the marks of time on its crumbling walls. Near
the doors, both outside and within, are Turkish soldiers in
semi-European uniform, and armed with the latest pattern
of breech-loading muskets. They conduct themselves with
a dignity befitting the rulers of the country, and it must
be said to their credit, that neither here nor elsewhere in
Syria has any one ever asked me for *baksheesh*, though
I will not go so far as to say that they would not accept
it if offered. It is a mortifying reflection that here, where
the Christian religion had its birth, these Mahometan guards
are required to prevent the rival sects of Christians from
shedding each other's blood, within the walls of the building held by them as the most sacred on earth.

Just inside the doors is a flat marble slab called the
"stone of unction," on which the Lord's body was anoint-
ed for burial, and near by is a circular stone where the
Virgin Mary stood during the anointment. We pass a
little farther on and stand beneath the great dome, in
front of a building about fifteen feet square, embellished

THE HOLY SEPULCHRE.

with all that wealth and superstition can supply. Outside and within are scores of lamps of gold and silver—the gifts of kings and queens—kept constantly burning. It is divided into two apartments, the inner one, about six feet by seven, containing the white marble sarcophagus in which they believe the body of the Saviour was laid. There is a constant stream of pilgrims, many of whom have come thousands of miles, and they are admitted three or four at a time within the sacred precincts, crawling on bended knees, kissing the marble floor and the tomb, and often with the tears streaming from their eyes. It is a scene hard to look upon unmoved; but with me it was rather pity for these poor, ignorant creatures, than reverence for the spot to them the holiest upon earth.

The church covers a large area and is divided between the Armenians (native Christians), the Latins (Roman Catholics), and the Greeks (or Russians). The latter control the spot called " Calvary," where Helena, the mother of Constantine, discovered the three crosses hid beneath a rock. Here you are shown the holes in which the crosses were fixed, and the fissure in the rock caused by the earthquake. In the center of the richly decorated Byzantine Chapel adjoining, is a small pillar which they call " the center of the world,"—from this spot they say the earth was taken from which God created Adam. It would require too much space to describe half the " sacred places " —over forty in number—which are located within this church. I will only mention the spots where Mary Magdalene and the mother of Christ stood during the crucifixion, and where Christ appeared to them; the tombs of Joseph, Nicodemus, and Adam; the pillar of flagellation, etc. I took in my hand the sword and spurs of Godfrey de Bouillon, the first Christian king of Jerusalem—doubtless genuine relics, and still used in the ceremony of investing the Knights of St. John. During all the time we were in the church, services were being held in many different chapels, and processions of priests and devotees were passing to and fro, bearing candles and burning incense.

Leaving the church, we walked through the "Via Dolorosa," where our Saviour bore the cross on His way to Calvary, under the arch of "Ecce Homo," past the house of Pilate and the "Hall of Judgment," and the spot where St. Veronica offered the handkerchief for wiping His face. Upon it is impressed the picture of the Lord's face in blood, and it is now one of the most sacred relics in St. Peter's at Rome.

The Mosque of Omar, to the Mahometan the most sacred place in the world except Mecca, was formerly very difficult of access to all but the "true believer," and permits can now only be obtained from the Governor at the request of the foreign Consuls. When I was here before, these cost twenty francs each, but the price is now reduced to five. Our shoes had to be replaced by slippers, in obedience to the injunction, "take thy shoes from off thy feet, for the place whereon thou standest is holy ground." The enclosure is one thousand five hundred by one thousand feet, planted with cyprus and palm trees, and surrounded by a high wall. Upon a broad marble platform in the center, stands one of the most beautiful of mosques. It is built upon the foundation walls of Solomon's temple, and covers the "holy of holies." The building is octagonal in form, about sixty feet each side, supporting an elegant dome. In the center, under a canopy of the richest silks, is an irregular stone, nearly fifty feet in diameter, called the "rock of prophecy," which the Mussulman believes to have fallen from heaven. When the prophets fled for safety to other lands, this rock was about to follow, but the angel Gabriel seized it in his mighty hand and held it fast until Mahomet arrived, who fixed it eternally on its present site. The print of the angel's hands and of the prophet's foot as he ascended from it to heaven, are shown upon the stone. Beneath it is a cave, about eighteen feet in size, where Mahomet rested after his flight from Mecca to

THE GOLDEN GATE.

Jerusalem in a single night. It is believed that this rock is immovably suspended in the air, quite independent of the pillars under it, which are only there in case of accident! Every prayer uttered in the cave beneath will be granted. At the bottom is a deep well, where, they say, are all the souls of the departed waiting the resurrection.

Another mosque, within the same enclosure, was once a

7

Christian church during the occupancy of Jerusalem by the Crusaders. It contains the "tombs of the sons of Aaron," the "foot prints of Christ," and the "pillars of proof,"—two marble columns standing side by side, with a space of but nine inches between them. Through this space a good man may pass regardless of his size, but a wicked person cannot possibly squeeze through, however slender he may be. Although I have twice passed through without the slightest difficulty, I shall not set up for a saint.

On one side of the enclosure we see the interior of the beautiful "Golden Gate," through which Christ passed when he triumphantly entered Jerusalem on Palm Sunday. It is now walled up, as the Moslems believe that when the Christians again obtain possession of the Holy City, they will enter by this gate. Many other curious places were shown us here, which I have not space to describe. The good-natured Sheik who attended our party through the grounds, was very civil and polite, and in consideration of some extra *baksheesh* gave me a small piece of the tile lining of the interior of the mosque, which I shall add to my collection of relics.

## CHAPTER VIII.

### JERUSALEM, AND OUR RETURN TO JAFFA.

Visit to the Mount of Olives—A View Unequalled in the Holy Land—The Stolen Footprint—Bethany—Tomb of Lazarus—House of Martha and Mary—The Identical Fig Tree—The Scene of the Last Supper—Armenian Convent—A Beautiful Missal—The Jews' Wailing Place—Farewell to Jerusalem—The Octroi Duty—Last View of the Holy City—A Dismal Ride—A Sinner on his way to Confession—I Assume the Rôle of a Preacher—He becomes humble and Penitent—Once More Entertained at the Gateway to the Plain—Human Nature Not Totally Depraved—The Russian Convent at Ramleh—Hospitality of the Monks—Morning Ride to Jaffa—The Decoration of the " Red Jerusalem Cross."

 UR visit to the Mount of Olives, and to the village of Bethany, was one of the pleasantest of our Jerusalem experiences. Leaving the city by the Damascus Gate, then turning to the right, we wind round the ancient walls, and descend the steep hill to the valley of Jehoshaphat. Our faith grows stronger as we leave behind us the foolish myths and absurd traditions of both Christian and Moslem, which meet us at every turn within the walls. We stop for a few moments to enter a small square enclosure which is called the " Garden of Gethsemane." If not the

identical spot, it must be very near the site of the Garden where our Saviour passed the night of agony.  Here are six olive trees said to be fifteen hundred years old ; certainly the oldest, most gnarly and knotted specimens I ever saw of this long-lived tree. and their being here gives an air of genuineness to the place.  This valley has from time immemorial been the great burial place of the Jews, and there are now in the city many very old and wealthy descendants of Abraham, who have come from distant foreign lands, that their bones may be laid in the tombs of their forefathers.

Here we see the quaint and antique tombs ascribed by tradition to Absalom and Zachariah.  In olden times every man passing by, cast a pebble at the former, and it is now half buried in loose stones.  The day was quite warm and pleasant, and we passed many parties of both Jewish and Moslem women and children out for a walk. One party we noticed, were kneeling and throwing flowers over a recent tomb, perhaps of some near relative, and we make a detour, that we may not disturb their grief. " One touch of nature makes the whole world kin."

We reach the summit of the Mount of Olives, and from the tower of the mosque we enjoy a view unequalled in beauty in all the Holy Land.  For the first time we seem to be in a land sacred to holy memories.  Before us lies the " City of our Lord." the bright sun gilding alike the domes of mosques and temples.  In the foreground we see women drawing water from a well, and balancing, on their heads, the jars in form identical with those used three thousand years ago.  A long train of camels are slowly winding along the road from the South, their attendants wearing the same loose, flowing robes as in the time of the patriarchs.

In the far distance on our left, are the Mountains of Moab, and the Dead Sea, that looks like a vast lake of

JERUSALEM FROM THE MOUNT OF OLIVES.

molten lead. We trace the Jordan, like a silver thread, through a green valley amid the sterile rocky mountains. Though more than twenty miles away by the road, it seems scarcely half that distance in a straight line. It is over four thousand feet below the point on which we stand. Descending from the tower, we merely glance into the church at the rock on which a large indentation is shown as the footprint of our Saviour, from whence he made the Ascension. They say there were originally two prints, but the Moslems stole one of them. Such nonsense is not in harmony with the scene, and we hurry away.

Following a rough foot-path over the hills, a half hour's walk brings us to the village of Bethany, now a half deserted collection of mud-colored huts, surrounded by groves of almond, fig, and olive trees. An old Arab, who has watched our coming, leads the way and conducts us to what is supposed to be the tomb of Lazarus. He lights tapers, and each taking one, we follow him down steep, dark, winding steps to a cave twenty feet or more below the ground. A very short stay was enough, and with a glance at the so-called house of Mary and Martha, and the identical fig tree which Jesus cursed, we leave the village, followed by a crowd of Arab children screaming for *baksheesh*.

We return to Jerusalem along the main road, around the south side of the Mount of Olives, probably the same pathway by which our Saviour rode on that humblest of animals, while the people strewed the way with garments and branches of palm.

Another day was spent in making a circuit of the walls, in visiting the " Tombs of the Kings " and the " House of David " on Mount Zion, beneath which is his tomb. A large upper room in this building, which is outside the walls, is shown as the scene of the " Last Supper," and where Christ appeared to the Apostles after the Resurrection. The Mahometans are in possession of this place, and hold it very sacred, as they consider David one of their prophets. The Armenian convent is close by but within the walls, and was the " House of Caiaphas," the High Priest. It is very rich in decorations of gold and silver, and claims among its relics the stone which closed the door of the Holy Sepulcher, and the rock on which the cock crew when Peter denied his master ! Far more interesting to me was a most beautifully illuminated missal I there saw. Every page of the parchment was decorated with coloured illustrations on the margin, and it must have been a labor of love for many years to the old monks, who ages ago have turned to dust ; rubies, sapphires, and diamonds glistened on the covers, and the heavy clasps were of solid gold. The gray-bearded old monk watched it with jealous care while it was in my hands, and seemed relieved when he returned it to its case of rich velvet, and replaced it on the altar. As we left the church, he sprinkled us with holy water and gave us his blessing.

At the " Jews' Wailing Place," in front of some large stones built into the outside wall of the Mosque of Omar and which are supposed to be part of the foundations of Solomon's Temple, is a very affecting scene every Friday afternoon. Here they congregate, young and old, and utter the most plaintive cries and lamentations. The stones are worn away with their kisses, and they mourn as if their hearts would break.

I shall not attempt here to describe the curious scenes that I witnessed three years ago, during " Holy Week," the procession on " Palm Sunday," and the " washing of feet " by the high church dignitaries. I then made a most interesting excursion to the Jordan, the Dead Sea, and to Bethlehem.

Our present trip was limited to two weeks, and we were obliged to hurry back to Egypt to join the steamer for our voyage to Persia and Bagdad.

The sky was overcast with clouds, and every appearance indicated a dreary, drizzly journey before us, when my friend F—— and I said farewell to the pleasant companions of our pilgrimage, and mounted our horses to return to Jaffa. As we passed under the heavy archway of the Jaffa gate, we noticed that the Turkish soldiers levied an *octroi* duty, in kind, upon all the country products brought into the city for sale. Every market-man

THE OCTROI DUTY AT THE JAFFA GATE.

was relieved of a part of his load, seemingly at the discretion of the guards. Beside them were piles of fuel, vegetables of all kinds, eggs, and poultry. Whether these were sold for the benefit of the government or appropriated for the use of the guards, we were unable to ascertain. Our dragoman, Hassan, had been sent forward in advance with the pack-mule, and we slowly ascended the heights that overlook Jerusalem on the north, past the Russian convent, and several neat and well built dwellings.

As we reached a point where a bend in the road would hide the city from our view, we halted for a few minutes and turned in our saddles to take one last look at the Holy City. The impression left on my mind by this second visit to the holy places, was one of sadness, relieved only by our one day's excursion to Olivet and Bethany.

Slowly and without exchanging a word, we turned our horses' heads towards the sea, buttoned our overcoats more closely against the chilly wind, and cold penetrating rain that beat in our faces, and with loosened rein allowed our beasts to pick their way along the stony road down the steep hill. For the first hour we were constantly meeting donkeys laden with twigs and roots for fuel, and men, women, and even half grown children plodding along under heavy burdens towards the city. As we passed them they invariably looked up at us with faces sad and weary, as if life had to them no happiness in the present, and no bright hope in the future. The steadily falling rain was making the road more muddy at every step, but we gradually threw off our depression, determined to take a " Mark Tapley " view of the situation, and be as " jolly " and cheerful as we could under the most adverse circumstances.

Two hours after leaving Jerusalem we descried a solitary traveler approaching us on horseback, and as he drew near, we recognized our rascally host of a few days before at Bab-el-Waud. He was dressed in his best gaberdine, over which he wore a striped *abbah* of goat's hair, which is almost impervious to water. It was the Jewish Sunday, and he was evidently on his way to Jerusalem to worship. We stopped our horses and confronted him with a salutation more emphatic than complimentary. In a few plain words we reminded him of his dishonesty, and intimated that if he was now about to square up the weekly account of his iniquities, the best proof his sincerity and repentance would be to make restitution of his ill-gotten gains. As he glanced at our faces and saw that we were in earnest, his *nonchalance* deserted him and he looked as humble as became a great sinner going to confession. He assented to our proposal, and wrote some words in Hebrew upon a dirty scrap of paper, which he said was an order to his brother, whom he had left at the inn, to give us a lunch free of charge. His meekness and seeming penitence disarmed our resentment, and we allowed him to proceed on his journey, a sadder and I trust a happier man for this one burden of transgression lifted off his conscience.

A few hours later we descended the last of the Judean hills and halted at the "gateway of the plain." The brother came out from the Inn and we presented the paper with some misgivings that we had been *sold*. He read it, then courteously invited us to dismount, and in a short time placed before us a very fair lunch. As we rose from the table he presented the identical box of cigars. To test his sincerity I took out my purse and offered to pay for them, but he refused any compensation. We shook hands quite cordially at parting, and rode away with a far better opinion of human nature than before—for our former experience at that place had indicated that it is sometimes almost totally depraved.

After leaving the hills, our ride across the alluvial plain was very disagreeable. The rain was incessant, and the road knee deep in mud. We were glad to reach Ramleh before dark, and passing by the hotel of the would-be American Consul, we sought the Russian Convent, where we were kindly welcomed. I had stopped here one night three years before, and to my surprise I found I was recognized by the priests and their wives. The clergy of the Greek Church are permitted to marry, and the presence of women and children seemed quite inconsistent with our usual associations of a convent or monastery.

During this visit to the Holy Land, I have been saluted by several hotel keepers and dragomen, with evident marks of surprise, both at Jaffa and Jerusalem. These people have a wonderful faculty of remembering faces. If any of them swindled me before, I have long ago forgiven them, and brought back with me no malice. This time I have been treated with especial kindness and attention, for they seem to think that I shall hereafter be a regular visitor at intervals of two or three years.

The ground floor of the convent was a stable, where our jaded horses were well cared for, and we climbed by an outside stairway to the apartments above, where we were shown to a chamber plainly but comfortably furnished. After changing our rain-soaked garments we were summoned to a substantial supper, served on English blue delf ware of the old fashioned "willow pattern." Everything was scrupulously neat and clean, and we were the only guests. The building, like all in this country, is of stone, with thick walls, arched ceilings, and no wood work except the doors and window frames. During the rainy season, these vaulted, cell-like rooms must be dark and damp, but in summer they are cool and agreeable. At Ramleh there are two convents, the Russian (or Greek) and the Latin (or Roman Catholic), both of which, for two months in spring are crowded by pilgrims, mostly of the poorer classes, from Europe. The pilgrimage culminates during

" holy week," when there are frequently ten thousand Europeans in and around Jerusalem. These two months embrace the only proper time to travel in Palestine. Before the middle of March the weather is unsettled, and too cold and rainy for tent life. Later than the fifteenth of May it is usually too hot for comfort.

After our fatiguing ride we retired early, and although the beds were hard, and our doors and windows without fastenings, we slept as soundly and as securely as in the most luxuriously furnished modern hotel.

The next morning our kind hosts gave us an early breakfast, and accepted with profuse thanks the money we offered for our entertainment. At these convents the poorer class of pilgrims are fed and lodged free of charge, but travelers, like ourselves, are expected to pay whatever amount they please, or if they go away without paying at all, no fault is found.

Our morning ride of twelve miles to Jaffa, with a bright sun and clear sky, was in strong contrast with yesterday's experience, and when we reached the town we were glad to see the smoke of an " Austrian Lloyd " steamer approaching from the eastward, on which we were to embark for Port Said.

There are three lines of steamers along the Southern coast of the Mediterranean,—the " Messageries Maritimes," the " Austrian Lloyd," and the Russian. They touch at nearly every port, and are all comfortable and well-appointed. But the French line is usually preferred, the steamers being larger and the service more efficient.

The "true believer " who makes a second pilgrimage to Mecca, is entitled to certain rights and privileges among the followers of the Prophet. But what honors properly belong to one who has made a second pilgrimage to Jerusalem, I have been unable to ascertain—perhaps the case

has no precedent—so I shall claim the distinction of having the end of my trunk decorated with a Red Jerusalem
Cross.   As the founder of this new Order, I hold myself
ready to bestow the decoration upon all Americans who
may show themselves entitled to it.

STREET IN JERUSALEM.

# CHAPTER IX.

## THE SUEZ CANAL.

An Accomplished Fact—Sketch of its History—Reasons Alleged for its Failure—Bugbears Exploded—Is it a Financial Success?—Rates of Toll —New Lines of Steamers—The Business of 1873—The Tides—Width, Depth, and Rate of Speed Allowed—Lake Menzaleh—Mammoth Dredging Machines—A Unique View—A Ship in the Desert—Lake Timseh— The Bitter Lake—A Ready Made Canal—We Reach Suez—A Town as old as the Pharaohs—No Pleasant Greeting to the Red Sea—Why Called "Red"—The "Crescent and Star"—The Water never Smooth and Clear —Pharaoh's Chariot Wheels not to be Seen.

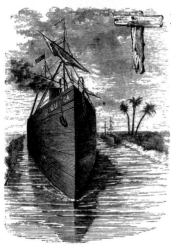

HE Suez canal, one of the greatest achievements of the century, was opened at the grand *fête* in November, 1869, at which the Empress Eugenie assisted. It was then fully described by special correspondents from all over the world.

As we are now about to pass through the whole length of the canal, I propose to give a short sketch of its history, and such information as I have been able to gather, as to its present condition and practical working, a matter which, six years ago, was all conjecture, and about which the letter-writers differed so widely. That it is now an accomplished fact, and a success, no one with his eyes open can deny. As Lardner scouted the idea of ships propelled by steam ever crossing the Atlantic, so Stephenson, the great engineer, and the English generally, for years insisted that the Suez canal would be a failure. Perhaps " the wish was father to the thought." The English government, too, must now feel heartily ashamed of its intrigues with the Sultan to throw obstacles in the way of this great work, on the ground of philanthropy in behalf of the forced and unpaid labor of the Egyptians—for no nation is now reaping so much benefit from this new route of steamers to India, as the English people themselves.

The first great bugbear was the fancied difference in level between the Red Sea and the Mediterranean, by which locks would be required, in accordance with the report of a commission sent out by Napoleon I. in 1798. This idea was exploded by more accurate surveys made fifty years afterwards. The next objection was, that the channel would have to be made through hopeless quick-sands at the southern or Suez end, and through centuries of Nile ooze at the northern part near the Mediterranean, where no channel could be made permanent, but the more you dug and dredged the worse it would be. This obstacle disappeared when it was proved that for most of the route, the banks of the canal would not be of fluid sand, but of mud, clay, and shelly earth—that below the Nile ooze and slippery mud of Lake Menzaleh, there was a " hard pan " of clay, which, thrown up, gave solidity to the banks—and that so small a portion of the route passed through loose sand, that no real trouble threatened the canal from the instability of its banks. These objections being disposed of, it was then urged that the sand drift from the siroccos of the desert would refill the canal as fast as it could be removed, thereby causing such immense expense in keeping the channel open, as to ruin the great enterprise financially. But it has been demonstrated by experience that not more than five miles of its entire length is liable to this drifting in of the sand ; and at these places the encroachments of sand never exceed two yards in depth a month, which the company has contracted to be removed, at no great expense, as fast as it accumulates.

To Ferdinand de Lesseps, the world is indebted for having pushed through this magnificent work in the face of every obstacle, real and imaginary. With perfect faith in the eventual success of the enterprise, like Cyrus W. Field, of Atlantic cable memory, he persevered when less sanguine men would have given up in despair ; and to him belongs the credit of having opened this second Gibraltar inlet and outlet, to the commerce of the world.

It is true that the Suez canal is a French work, but it is not owned nor in any way controlled by the French government. Of the 400,000 shares representing the stock, 176,000 belong to the Viceroy of Egypt, Ismail Pasha, without whose active and energetic assistance it never could have been completed. The balance of the stock belongs to individuals, mostly Frenchmen. The first " Act of Concession " from the Egyptian government for a canal across the Isthmus of Suez, was granted in 1854. Then followed five years of preliminary surveys and preparation, and the first ground was broken at Port Said in 1859. The Red Sea entered and mingled with the waters of the Mediterranean on the 15th of August, 1869. But it was not until about the 1st of January, 1870, that this thoroughfare, which all ages have wished for, but till now in vain, was opened as a highway to the commerce of the world.

And now, after five years' trial, it will be asked whether this costly work is a financial success. Probably not, as yet. The preferred stock last issued was guaranteed five per cent.—but to realize this dividend on its whole cost, requires an income of five million dollars a year, and over two millions more for running expenses, repairs, and management. The rate of toll is two dollars a ton register on every steamer, and two dollars for every passenger; sailing ships half that rate, besides pilotage, etc. It costs the steamer I am on, $1,600 for passing through the canal, which seems a large sum for one day's toll, but it is a trifle compared with the expense of sending her around "the Cape." To make the canal pay from tolls alone, would require at least five steamers to pass each way every day; and at present I am told that the average is about half that number. But the Suez Canal Company has other sources of income. The Viceroy made liberal grants of land to the company, a part of which have since reverted to him in consideration of a large sum of ready money; but fifty per cent. of all land sales in the towns of Port Said, Ismailia, and Suez, where the company owns large tracts of valuable property, comes into its treasury. And since the opening of the canal, new lines of passenger and freight steamers have been established, by which Russia, Austria, Italy, and France are coming into competition with England, for the trade of the East.

The business of the canal has steadily increased since it was opened, but not so rapidly as was anticipated. The income from tolls in 1873 was over $5,000,000 from the 1,200 steamers passing through. The expense of its administration, including the cost of dredging, about $2,250,-000. Capital stock $100,000,000, and a bonded debt not very large, mostly held by the Viceroy of Egypt. The surplus income is being absorbed at present by the extension of the breakwater into the sea at Port Said, 6,000 yards, to prevent the silting up of the harbor.

All measurements and distances being in French meters, kilometers, and hectares, I will, for the convenience of the reader, reduce them to English. Our steamer draws sixteen feet, but under her keel is six feet to spare, which is increased about two feet more at high tide. And here I may as well explain the matter of tides. The ordinary rise and fall of the tide at Port Said, on the Mediterranean, is one and a half feet, and at Suez three and a half feet. At the Equinox the maximum rise and fall is about double.

There being no gates or locks to interfere with the free inflow and egress of the ocean at either end, the tides slightly affect the depth of water in the canal, and produce a current which never exceeds two miles an hour, and is lost in the lakes which form over one-half the whole course. At the water line the width of the canal when finished according to its enlarged scale, will be three hundred feet, the depth thirty feet, and the breadth at the bottom seventy feet. This will give space enough for the keels of two large ships to pass each other without inconvenience. At present the average width is about two hundred feet, with not less than twenty-four feet of water in the shallowest spots. At frequent intervals there are wider basins where ships can meet and pass each other. The management is by telegraph, and every few miles we see upon the banks a neatly fitted up telegraph station, from which the position of every ship in the canal is reported at headquarters. The maximum speed allowed is eight miles an hour, which would take a ship through the ninety-six miles between Port Said and Suez by daylight, as no steaming is allowed after dark.

The first twenty-six miles from the Mediterranean, the canal runs through the shallow water and deep mud of Lake Menzaleh. This formed a part of the Nile delta, and was originally one of its outlets. To excavate a ship

8

canal through the soft, slippery mud of this marsh, with banks that would stand the rush of the Mediterranean within, and the occasional storms on the lake outside, for a long time baffled the utmost ingenuity and skill of the engineers. But when, as has before been stated, it was discovered that by going deep enough they would come to a strong, tenacious clay, underlying the centuries of Nile ooze, which being thrown out and mixed with the mud would form a solid bank, this difficulty was overcome.

These double dykes are about four feet high, and within them are buried the iron pipes through which the great "*Pompe-a-feu*" (steam pump works) at Ismailia forces all the water supply for the city of Port Said.

A STEAMER IN THE DESERT.

Moored to the banks we notice the mammoth dredging machines, which are built entirely of iron. These were not only constructed but invented by the contractors, to meet the special difficulties and requirements of this service. Ten of these gigantic machines, the use of which I never should imagine if I had seen them anywhere else, cost eighty thousand dollars each, and twenty-five steam barges to carry off the dirt brought up by the excavators, cost fifty thousand dollars each. That these were built by the contractors, will give an idea of the magnitude of the work.

Leaving Lake Menzaleh, the canal passes through nineteen miles of sand, to the next lake in the chain.

From the deck of our steamer the view is unique. We are high out of the water, and I can see over the top of the banks a desert of sand stretching away as far as the eye can reach.

We now come to Lake Timsah, six miles long, upon the western shore of which is the new desert-founded city of Ismailia. The water of this lake is deep and clear, but very salt. We next enter another section of the canal proper, eight miles long, which connects Lake Timsah with Lac Amer, or the "bitter lake."

This was an oval depression in the land, directly in the track of the proposed canal, and is supposed to have been originally the head of the Gulf of Suez. The receding of the water of the Red Sea left it an inland basin, from which the water has long ago evaporated. Upon the bed of this hollow was a layer of salt, in many places several feet in thickness. When the water of the Red Sea was again let into this bed it formed a ready-made canal, twenty-one miles long, in the widest part ten miles across, and deep enough for the largest ship. The salt accumulated in the bed of the lake makes the water very bitter, and hence the name given to it.

Steaming more rapidly through this we once more enter the canal, and three hours after we enter into the harbor of Suez, and before dark are comfortably quartered at the "Peninsular and Oriental Hotel."

We shall be detained a few days at Suez waiting the arrival of our steamer, and have an opportunity of seeing whatever is interesting in this old town, which, within a few years, has taken a new lease of life.

The harbor is mostly artificial, and a splendid dry-dock of stone has been built by the Khedive, the only one, I believe, on the waters that flow into the Indian Ocean, this side of India. From the flat roof of the hotel, I can count ten war steamers flying the Turkish and Egyptian flag, the "Crescent and Star."

It is now more than three years since I landed here, coming from India. I then said good-bye to the treacherous waters of the Red Sea, without regret, and I greet them now with no anticipations of pleasure. Why this sea is called "Red" is a mystery. I could never see any roseate hue in its stormy waves, bleak, sandy shores or volcanic rocks. I have read somewhere that when the water is smooth and clear—(*which it never is,*)—the chariot wheels of the Egyptian hosts may be seen beneath the waves. But travelers unanimously agree with old Pharaoh, that the Red Sea is the most disagreeable and treacherous piece of water upon the face of the globe.

# CHAPTER X.

## ON THE RED SEA.

Dangerous Navigation—The Gateway of Tears—The Wind Always Ahead
—Our Steamer Named after a Hindoo Goddess—Mount Sinai in Sight—
"Dolce Far Niente"—Jeddah, the Port of Mecca—Yusef Effendi—The
Sacred Banner—Mohamet Benaji—Pilgrimage to Mecca—We Visit the
Governor and the Prince of Zanzibar—Elaborate Speeches—The Tomb
of Eve—A Moslem Tradition—The Prince and his Harem come on board
—Not Visible to Outsiders—The Persian Pearl Merchant—Pearls of Great
Price—The Prince's Treasures—"Right, Left, and Ace"—I Decline an
Invitation to Zanzibar—Mocha, the "Coffee City"—How the English
Acquired Perim, the Key to the Gateway.

HEN the new route to India
was opened across the Isthmus of Suez, it was supposed
that sailing ships would no
longer plod their weary way
round the Cape of Good
Hope; but five years' experience has shown that only
ships propelled by steam can
navigate with any degree of
safety, the treacherous current and dangerous reefs of
the Red Sea. There are but
few lighthouses, and many
valuable ships are lost every year upon the sunken reefs,
in spite of the utmost care of officers and pilots.

The native Arabs never start out on a voyage across
the Red Sea in their trading boats or *bugalahs*, without

putting up a prayer to Allah for safety. They call the narrow straits at its foot, Bab-el-Mandeb—" The Gateway of Tears." It is fourteen hundred miles from Suez to Aden, which is situated ninety miles beyond the Gateway opening into the Arabian Gulf. Its greatest width is two hundred miles, and the shores everywhere seem lined with sandy deserts or sterile rocky mountains. No rivers empty into this vast caldron, and very little rain falls upon its parched and desolate shores.

The wind blows in from the north through the Gulf of Suez, and from the south through the straits of Bab-el-Mandeb, but near the middle of the Red Sea it is generally calm. Here the heated air seems to rise into an immense funnel, and the temperature is almost intolerable.

That the navigation of the Red Sea is both difficult and dangerous, is testified by the many wrecks scattered along its coasts, from Suez to the Indian Ocean.

As we pass a high volcanic island called Jubaltare, we are shown where a magnificent steamer of the Peninsular and Oriental Steamship Company, from Bombay, with over two hundred passengers, was lost with all on board. The channel is not wide, and near the shores are many dangerous rocks and treacherous currents. They say the wind on the Red Sea is always ahead, whether the vessel is bound up or down. The shores, which are either barren, sandy deserts, or sparsely inhabited by hostile tribes of Arabs, offer no hospitable reception to the shipwrecked sailor.

Our steamer bears the name of a Hindoo goddess whose home is on the Ganges. She is of iron, strong and swift, English built and manned. Our captain is a jolly sea-dog, a thorough John Bull, a careful navigator, and on the bridge night and day, almost sleepless in his anxiety for the safety of his ship. As the " Gunga " is to be our home for a month or more, we came on board with no little solicitude as to our accommodation and comforts for so long a voyage. We find ourselves the only cabin passengers, and in very pleasant quarters. But our bright prospects are somewhat clouded by the announcement that the steamer is to stop at Jeddah, the port of Mecca, about half way down the Red Sea, and take on board three hundred pilgrims on their way home to the several ports in Arabia and Persia. But an old traveler will never borrow trouble. So we enjoy to the utmost the few days that we have the ship all to ourselves. The Hindoo goddess glides steadily and rapidly through the smooth water, the weather being perfect, and the Red Sea seems inclined to redeem its bad name—or perhaps is lulling us on, to show its teeth by-and-by.

On our second day from Suez, Mount Sinai was seen far away on our left, its summit wreathed in fleecy clouds; but between us and its base is a long stretch of sand hills and barren desert.

To pass away the time, we read a little, write a little, smoke a little, and sleep a good deal. We lie on deck under the awning and gaze for hours over the smooth, dark blue water, where it meets the lighter blue of the sky in a clear, sharply-defined horizon. It is a *dolce far niente*, only to be matched on the Nile. Tired of gazing and dreaming, we read aloud from the only two books we could find in Cairo that seemed adapted to our proposed journey—" The Arabian Nights " and " The Koran."

The fourth day we slacken speed, as we are approach-ing the port of Jeddah. For twenty miles out, the charts show long series of coral reefs, and the channel between them is very intricate. There is no light-house, and a ship would not venture to approach the coast by night; but on some of the most prominent reefs, the Turkish government has erected beacons of white-washed stones. The Arab pilot directs our zig-zag course, making several very sharp turns, sometimes so near that we can toss a biscuit into the seething water that breaks in long lines over these treacherous sharp points of coral, that would punch through our iron plates like pasteboard. We drop anchor in front of the town, near a dozen other steamers, English, Turkish, and Egyptian, and one an " Austrian Lloyd," from Trieste. In the inner harbor, protected by a long, sandy spit of land, we see a fleet of Arab *bugalahs*, with high poop decks and lateen sails, like Chinese junks. These native craft are from fifty to two hundred tons burden, and run boldly in and out among the reefs along the whole coast of the Red Sea. Several hundreds are engaged in transporting pilgrims, more than twenty thousand of whom come every year to Jeddah from the African coast alone. The city has an imposing effect from the sea; its tall, clean-looking, white buildings, extending for a mile or more along the beach, with a background of high mountains, beyond which, fifty miles inland, lies the sacred city of Mecca. A high wall encloses the town, with towers at intervals, and two strong forts at the angles towards the sea. Gates on three sides are open to all, but to the east is the Mecca gate, through which none but Mahometans are allowed to pass.

A boat with a Turkish flag comes alongside, and the health officer holds up a tin fumigating box, into which our ship's papers are dropped. These being found satisfactory he comes on board, followed by the ship's agent, Yusef Effendi, who tells our captain that he has three hundred pilgrims, or *Hadjis* waiting passage, among them the Prince of Zanzibar, Sayd Hammoud, who has engaged all the vacant first-class cabins for himself and his harem. The prospect of entertaining a live prince and an uncertain number of princesses, stirs the loyal blood of our skipper, and the stewards are at once set at work to prepare the rooms for the royal party. My friend F. and myself are put into one state-room, which we do not grumble at, as His Royal Highness will go with us no further than Aden, where he takes another steamer to Zanzibar.

Yusef Effendi, though an Arab, speaks very good English, as well as French, Italian, and Turkish, and politely invites us to go on shore in his boat. This afternoon the silken screen which for the past year has hung before the sacred *Caaba* in the Temple at Mecca, and which is renewed every year, a present from the Sultan of Turkey, is to be taken with great ceremony on board a Turkish man-of-war, to be transported to Constantinople, where it will be cut up into small pieces and distributed as a most precious relic among the faithful.

We reach the shore just in time to see the procession pass through the streets, headed by the Turkish Governor or Pasha, and escorted by a large body of troops. A hundred camels, gaily decked with rich trappings, on which the " crescent and star " are embroidered in red and gold, are followed by a long cavalcade of horsemen, and behind them are thousand of *Hadjis* on foot. All business is suspended in the bazaars, and as the camel which bears the sacred banner passes, the head of every Mussulman bows to the ground. A few years ago an occasion like this was the scene of a fearful outbreak of fanaticism on the part of the pilgrims, and several hundreds of Christians were massacred. But we witnessed the show from an upper window in Yusef Effendi's house, and were in no danger of being molested. At the shore the banner, or carpet, as it is sometimes called, was placed on a barge covered with Turkish flags, which was towed by the man-of-war's boats to the ship, where it was received with a salvo of cannon.

After being served with *chibouks* and coffee, Yusef conducted us to the warehouse of his firm, and introduced us to his senior partner, Mohamet Benaji. I doubt whether any great London or New York merchant prince could have received us with more dignified ease and grace of manner. With true Oriental politeness, he places at our disposal his house and all it contains. Yusef says his word is " good as the Bank of England." He is a very fine-looking old gentleman, and is evidently held in great respect by all about the place. Every one who approaches him bows very low and kisses his hand. His rich turban, long, gray beard, and loose flowing robe of costly materials, give him a patriarchal appearance, while the urbane and dignified expression of his face would make him a model for a painter. Seated on the divan beside the patriarch, we are once more regaled with fragrant mocha and *narghilehs*, served on silver trays by black slaves. Yusef then shows us through large warehouses where are piled whole cargoes of coffee, rice, dates, and sesame or millet, packages of mother-of-pearl and tortoise shells, gum (arabic), and other products of this country, of which over $5,000,000 in value are shipped yearly from the port of Jeddah.

The streets and bazaars through which we pass, are the cleanest of any Arabian city I have ever seen; the buildings are mostly of stone, some four and five stories in height. There is no glass, but each window has a projecting lattice work of elaborately carved wood, which admits a free circulation of air, but hides from view the faces of the inmates. The business of Jeddah is largely dependent upon the pilgrims, of whom over one hundred thousand arrive and depart annually. The Koran enjoins upon every true believer, if his circumstances and health will permit, to make at least once during his lifetime, the pilgrimage to Mecca, and all who comply are promised certain immunities in this world, and a higher seat in paradise hereafter. The faithful come from every Mahometan country on the globe—from Persia and India in the far East, from the South coast of the Mediterranean and the Western shores of Africa, often accompanied by their wives and children. The thousands who cross the deserts in caravans suffer incredible hardships, and many perish by the way, but they believe that to die on a pilgrimage insures immediate entry to Heaven. The Koran permits them to do a little trading by the way, towards defraying the expense of these long journeys, but not so much as to distract their minds from their devotional duties, which must be most scrupulously observed. The opening of the Suez Canal has greatly increased the facility of reaching Mecca by water, and the English steamers engaged in this traffic find it very profitable. The sacred season at Mecca occurs usually in December or January, but the Arabian months being lunar, it varies from year to year.

The next day we were again invited on shore by Yusef Effendi and taken to the house of the Turkish Pasha, to whom we were duly presented. We were received with great politeness, but as he spoke only Turkish, our conversation had to be carried on through an interpreter. Arabic and Turkish are quite distinct languages; the latter being the dialect of the *Court*, is spoken only by the officials, who are all Turks; the former is the commonly spoken language of Arabia, and universally written and printed. I was introduced to the Governor as an " American Pasha and a great Traveler," and I know not with how many other titles Yusef magnified my importance. He was exceedingly civil, made room for me beside himself on the divan, ceremoniously presented to me some of his officers,

and ordered the inevitable "hubble-bubble" and coffee.
He then addressed me in some very complimentary
speeches, which I tried to answer in the same vein.

"A great traveler like yourself," he said, "who has been
all over the world and seen the wonders of China and India
as well as of Europe, must be a very wise and learned man."
I bowed, stroked my beard, and assuming a modest air replied, that "Allah grants wisdom to whom it pleases him,
sometimes more to those who stay at home" (here another
bow to his excellency,) "than to those who seek knowledge
in far countries."

I was obliged to decline his invitation to dine the next
day, on the plea that our ship was to sail in the morning.
The prospect of a few more such elaborate speeches was
too much for me, and with an apology for occupying so
much of his valuable time, we took a ceremonious leave.

Our next call was on the Prince, who was to be our
fellow passenger to Aden. We found him with his legs
curled up on a pile of soft Persian carpets, in the courtyard
of a large house, and surrounded by a dozen or more attendants. It is said that when the Queen's Embassador, Sir
Bartle Frere, was lately presented to the Sultan of Zanzibar, he was received by that shady monarch without rising.
But H. R. H. the Prince, pulled his bare feet from under
him, slipped them into richly embroidered sandals and
rose to shake hands as cordially as if I had been accredited
from President Grant. Then motioning me to be seated,
he called a very black negro, whom we came afterwards to
know as Mauritio, to act as interpreter. Prince Hammoud
is a pleasant looking fellow of about twenty-two years old,
with large, lustrous and beautiful eyes, (probably from his
mother) clear cut Asiatic features, and light coffee colored
complexion. He is quite fat, and looks lazy and good natured. His turban was of the gayest colors, his vest of

embroidered silk, and his *bernous* of blue cloth ornamented
with gold braid. An elegant silver mounted sword, of the
Damascus pattern, lay beside him on the divan. When it
was explained to him who we were, he seemed much

INTERVIEW WITH PRINCE HAMMOUD.

pleased, and we at once entered into conversation. As he
glanced at my guard chain rather curiously I took out my
watch, which he examined very carefully, then handed me
his own for my inspection. But nothing pleased him so
much as the half dozen card photographs which I call my
" family picture gallery," especially those of a very important little personage whom we know at home under the
familiar name of " Dumpling," and his mother. He called
his attendants around him to show these pictures, and
seemed incredulous of the relationship I claimed to young
D., although I pointed to my gray hair as proof.

I asked him by pantomine whether he had any children,

but he shook his head, and a shade of disappointment passed over his face. I then ventured to ask through the interpreter, how many wives he had. Mauritio looked shocked and declined to put the question. So my search for knowledge in that direction came to naught. A polite enquiry after the welfare of his harem would give mortal offense to a Mussulman, although he may be as proud and vain of his children as any Christian parent.

Leaving the Prince, after a pleasant interview, we went just outside the walls to see the Tomb of Eve, who, according to tradition, is buried here. When our first parents were cast out of paradise (which was located in the seventh Heaven,) they fell, Adam in the Island of Ceylon, and Eve in Arabia, near Jeddah. In stature they equalled the tallest palm tree, and the tomb of our great mother, which we see here, is sixty cubits long and twelve in width. They believe that after a separation of over two hundred years, Adam was, on his repentance, conducted by the angel Gabriel to a mountain near Mecca where he found his wife. The mountain is known to this day as *Arafat* ("Adam's Home,") and here they lived for many years as happily as could be expected under the circumstances.

To-day the pilgrims are coming on board in the native boats, bringing large quantities of baggage, and great rope-bound chests and bundles strew the deck like an emigrant ship from Holland. As they pass up the gangway ladder, the first officer takes possession of all their arms, consisting mostly of antique silver mounted swords and daggers, more for show than service, which some yield up with a bad grace. But this precaution is necessary to prevent trouble, and it is explained to them that their weapons will be returned when they leave the ship. We stand on the quarter deck watching the arrival of a large boat, in which are ten or twelve ladies, closely followed by another filled with luggage and servants. This is the Prince's family, and there is great curiosity to catch a glimpse of their faces. But their heads and forms are completely enveloped in folds of white cloth, and as they climb up the gangway and waddle across the deck to the ladies' cabin, we can see nothing to indicate whether they are beautiful as Houris or black as Erebus. But we notice as they shuffle along in clattering sandals, that their bare feet are guiltless of "balbriggans."

A row of sailors and firemen are curiously peeping over the ship's bulwarks. The captain scatters them with an angry (perhaps disappointed) growl,—" Get away there! didn't ye ever see a woman before ?"

The Prince himself with his grand vizier, who seems to be the Mentor in charge of the whole party, did not come on board until the next morning, just before we got under way. Besides the Zanzibar party, which consists of over sixty persons, including slaves and attendants, we have taken a wealthy pearl merchant with four ladies. They are bound to Busheer in Persia, and claim first class accommodations. A thick green curtain has been stretched across the after part of the main cabin, behind which they are to be located. But Abdul Azziz seems hard to please. The captain and Yusef assure him again and again, that his ladies will be quite secure from intrusion behind this screen. It is evident that he thinks his Persian " Lu-lus " to be " pearls of great price." In person Abdul is not attractive, having lost one eye, and in complexion he is quite dark. The curtains are carefully pinned together and secured, and at last he seems satisfied and immensely relieved when he has deposited behind them his precious parcels. It will hardly be safe for either of us to venture within ten feet of the curtain, unless we dare brave the scowl of that male dragon of a

Cyclops. So we leave him. "They may be young or old, dark or fair, we do not know nor do we care."

For three days we have now been quietly steaming down the Red Sea, since leaving Jeddah. The pilgrims, from prince to slave, have all become settled in their places. Most of the time is passed on deck, and the prince and I have become very good friends. He reads and writes Arabic, and has shown me his Koran elegantly bound in red morocco with clasps of gold, which he took from its silken case and touched reverently to his lips and forehead. But he would not permit me to handle it. He opened his trunks and displayed his treasures of jewelry, amber and pearl bracelets, etc., and boxes of perfumes of which all Orientals are very fond. He is quick to learn, and I have taught him to speak and write the numerals and several English words. Having seen Mr. F—— and myself play euchre, nothing would satisfy him until initiated into the mysteries of that fascinating American game. Last night at sunset when the *muezzin* called the faithful to prayers, Sayd Hammoud was playing his favorite game. At that moment a new deal had given him a "lone hand," right, left, and ace, so the line formed on deck with the *cadi* in front, facing towards Mecca, had to wait until the prince finished his game. I was showing him one day a small silk American flag. He took it and very deftly twisting it around my fez in the shape of a turban, exclaimed, "You Arab Americaine, go Zanzibar." But his invitation, afterwards several times renewed, I must decline. Familiarity has bred its proverbial result. It is of no use for him to urge that at Zanzibar I shall eat six times a day and soon grow as fat as himself. I have given him the photographs he admires so much, on which he has written his name and mine in Arabic, and with some beautiful coral ornaments as souvenirs, I shall have to say farewell to-morrow at Aden, to the good natured young Prince of Zanzibar.

Fifty miles above the entrance to the Indian Ocean, on the east coast, we pass within sight of the half deserted coffee city of Mocha. Its minarets glitter in the morning sun, and a few small native craft can be seen in the harbor, but it is no longer a place of commercial importance, the trade in its principal staple having been transferred to Aden.

The little British island of Perim, lies in the middle of the gateway at the entrance of the Red Sea. Here is a lighthouse and a fort, where a regiment of troops is stationed. This key which commands the gates is a rocky island some acres in extent, situated in mid channel, and we pass so near that a biscuit might be tossed from the high rock on board our steamer. The Suez canal being a French work, and Egypt under French influence, the seizure of Perim by the English was especially annoying to their neighbors. It happened in this wise : The French emperor had determined to take possession of the little island, and despatched a fleet for that purpose, which put into Aden for coal. The governor of course invited the French admiral and his officers to dinner, and regaled them with unexceptionable champagne. In the course of the evening some of the junior officers " let on " that they were bound to Perim. The shrewd old governor penciled a note to the harbor-master to delay the coaling of the French ships ; and the same night two British men-of-war left Aden and started up the coast. The next day after a ceremonious leave-taking and courteous farewell to their British hosts, the French fleet sailed for Perim. But when they arrived, to their great mortification and chagrin they found the British flag flying, and a great show of guns in position. Whether they put into Aden on their return, history does not say.

# CHAPTER XI.

## MAHOMET AND HIS RELIGION.

A Tempting Proposal, but Declined for the Present—Mecca, Mahomet's Birth-place—Medina, his Tomb—His Coffin Rests upon the Earth—The Descendants of Ishmael—Their Plea for Robbery—Traditions of Mecca—A Stone from Paradise—Early Life of Mahomet—His First Convert—Persecution and Flight—The Hegira—His Religion Enforced with the Sword—Its Rapid Spread Over the East—The Doctrines of the Koran——Its Sensual Teachings—"Bismillah"—Moral Precepts and Religious Duties—Practices and Ceremonies—The First Temperance Reformer—The Hadji's Prayer—A Dress Parade—Persian Poem—The Pearl Merchant—The Prince and the Howadji.

HILE I was at Jeddah, my friend, Yusef Effendi, to whom I am indebted for much information about the *hadjis*, or pilgrims, offered on my return to go with me to Mecca. His plan was to make the journey on horseback by night, and he assured me that if I assumed a Turkish or Arab dress, we could penetrate to the sacred *Caaba* itself, without detection. My complexion, which, thanks to an African sun, was assuming a rich mahogany color, would render the disguise quite easy—presuming, of course, that I should keep my mouth shut—and, besides, he urged, if any difficulty should occur, the influence of the wealthy old patriarch, Mohamet Benaji, would save me from harm.

This proposal, though rather startling at first, had its attractions, in view of the fact that, so far as I know, no American has ever penetrated to the holy city, although it has been visited and described by several European travelers, disguised as *dervishes*. And then, I must confess a fondness for adventure, (how else should I now be on my way to Bagdad?) and here was just enough of danger to give a charm to his scheme. So, without positively declining, I left the matter open for future consideration.

But I ought not to pass within a few miles of Mecca, the birth-place of one of the most remarkable men who ever lived, without giving a short sketch of his history, and the peculiarities of the religion he founded, which at one period seemed destined to over-run all Europe and extinguish Christianity. It may seem a strange incongruity that any educated, intelligent man can be a Mahometan. But I have met several such persons, and made the acquaintance, among others at Cairo, of Ali Hassan Effendi, to whom I am indebted for much information about the manners and customs of Mahometans. He was born in Egypt, and was sent when ten years old to England and educated at King's College, London. He speaks and writes English perhaps better than myself, is well read in ancient and modern history, as well as the current literature of the day, wears a dress all European except the fez—and it is difficult to realize that such a man believes the religion of the "false prophet," about which he discoursed without the least reserve, and defended with arguments to me quite novel. But I soon found that he no more believed the absurd superstitions of the ignorant Arabs, than an educated Protestant can receive as authentic the stories of miracles performed by relics of the saints.

It is a common but erroneous impression that Mahomet was buried at Mecca. His tomb is at Medina, a large city about two hundred miles to the north. It is held as a place of pilgrimage second only to Mecca, and its appearance was described to me with great exactness by a *hadji* who has been there. The absurd story of Mahomet's coffin being suspended between heaven and earth is, of course, a myth.

The Arabians claim to be one of the most ancient of peoples, their writers tracing their genealogy back to Noah. The wild tribes of the desert are descendants of Ishmael, the son of Abraham and Hagar. They excuse themselves for the frequent robberies of travelers and merchants, by alleging the hard usage of their father Ishmael, who, being turned out of doors by Abraham, had the open plains and deserts given him by God for his patrimony, with permission to take whatever he could find there. They therefore claim the right of levying contributions, not only on the descendants of Isaac, but on everybody else who comes in their way. Among themselves, however, they are strictly honest, and in tents and houses, where things are left open, theft is almost unknown.

Long before the time of Mahomet, the Arabians went in pilgrimage to Mecca to celebrate the memory of Abraham and Ishmael. But this was only a custom. In the Koran, Mahomet enjoined as a precept the journey to Mecca, and prescribes the religious ceremonies connected with it. In the center of that city is the holy temple called the *Caaba*, built by Abraham, and the burial-place of Ishmael. There are many curious traditions about this temple, one being that it was built by Adam after his expulsion from paradise, and modeled after one he had seen there—and in the last days of the world the Ethiopians will come and demolish it. Within the building is a celebrated black stone, set in silver, which is kissed with the greatest devotion by all pilgrims, and called by some, the "Right Hand of God on Earth." The fable is, that it is one of the precious stones of Paradise, and fell to the earth with Adam,—that it was saved at the deluge by the angel Gabriel, and by him brought back to Abraham when he was rebuilding the *Caaba*. On it the patriarch stood, and it rose and fell, a sort of moveable scaffold, as he was raising the walls. This stone was originally whiter than snow, but from the kisses of so many people, assuming the sins of mankind, it has become black. All pilgrims shave their heads at Mecca, leaving only a little tuft of hair on the crown, by which the Prophet is to lift them up into paradise. A part of the ceremonies, as prescribed in the Koran, is running a certain number of times around the *Caaba*,—sometimes stopping and looking about as if one had lost something, to represent Hagar seeking water for her son. Silly and ridiculous as many of these ceremonies are, they are no worse than one sees among the Christian *hadjis* at Jerusalem: and Mecca has this advantage, that the rival sects among Mahometans never quarrel or come to blows within their holy city.

That Mahomet was a man of no ordinary ability cannot be denied, but historians differ widely as to his character. Partial writers of his own faith are enthusiastic in praising his religious and moral virtues, his piety, justice, liberality, humility, and abstinence. His charity, they say, was so great that he seldom had any money in his house, hardly enough to support his family,—that God having offered him the keys to the treasures of the earth he refused to accept them.

On the other hand, the sudden spread of Mahometanism,

and the destruction of the Eastern Churches, once so flourishing, have inspired such a horror among the old Christian writers of this religion, that they represent the character of its founder and his doctrines in the most infamous light. Perhaps in no period in the world's history was such an opportunity as the seventh century offered to Mahomet. The great Italian politician has said : " without opportunities, it is impossible for any person to make himself a prince or found a State." At that period, the pure and simple religion of Christ had become confounded with the worst superstitions. Both Eastern and Western Churches were torn to pieces by disputes on points of doctrine. Emperors and bishops were ready to condemn a man to death for a slight difference in religious opinion, and according to some writers, Mahomet was raised up by God, to be a scourge to the Christian churches for not living true to the holy religion they had received from their divine Master. At that time, the divinity of the Virgin Mary was believed in by many so-called Christians, and she was worshiped as God. This was specially condemned in the Koran as idolatry, and gave Mahomet a pretext to attack the Trinity itself. His professed object in establishing a new religion was to restore the true and ancient worship of the One God, as professed by Adam, Noah, Abraham, Moses, and Jesus,—all of whom he calls prophets, himself being the last and the complement of divine revelation.

His father was a merchant, who died leaving his wife and infant son with no possessions but five camels and a black slave. He was reared by his grandfather, and as a merchant traveled all through Arabia, acquainting himself with the state of society, religious and political. His success in business, and his marriage to a rich widow, soon made him very wealthy, but he was forty years old before he promulgated his scheme of founding a new religion. His wife was his first convert, to whom he announced that the angel Gabriel had appeared to him, and told him that he was appointed the Apostle of God. Khedjah, like a sensible wife, had great faith in her husband, and received the news with great joy. Other relatives soon became his proselytes, among them his nephew Ali, afterwards his son-in-law and successor. But when he began to preach his mission in public he was bitterly persecuted and denounced. In the twelfth year of his career as a prophet, his enemies had become so powerful that they made Mecca too uncomfortable for him, and by the light of the " stars and the crescent moon " he fled to a cave in the mountains, from whence he afterwards escaped to Medina, where he had many adherents. This flight, or *hegira*, is the date of the Mahometan era, about 1250 years ago.

Assuming that Mahomet was sincere at the commencement of his career, persecution, which usually advances rather than obstructs the spreading of any new religion, had now made him a fanatic. He wisely had never professed to perform miracles, but he now announced that the angel Gabriel had taken him in a single night to Jerusalem, and thence to Heaven, where he had a special revelation from God. This absurd story, suggested perhaps by the account of Moses, was well received by his disciples, and added immensely to his reputation and influence. Up to this time he had used only persuasion to propagate his new doctrines ; but now, embittered by persecution, he announced that God had given him permission to defend himself against the infidels, and extend the true religion by force of arms.

One of the most convincing proofs that Mahomet was an imposter, and the doctrines he taught a human invention, is the fact that for its progress it was indebted almost entirely to the sword, while the divine origin of Christianity has enabled it to prevail against all the powers of the world, by its own inherent truth. At the head of a large army of fanatical followers, to whom he promised immediate entrance to paradise if they fell in battle, he returned and captured Mecca. So rapidly did his religion spread, that at his death, which occurred six years after, all Arabia, from the Persian Gulf to the Mediterranean, and from Egypt to Persia, had submitted to his authority. Ali, who was married to his favorite daughter, Fatima, conquered Egypt and Persia, and at the close of the fourteenth century, the Mahometan empire had extended over India and all northern Africa, had conquered Constantinople, and, crossing the Bosphorus, was only checked under the walls of Vienna; while from the west, Europe was threatened by the Moors, who had crossed the Mediterranean, and occupied the most fertile provinces of the Spanish peninsula.

To describe, other than very briefly, the peculiar doctrines of the Koran, will require too much space. This book, which to a Mahometan is much more sacred than the Bible to Christians, is made up of a series of revelations, professedly received by the prophet from the angel Gabriel, from time to time, as suited the exigency of the occasion. Each chapter commences with the word " *Bismillah*," " In the name of the most merciful God." And to this day you never enter a pious Moslem's house, partake of food, or accept the slightest service, without the invariable greeting of " *Bismillah*." In Bagdad, I was once following a European through a very muddy street, picking our way close to the wall, when we came plump upon a native; my friend halted, and motioned to the man to get out of the way. This he declined to do, but with a graceful *salaam* he pointed to the mud and ejaculated, " In the name of the most merciful God, take the mud yourself."

The Koran not only prescribes all the doctrines relating to faith and religious duties, but contains also a complete code upon which is based the civil law of all Mahometan countries. It varies but slightly from the Mosaic code, in all that relates to marriage, divorce, and inheritance. It acknowledges the divine authority of the Pentateuch, Psalms, and Gospel, but Mahomet claimed that these books had undergone so many alterations and corruptions, that no credit should be given to the present copies in the hands of Jews or Christians ; that the true versions contained many passages concerning himself, which have been suppressed; and the revelations of God through him, in the Koran, being the " seal of the prophets," no more are to be expected to the end of the world.

The great doctrine of the Koran is the Unity of God, to restore the worship of whom, Mahomet professed was the chief end of his mission. Its style is usually beautiful and fluent, especially where it imitates the prophetic manner and Scripture phrases. It abounds in bold figures after the Eastern taste, and some passages describing the majesty and attributes of God, are really grand. It teaches resurrection and judgment; and the torments of hell, as well as the delights of paradise, are minutely described in all the glory of Oriental imagery. The poor are to enter paradise, five hundred years before the rich, and the prophet says that when he took a look into paradise, he saw the majority there to be the poor on earth.

It is difficult to convey to the common mind the idea of spiritual pleasures, without the use of sensible objects. This was especially true in the early ages, and the Scriptures describe the mansion of the blessed as a glorious city, with streets and gates of gold and precious stones. But

TAN–J

the Bible has no intimation even of the sensual delights of the Mahometan paradise, so minutely described in the Koran, inflaming the imaginations of these Eastern people, who are more given to the pleasures of sense, than the cooler blooded nations of the West. The law of predestination, that whatever is to happen has been fixed by God's irrevocable decree, was used in the Koran to urge his followers to fight without fear and with desperation. This idea of fatalism is so characteristic of Mahometan minds, that it stands in the way of all progress or enterprise.

The common idea, that Mahomet allowed an unbounded plurality of wives, is a mistake. The Koran expressly limits the number to four, and adds the very sensible advice, " if a man shall apprehend any inconvenience from so many as that, he shall marry one only." In Mahomet's time, unlimited polygamy was common among the Arabians, so that this feature of his religion offered no attraction to the sensualist to join his ranks, as Mormonism has done in a later and more civilized age. The use of wine, and all games of chance, are specially forbidden, and the Koran put an end to the inhuman custom, then practised among the Arabs, of burying their daughters alive, to be freed from the expense of providing for them. Resignation to the will of God, charity, honesty, hospitality, fasting and prayer, are enjoined in many parts of the Koran. This last was taught as so necessary a duty, that Mahomet calls prayer the " pillar of religion and the key to paradise." In another place he says, "there can be no good in that religion wherein is no prayer." Five times a day his followers are called upon to pray—in the morning before sunrise, at noon, in the afternoon, at sunset, and before retiring at night; and during these devotions, the face must be turned towards the sacred *Caaba* at Mecca. Nor is the mere outward observance of these forms of any avail, if performed without due attention, reverence, and devotion. On such occasions, sumptuous apparel and costly ornaments must be laid aside. The women are not allowed to pray in the mosques at the same time with the men, lest their presence should distract the minds of the devout from the worship of God. Before prayer, every Moslem must wash his face, hands, and feet, or if so situated that water cannot be had, as in the desert, he is permitted to use clean, dry sand. In a hot climate, frequent ablution is conducive to health, and Mahomet was wise in making the free use of water so important a religious observance.

I might go on and describe the religion of the " false prophet of Mecca" at much greater length, but I fear that my imperfect sketch has already occupied too much of the space that I should have devoted to personal observations and incidents of travel. My only apology is, that, although this subject is familiar to scholars and theologians, the great mass of the people have no definite ideas as to what Mahomet taught, and the religious observances of his followers, and as this journey is through Moslem countries, some scenes hereafter to be described, may, perhaps, be the more intelligible to the reader.

My experience among the *Hadjis* at Jeddah, and on our steamer, has made me so familiar with the outward forms of their religious exercises, that I shall need but little instruction, if I should accept Yusef Effendi's proposal to visit Mecca. Being on the pilgrimage, they are very strict in their ablutions, prayers, and prostrations. During the day they are scattered over the deck, and spend their time in eating, smoking, sleeping, and reading the Koran. At the stated hours of prayer, we hear the shrill call of the *muezzin*, who is perched on the highest point of the forecastle, instead of his usual place in the gallery of a min-

aret. Then all is bustle and confusion. The sleepers
awake and rub their eyes, *chibouks* are laid aside, water is
drawn from the side of the ship for ablution, and here on
the quarter deck where the *quality* is located, it is poured
by the slaves over the hands of their masters. I should
not call these black servants *slaves*, for having been to
Mecca, by the Mahometan law they have become free.
Having combed their beards, and made their toilets, each
one spreads before him a clean mat or carpet, kept for this
purpose. The Prince has laid aside his richly embroidered
robe,—for before God, prince and peasant are alike,—and
they range themselves in line with faces towards Mecca.
The *moollah*, or class leader, stands a few feet in front,
and all being ready, what we irreverently term the " squad
drill" commences. They do not mind in the least our
watching their performances, but seem rather proud, than
ashamed of their religious exercises. The " dress parade"
at sunset is the most showy affair, and if any prayer has
been omitted during the day, it is now made up. First
each man strokes down his face and beard a few times, and
holds his open hands before his eyes, thereby seeming to
shut out the world from his thoughts, and exactly follows
the *moollah* in all his motions. Then with closed eyes
and every appearance of devotion, he repeats in a low
voice, the prescribed formula of prayer. This is the first
chapter of the Koran, and answers to the Lord's Prayer
among Christians. In it the words " There is no God
but God, and Mahomet is his prophet" frequently occurs.
It is first said standing erect, then stooping forward with
the hands resting on the knees ; the third position is upon
all fours, with the forehead touching the ground, and resting upon a small piece of stone brought from Mecca.
Then sitting up, they say a shorter prayer, which they repeat with their heads again on the ground. This perform-

ance occupies about fifteen minutes, and then all rise to their feet, open their eyes and look about with a complaisant air, as if they had done their duty, and would be entitled to a record therefor in the world to come. Some

MAHOMETAN AT PRAYER.

very devout ones, and others who have been remiss during the day, go through the same programme two or three times in succession. The less reverent drop out from the ranks, carefully roll up their carpets, resume their *chibouks*, and settle down for a pleasant chat among themselves, or with the *Howadji*, who has been a curious spectator of the scene.

They usually retire early, but one bright moonlight night, a party of Persians collected on the quarter deck, and one of their number recited in a musical voice a long poem in blank verse. It was described to us as a " love story," and from the frequent peals of laughter, must have been full of humorous passages which were highly enjoyed by the auditors. The pearl merchant, Abdul Azziz, seems to be the chief Sheik among the Persians—but, poor fellow, the responsibility of his harem, behind the green curtains in the after cabin, causes him great care and anxiety. He is constantly running below, scolding the attendants, or peeping from the deck through the skylight which commands a view of the cabin. The Prince, on the other hand, jolly and fat, takes the world easy. With his grand vizier he sleeps in the room opposite mine, with doors wide open, and quite neglects the ladies of his suite, who are shut up in the ladies' cabin. He sleeps soundly too— thanks to a clear conscience and good digestion. Listening to his loud breathing, the *Howadji* lies awake through the long watches of the sultry night, and his thoughts wander across the two oceans that separate him from the dear ones at home.

# CHAPTER XII.

## ADEN.

S we steam into the land-
locked harbor of Aden, over
which tower high volcanic
mountains, their rocky sides
unrelieved so far as the eye
can reach, by a single green
tree or a blade of grass, we notice the flags at half mast, and
a steamer just arrived from
Zanzibar, in naval mourning,
viz: a light blue streak along
her sides, and a broad band
of the same color around her
funnel. She has on board
the remains of one of the most famous travelers and explorers of modern times, the lamented Dr. Livingstone, on
their way home to be placed at rest in Westminster Abbey,

beside the dust of England's greatest warriors, statesmen, and scholars.

Lieut. Murphey, of the Royal Artillery, who was one of the party that had penetrated for his relief, as far as Unyanyembe, and there met the Doctor's faithful servants with his dead body, has come thus far, and now returns to Zanzibar.

As soon as our anchor was down I went on board the "Calcutta," where I had a very interesting interview with his faithful and devoted servant, Jacob, a "Nassick boy" who has been under the tuition of the English missionaries at Zanzibar, and can speak and write English. He is very black, with short curly hair, intelligent and very communicative. He goes on with the body to England. He has kept a diary of all the events connected with the Doctor's death, and of his adventures on his way to the coast, which have been published.

Dr. Livingstone died in May, and Jacob says that they were afraid if they did not bring away his body they might be accused of killing him. They had a small quantity of spirits and some salt, and Jacob used these in preparing the body for its last long journey. They packed it in the bark of a tree, and for over seven months toiled through a wilderness of jungle, and past many hostile tribes to Unyanyembe. From here they were two months more on their way to Zanzibar.

In passing through the territory of some powerful chief, he told me they were stopped, and a large sum of money demanded as a ransom. This they did not have, and for a time he was in despair. At last he got away by stratagem. Pretending to bury the body with great ceremony, they secretly took it out from its case of bark, and repacked it like a bale of goods.

The toils and hardships they passed through would fill

a volume. Two large cases, containing the Doctor's papers and charts, accompany the body to England. Jacob entirely confirms Stanley's account of meeting Dr. Livingstone, and sets at rest all controversy on that point. His account of the Doctor's death was most touching, and the tears which came to his eyes, showed how devotedly he was attached to his master. His own efforts and labors were told in a modest, unassuming manner, and I was much prepossessed in his favor. He will doubtless be made much of when he reaches England. The mail steamer left the next day for Suez, with the remains of one of England's bravest sons, faithfully guarded by his devoted servant.

Aden, the great half-way coaling station between the Mediterranean and India, is situated on a peninsula that juts out from the Arabian coast, and in appearance, is the most desolate, barren, and forbidding place, that it is possible to conceive of. Naked cliffs and volcanic ridges surround it on every side—some rising to the height of eighteen hundred feet—while forts mounting heavy guns, crown every peak, and water batteries command every part of the harbor and its entrance. Six years ago, during the Abyssinian war, Aden was the base of supplies for the English troops operating against King Theodore. Then the harbor was full of ships-of-war and transports. Annesley bay, where the British disembarked to march against Abyssinia, is about three hundred miles up the coast, full of small, rocky islands, and very difficult and dangerous of access. At Aden, there are daily arrivals and departures of steamers, plying through the Suez canal between Europe and India and China. It is ninety-six miles from here to the entrance of the Red Sea, and this lonely, barren rock, this treeless, grassless, black ruin, which can most expressively be described as "Hell with the fires put out," where not a

10

drop of fresh water can be had, except that which is caught
from the clouds or condensed from the sea, is growing into
a busy town, with a population of thirty thousand people.
A score of small native craft are in the inner harbor, and
anchored around us are five or six large steamers, and
as many sailing ships.

Besides its importance as a coaling station, Aden has
secured to itself the export trade in Mocha coffee, amount-
ing to twenty thousand tons a year.

Notwithstanding its desolate and oven-like appearance,
this place is said to be quite healthy from October to April.
If the " fires are put out" during the winter months, the
terrific, scorching heat of summer, must give the inhabitants a foretaste of the lower regions with the fires at full
blast.

Aden is very strongly fortified, and cannon bristle from
every point commanding the harbor. It has been held by
the English about thirty-five years, and its importance has
increased immensely since the new route to the East was
opened across the isthmus. Half way between Europe and
India, every steamer here replenishes its supply of fuel,
and from its position, it commands the Red Sea trade, as
Gibraltar does the Mediterranean. The warlike tribes on
the neighboring coast, have several times attacked the place,
but for the past ten years, their chiefs have rested quiet,
with the annual stipend allowed them by the British Government. The garrison consists of one European and
two native regiments of Sepoys from India.

Our steamer is soon surrounded by a fleet of tiny boats,
or "dugouts," each containing a shining little Arab, in
most primitive toilet, who clamors for the privilege of diving for any coin we may throw into the water. They seem
more than half amphibious, and as they slip in and out
their canoes, diving and sporting in the clear sea, their

smooth, glossy black skins, remind us of a school of porpoises.  We throw them a bright sixpence, and a dozen at
once go for it.  We see them kicking and struggling deep
under water, then the victor rises to the surface with a grin,
shows the coveted coin between his teeth, and shakes his
woolly head like a spaniel.  Other boats contain the dealers in ostrich feathers, red coral and curious shells.  These
are mostly sharp fellows, and if they do not sell their own
wares, are sure to steal whatever they can lay their hands
on.  They are not allowed to come on board, but sometimes
will smuggle themselves up the ladder, and if discovered,
the sailors take great delight in  playing upon them with
the hose, or unceremoniously pitching them, feathers and
all, into the sea.

OSTRICH FEATHER DEALERS AT ADEN.

We  spend  the  days  on  shore  but  find  it  more  comfortable  to sleep at night on the ship.  At the landing we

are surrounded by a crowd of *gamins*, real street Arabs, who follow us everywhere, clamoring for *baksheesh*,—offering to procure for us a carriage, or donkey, or to get up a fight for our amusement. Words being of no avail, we have to use our sticks freely, to keep them off, but nothing daunted, they follow us at a little distance, watching their opportunity. We sit down for a moment, to rest in the shade, and one comes up stealthily behind and commences fanning me with a *punkah*. This delicate attention meets its reward, and the *baksheesh* is won. There is said to be over five hundred of these little fellows in Aden, from ten to fifteen years old, who come from the neighboring tribe of *Abdalees*, on the mainland. They have a community of their own, and live upon a small rocky island in the harbor, or in caves on the mountain side.

Along the *bund* facing the water, are immense piles of coal, several large stores and warehouses, and two hotels. The most important personage here, is a Parsee merchant, Cowasjee Dinshaw. He is the agent of several lines of steamers, and the broad veranda in front of his place, is a general rendezvous for strangers. His warehouse is crammed with a most varied and heterogeneous stock of merchandise. It is a "variety store" and "curiosity shop" combined. Japan, China, India, France, Germany, and England, all are represented on his shelves, and there, too, can be found Cleveland petroleum and Connecticut clocks. He will fill your order for anything you may desire, from an elephant to a paper of pins, only you must expect to pay handsomely for whatever you buy of "Old Cowasjee."

This is called the "Harbor Landing;" the town and cantonments of the troops are situated in a hollow among the volcanic hills five miles away.

From the many dilapidated vehicles at the landing, we

selected the most promising one, but it had evidently
served out its full term in some European city before being
transported to another continent.   The horse was wild and
half broken, the harness supplemented with pieces of rope,
and the native driver seemed in keeping with the establishment.   I must, however, do him the justice to say that whatever he may have lacked in wearing apparel, he was not
wanting in activity and energy.   He rode sometimes on the
shafts and sometimes on a seat perched in front of the vehicle—and was continually jumping off to run alongside,

DOWN GRADE.

and urge the horse to greater speed.   He always rode up
the hills, but when we came to a steep descent, he would
jump off and help hold back the carriage.   We noticed
that the vicious beast at such times, laid back his ears, as
if not satisfied with the hold-back arrangements, and
seemed inclined to throw his heels in the air, which would
not be pleasant to a driver directly in the rear.

The road was hard and smooth, and for two miles wound along the shore, then turning inland with many sharp curves, through ravines and round the base of high cliffs, on which not a particle of vegetable life could be seen. The scenery was unique and grand, but the very picture of desolation. We were in high spirits, like a couple of sailors taking a run ashore, after a long sea voyage. We met long trains of camels, some laden with bags of " Mocha," others carrying goat skins of water, from a small stream fifteen miles away on the main land.

These ungainly beasts, with crane-like necks and awkward gait, plodding along in single file, each one surmounted with a black urchin, perched high in the air, were in strong contrast with the little donkeys, scarcely bigger than a Newfoundland dog, and carrying burdens larger than themselves, or mounted by natives whose feet dangled to the ground. The people here, are of every race known in the East, and we met one unmistakable " Johnny" with pig-tail and slanting almond eyes, who told me in " pigeon English" that he was cook on a steamer in the harbor. But most of the natives we met, were Abyssinians, very black, with Asiatic, not negro, features, and hair cultivated in long corkscrew curls, sticking out in all directions, and by the application of lime, faded out from black to a dingy brown. These shock heads, in which both sexes seem to take great pride, were not unlike the prevailing style of young girls' hair at home. The appearance of the women was by no means attractive. All wore enormous silver ear ornaments and nose rings, strings of glass beads, and anklets and armlets, more massive than ornamental. One couple especially attracted our attention. They were gotten up in the most exquisite style of Abyssinian art, especially the young woman, and seemed to create quite a sensation on the road. She was profusely decorated, and wore in her nose a large ring with the three pearls, indicating that she was a bride. Her " fellar's" wool, originally black, had been colored to a dingy blonde, and was elaborately curled until it would fill a half bushel measure. The lady rode a donkey, and the groom walked by her side (barefooted, of course), and so absorbed were they in each other, that we drove slowly by and stared at them, without attracting their notice.

The entrance to the town is through a deep gorge, where for a space of one hundred yards the walls rise from eighty to one hundred feet in height, on each side. A massive gateway and cannon, guard the entrance, and a squad of native soldiers in red coats (Sikhs from India), presented arms as we passed. Emerging from the narrow ravine, the town was before us, occupying a basin about a mile in diameter, evidently the crater of an extinct volcano. A circle of jagged peaks surround it, some of them covered with forts and batteries. Several regiments of troops are quartered here in airy stone cantonments, forming a large fort in the center of the town.

The most curious feature in Aden is the tanks or reservoirs, for supplying the town with water. The fall of rain is very slight, sometimes not a drop for three or four years. There are no springs, and the nearest fresh water on the mainland, is fifteen miles off. These magnificent cisterns, date back to the sixth century, and as originally constructed, had a capacity of over thirty million gallons. They are excavated in part out of the solid rock, and lined with a hard white cement, having the appearance of marble. When the British took possession of Aden, they were in ruins and filled with rubbish. Within the last fifteen years, a large sum has been expended on their restoration, and they are now capable, when filled, of supplying the town for over a year. It is very difficult to give a description of these great works, intelligible to one who has never seen them. The range of hills forming the walls of the crater, is nearly circular, the inner side of these hills is very steep, but the descent is broken by a large plateau, about midway between the summit, and the sea level. This table land is intersected by numerous ravines, nearly all of which converge into one valley, which thus receives the drainage of a large area. The steepness of the hills, the hardness of the rocks, and the lack of soil upon them, prevent any great amount of absorption, and a moderate fall of rain sends a tremendous torrent of water down the valley; and here the reservoirs are built. They are very fantastic in their shape, which is made to conform with the natural walls of rock on either side. Some are built like dykes, across the gorge of the valley, and every feature of the adjacent rocks is taken advantage of. The overflow from each is conducted into the succeeding one, and a complete chain is thus formed, reaching to the very heart of the town. The edges of these great basins are protected by iron railings, and stone steps lead from one level to the next. Everything about them is kept scrupulously clean, and the glare of the mid-day sun upon these white walls was exceedingly painful to the eyes. When I was here three years ago, they were nearly full, but now they contain very little water, which is not surprising, as it has not rained during all that time. The British government, which never does anything in the way of public works by halves, not satisfied with expending an immense amount of money on these great cisterns, has also constructed large condensing works, by which the sea water is rendered fit for use, and is now building an aqueduct to convey the water from the main land to the town.

From the tanks, we drove through the bazaars, which are very filthy and mean, with more gew-gaws of European manufacture than native goods. The specialties of Aden are ostrich and marabout feathers, ostrich eggs, leopard and lion skins ; which we found very cheap.

We have spent some days at Aden, and said good-bye to the Prince with many expressions of regret. At parting he repeated his offer of hospitality at Zanzibar, with six or any number of meals a day, not to be eaten with the fingers after the native style, but with knives and forks and other civilized appliances.

But Zanzibar even with these attractions must be declined, for it is close under the equator and the climate is too hot for a summer campaign.

While here we called by invitation on the English officers of the " Artillery Mess," whose bronzed faces showed long service in the East. Here, as in India, the visitor is always welcomed with a " peg," which means brandy and soda, and a *peg* it has proved in the coffin of many a poor fellow who has measured his length in a foreign soil, before the expiration of his seven years service, which would entitle him to a furlough home.

# CHAPTER XIII.

## ON THE ARABIAN SEA.

 E are not sorry when the "Gunga" leaves behind her these desolate peaks, and turns her prow to the northeast, for a long stretch of thirteen hundred miles across the Arabian Sea towards Muscat. The monotony of our life at sea is unvaried by storm or rough weather. All day we watch the flying fish, or peer through the glass at a faint line of smoke far away on the horizon, which betokens a passing steamer. One morning the captain called our attention to a "Yankee sea serpent." Crossing our bow, half a mile off, was a long procession of benetas, a large black fish. At regular intervals, they leaped a few feet above the water in graceful curves, which might easily be mistaken for the long folds of that fabulous sea monster.

At night we lean for hours over the rail, watching the schools of porpoises that sport around us, darting through the phosphorescent sea like streaks of silver.

After six days steadily steaming, with no land in sight, we approached the coast of Muscat. This is a province in Arabia, ruled by an independent Sultan or King, and extending several hundred miles along the coast, and inland an indefinite distance, depending upon the ability of the Sultan to enforce his authority over the wild and restless tribes of the interior. Under the late Sultan, Zanzibar and Muscat were united in one kingdom, but at his death, the two elder sons divided these provinces between them. Our young prince, Sayd Hammoud, is their brother. The city of Muscat has about sixty thousand inhabitants, and presents a very picturesque appearance when approached from the sea. The coast line is bold and rocky. We sail close in shore, passing several lofty headlands,—on one of which is a dilapidated fort,—and suddenly the town opens to view at the bottom of a deep cove, the houses built along the beach, with a background of precipitous rocks, and so close to the water, that the sea washes against them at high tide. In front of the town the shipping lies at anchor, and on every peak and crag, are formidable-looking forts, mounting iron guns of small calibre, over which flies the red flag of Muscat.

The Portugese held this place for one hundred and fifty years, and their commerce made it a very important port. They built these fortifications—some of them perched upon the summit of almost inaccessible cliffs—according to the best military experience of their day. But in 1648 they were expelled from all their possessions in Arabia, by a simultaneous revolution among the Arabs.

As our stay here will be short, we hasten to go on shore and see the town. The boats are long and narrow, shaped like an Indian canoe, and almost as easily upset. We sit flat on the bottom, and, holding on to the sides with both hands, are quickly propelled by paddles shaped like mustard spoons, to the landing place. Here we find a native guide who speaks a little English, and we follow him through narrow crooked streets to the British Consulate, where I post a letter for home. It must travel over ten thousand miles, and be two months on the way ; and I feel somewhat doubtful whether it will ever reach its destination. He then leads us through the bazaars, unpaved, very crooked and dirty, that remind me of a Chinese city. They are scarcely four feet wide, and the shops are crowded with all sorts of merchandise, among which I recognize articles of Yankee manufacture. Muscat is the only port in this part of the world, that has any trade with America. Three or four sailing ships come here every year, touching at Zanzibar, and return laden with coffee, dates, ivory, and gums. In front of the market place is the Sultan's palace, and we step inside the gate, where a magnificent African lion is pacing up and down his wooden cage. Lounging around the court yard, we see about a hundred soldiers— and such soldiers !—no attempt at uniform, some armed with matchlocks, some with single or double barreled shot guns, and others with long spears. Hanging against the palace walls, are round, antique looking bucklers or shields, which are carried upon the left arm. The Sultan, though nominally an independent prince, with whom England and other European countries have treaties, is in reality but a dependent of Great Britain, and protected by that power. Two English gunboats are now in port, having just returned from an expedition down the coast, some fifty miles, where, at his request, they knocked to pieces a strong fort held by some of his rebellious subjects, whom he was unable to subdue. Political matters are just now in a very

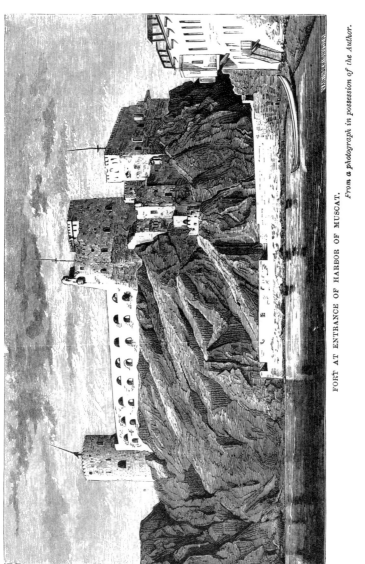

FORT AT ENTRANCE OF HARBOR OF MUSCAT.

*From a photograph in possession of the Author.*

unsettled condition in Muscat, and the lives and property
of the natives are so insecure, that trade is deserting the
place. To assassinate a Grand Vizier is no uncommon
occurrence, and everybody seems armed. Even the fruit
seller of whom we bought some dates, wore in his belt an
ugly looking, crooked sword called a *creese*. We saw lounging through the streets, many dark skinned, wild looking
Arabs, with fierce, restless eyes, long black hair, and
armed with swords and matchlocks. Their lithe forms
and savage looks, reminded me of a tiger, who would be a
far less dangerous animal to meet alone in the desert.
These are Bedouins belonging to the wild tribes in the
interior. We are told, that the Sultan rarely dares show
himself outside the palace walls, for fear of being assas-

SWORD AUCTIONEER AT MUSCAT.

sinated. Uneasy must rest the head that wears the crown
of Muscat.

While in the bazaar, we witnessed a novel auction sale.
A man came along singing at the top of his voice the
praises of an old, but very handsome sword, the scabbard
and hilt richly ornamented with silver and gold.   It was
a curious and valuable relic, and I wanted very much
to add it to my collection of weapons.   The highest bid
so far was sixty-four rupees—about thirty dollars.   The
auctioneer will carry it around in this way for three days,
and our guide said it would probably sell for one hundred
rupees.   These Eastern people are very fond of showy
weapons, and great sums are lavished on swords and
daggers, which are ostentatiously worn, not so much for
use as ornament, and as marks of rank and distinction.
They are handed down as heirlooms, and will only be
parted with in case of urgent necessity.

On our way back to the landing we passed one of the
forts which looked so formidable at a distance.   A nearer
view showed it to be much dilapidated, and the guns old
and rusty.   Workmen were busy patching up the holes
made by shot at a recent bombardment.   There is a Portuguese inscription over the inner gate, and the date 1588.
Not wishing to tarry after dark within the town, we called
our boatman and were quickly paddled back to the steamer,
passing close to an old thirty-six gun frigate, and some
armed *bugalahs*, which comprise the Muscat squadron.

From this place our course is to the entrance of the Persian Gulf, through a narrow strait, and past many high
rocky islands, on one of which is the grave of Captain Baffin,
the English navigator, who gave his name to a bay in the
North Atlantic.   We pass the island of Ormus, just as the
sun is setting behind its rocky hills, lighting them up with
a glow of gold and sapphire.

This is the " Ormus and Ind," whose wealth was once
proverbial.   In olden times a very rich and populous city

stood upon the plain between the hills and the sea. It commanded the richest commerce of the world, from India up the Persian Gulf and the Euphrates. The ruins of a strong Portuguese fort, and a population of four hundred fishermen, living in mat huts, are all that remain to mark the spot.

We approached the town of Bundar Abbas by moon-light, and signaled with rockets for boats to take off the native passengers and freight. This place was once of great commercial importance, and the remains of large European warehouses are yet to be seen. It is defended by a wall with towers at regular intervals, and has now a population of about twelve thousand. The only foreign resident is the agent of the " British India Company," to whom our steamer is consigned. He seemed heartily glad to meet English faces ; to him the only connecting link with the civilized world.

The next day, we anchor off the town of Lingeh, one of the most flourishing places on the Persian coast. Its appearance from the sea is very pleasant, the houses being built of white stone, and surrounded by date trees. From a high building in the center of the town, the residence of the governor, the flag of the Shah of Persia, the " lion and the sun," is flying, and at the masthead of a native *bugalah* we see the favorite banner of the Persians, —the two-bladed sword of Ali, on a white ground with a dark green border. Here we land sixty more of our pilgrims. The greeting to the new-comers is quite affectionate. Dark, black-bearded men kiss each other on both cheeks, and the pilgrims are addressed with the honorary title of " *Hadji*" prefixed to their names, which they ever after retain. Bands of music and processions wait at the landing to escort them to their homes. They have been absent on the pilgrimage over four months, and if called

upon to thank their friends and neighbors for this kind
reception, they can truly say that this is the proudest and
happiest moment of their lives.   The pearl merchant
leaves us here, and his four ladies, closely wrapped from
head to foot, are safely deposited in the boat.   So carefully
has he watched over his precious charge, that not one of
the passengers or officers has been able to catch the slightest
glimpse of their faces, during the two weeks of their sojourn
behind the green curtain.   Abdul at times has been quite
sociable.   In the moonlight evenings, he would sometimes
bring on deck his elegant *chibouk* with an amber mouth-
piece of immense size, and pass it around for our delecta-
tion.   His servant would keep it filled with delicious " tum-
back," and under its tranquilizing influence he would for a
while forget his dread responsibilities as a family man, and
tell us about the pearl fisheries, in which he is largely interested.   He is the Sheik of the Island of Gais, near
Lingeh, which is the most important place for pearls on
the Persian Gulf.   He has fifty boats and several hundred
divers, whose pay, he says, is the dates they eat and the
clothes they wear, while a few rich men enjoy the proceeds
of their dangerous calling.   They are dropped down with
ropes under their arms and weights tied to their feet, in
water from thirty to fifty feet deep, collect an armful of
the oysters and are drawn up to the boats.   Long practice enables the diver to remain under water from a minute
to a minute and a half, and while on the bottom he must
stir round lively.   They are armed with knives, and sometimes have desperate encounters with the sharks that
guard, like fabled genii, the treasures of the deep.   The
oysters, which are as large as ordinary breakfast plates,
are carried on shore at night and delivered to the Sheik.
At sunset all assemble for evening prayers, the Sheik
especially praying to Allah for a lucky haul.   At daylight

the next morning the oysters are opened and the pearls carefully collected. They vary in size, from a pin's head to a large pea, and the result of a day's fishing is very uncertain.

The shells, as mother of pearl, are worth in Europe about twenty dollars per hundred weight, and the pearls are packed in an envelope of dark red cloth, the parcel being made the exact size and shape of a pomegranate. A bit of red sealing wax secures the end, and the valuable fruit is forwarded to Bombay, where it will sometimes bring twenty-five thousand rupees.

Abdul had no pearls with him, but had taken quite a valuable stock when he started on the pilgrimage, and combining business with piety, had disposed of them to good advantage in Mecca. If the rumors were true, he had invested a part of the proceeds in a beautiful young Circassian—one of the four just now safely landed at Lingeh. As he stepped into his own boat and pushed away from the ship, he waved to us on deck a parting salute, and his one eye seemed to gleam with an expression of joy and triumph. We imagined him humming the popular air,—

"Lu-lu is my darling pride—Lu-lu bright! Lu-lu gay!"

From Lingeh it was two days' sail to Bushire, the principal seaport of Persia, and the largest city on the gulf. But my impressions of the territory of the Shah must be given in another chapter.

11

# CHAPTER XIV.

## PERSIA.

HE Persia of to-day, ruled by the Shah, who still assumes the title of "King of Kings," seems on the map but a small province, compared with the magnificent empire that once extended from the Mediterranean to the Indies. Its sovereign owes his throne to the successful raid of a Kurdish chieftain, a few generations ago, and is no more a descendant from Darius or Cyrus, than his capital is to be identified or compared with ancient Persepolis, the glories of which are handed down to us by the "Father of History," or deciphered from the inscription on its ruined walls.

The names Arabia and Persia are not those by which these countries are known to their inhabitants. The Arabs call their country *Jezeret-al-Arab* "country of the Arabs." The Persians call it *Arabistan*. The word Persia comes from the Greek *Persis*. Their own name for their country is *Iranistan*. The climate of that part of Persia bordering on the Gulf and extending up to the mouth of the Euphrates, is exceedingly trying to Europeans, though perhaps not quite as unhealthy as India. The intense heat of summer is aggravated by the humidity of the atmosphere. In winter the winds are very cold and piercing. The saying is, that there is always too much wind or none at all.

The small towns are all very similar—a square fort of rough stone, with loop-holed bastions at the angles, or several detached round towers; the Sheik's house, and a few more of stone; others of mud, or mats made from date leaf stalks; a grove of date trees in the immediate vicinity, and a detached tower or two near the walls. These are the invariable features. The larger towns are walled round, and have a greater proportion of stone buildings. Nowhere is there the slightest pretense at ostentation on the outside of their buildings, public or private. Luxury and wealth may be profuse inside their homes, but none is shown to the public as a temptation to the spoiler.

The people are Mahometans, with a small sprinkling of Jews and native Christians. They belong to a sect quite different from the Arabs, and revere the memory of Ali almost as much as Mahomet. His tomb, near Bagdad, is one of their sacred shrines.

The common dress of the Persians, as seen in the streets, differs somewhat from any we have heretofore seen. A hat of black felt, without brim, or a large turban,

takes the place of the Arab *kaffeah*. Instead of the long
striped *abbah* of camel's hair, they wear a loose robe of
cotton or silk, with long sleeves, and a shawl tied around
the waist, in the folds of which they carry their money and
valuables. The wealthy have richly embroidered under
vests, the outer robe being open from the throat to the
waist. The women wear the universal loose, baggy gown,
of white or dark blue cotton, and over the face a white
mask in which is a small open-work space for the eyes.
The disguise is so complete, that one might pass his own
wife or sister in the street without recognizing her. It is
said that this offers the greatest facility for intrigue, to
which these Mahometan women are very much inclined.
In the bazaars, especially those devoted to silks and wearing apparel, you see great numbers of females chaffering
with the shop keepers. But the men pass them by without notice, as it is impossible to tell, unless they choose to
raise the corner of their veils, whether they are white or
black, ugly or beautiful. At home in the harems, the
wealthy ladies are said to be very richly dressed, with a
profusion of jewels and ornaments. In my travels in
Mahometan countries, I have never yet seen a really beautiful woman. Circassian and Georgian females, who are
especially admired for their large, liquid black eyes, and
long silken lashes, over which the Persian poets go into
ecstacies, are but handsome-faced animals, without education or intelligence. Refinement and intellect are attractions to them unknown, and would be unappreciated by
their sensual masters. The children are remarkably
pretty, with fair complexions, and very precocious.

I find myself in Bushire, the guest of an English merchant, whose house is three miles outside the walls, to
which we ride out every night and return in the early morning. Bushire is the largest seaport in Persia, and has a

popuiation of about twenty thousand. It is built upon a low point of land, and the water in the harbor is so shallow that all large vessels have to anchor three miles from the town. It is guarded towards the sea by many round detached towers. During the war with Persia in 1856, Bushire was bombarded and captured by the English, and these fortifications were badly shattered. They have never been repaired, and now seem utterly useless as a means of defense. A wall extends across the land side of the town, but it is half in ruins, and we ride out upon the plain through a gap made by British shot and shell.

The buildings are of a light, porous stone, the principal ones being the English Residency and the Persian Governor's palace. The latter personage is called by the sonorous title of *Darya-Beg*—" The Lord of the Sea." He is a near relative of the Shah, and rules with despotic sway over a large province. He has a garrison of regular Persian troops, and a few light field pieces. My guide took me one day to the arsenal near the palace, and pointed with much pride to a row of old iron cannon of European manufacture, mostly ship guns, mounted on rickety carriages of very primitive construction.

I am not well versed in artillery, but my impression is that there would be more danger behind than in front of them. I should think about half the charge would escape through the vent. There was, however, one very fine bronze six-pounder, on a modern carriage, with an inscription showing that it was a present to the Sultan of Muscat, from a firm of Boston merchants. How it came into the possession of the Persians I was unable to ascertain. I have noticed in several places the habit they have of posting several cannon quite unprotected, outside the walls of their forts, which seems about as sensible, in a military point of view, as digging a ditch inside the walls.

The soldiers are said to be patient, quick to learn, and all I have seen are tall, athletic-looking men—good material for a fine army. But their officers are unskilled and careless, and the discipline and drill are very bad. One regiment is posted outside the walls, and we passed it one evening at dress parade. Their arms are flint-lock muskets, and their uniform very shabby. They have not been paid for three years, as the finances of the country are in a chronic state of disorder. This part of Persia suffered frightfully during the famine three years ago, and the country is poor from successive short crops, so that the people cannot pay their taxes. The Governor is now absent in the interior, with a body of troops to enforce the payment of taxes due from some of the Sheiks, or local chiefs.

A regiment sent out not long ago on a similar mission, came back without any money for the Governor, but the officers and men had a valuable *loot* which they had appropriated to their own use as back pay. There are a few hundred Armenians in Bushire, who have the only Christian church, and within this enclosure, are the graves of several Englishmen. There are about twenty-five foreigners living here, inclusive of the British diplomatic Resident and his suite, the telegraph corps and one firm of English merchants. The restrictions placed by the government officers on the foreign trade are very annoying, although one principal source of revenue is the duties levied on imports. They are very jealous of the encroachments of foreigners, and with the history of India as a warning, they will not permit any but a native to acquire a title to real estate.

One peculiar feature in Bushire is the wind towers, rising like large chimneys ten or twelve feet above the flat roofs. These have openings towards the prevailing winds in summer, and conduct currents of air into the sleeping rooms below. Many houses have a frame work of poles, covered with mats, upon their roofs, under which they sleep during the hot season. The air is full of moisture, and the fall of dew is so great that no one can sleep in the open air without some protection.

The India cable is landed here, and one line controlled by the English is carried overland to Teheran, the capital, and thence to Europe, while another cable connects Bushire with Fāu, at the mouth of the Euphrates, whence the Turks have a line through Bagdad to Aleppo and Constantinople. Reuter's telegrams pass through here to India, China, and Japan. As I listened to the click of the instrument working a through circuit to London, I was tempted to send a message, via London and New York, to Cleveland. The manager very kindly offered to send it at once ; but when I came to count the cost—nearly forty dollars for ten words—I was obliged to decline.

The bazaars here are quite interesting and in many respects peculiar. The Persian merchants are active and enterprising. These people are very fond of sweets, and there are many stalls where "lollipops" are sold. I must confess a weakness for such things, which I never expect to outgrow. The variety and cheapness of these preparations, for which I can give no English names, and their delicious flavor surpassed anything I have ever seen in Europe or America. Human nature has many characteristics which can be recognized the world over. I thought of this, as I watched a bright-eyed little boy standing in front of the stall, with a copper coin in his chubby fist, and gazing wistfully up at the treasures, seemingly unable to decide in which one to invest.

The carpet bazaar, too, is very attractive. They spread out before me those beautiful fabrics, thick and soft, with that marvelous combination and blending of colors, which in Persian carpets is the admiration of the Western world, and causes the patterns to be copied in the looms of Europe and America. Like the shawls of Cashmere these carpets are made by hand in the interior villages, the wools being drawn through and through, as in the quilting days of our grandmothers, and the surface cut and shaved smooth and soft like velvet. It is one of the wonders of the East, that people so rude and uncultivated, should have such skill and taste in forms and colors. But nature here is prodigal in graceful shapes and colors pleasing to the eye. The feathery palm and the bright tints of tropical flowers and plants, are a constant suggestion of beauty to those who have no conception of what we call art.

In my investments, I ventured to offer not more than half the prices asked, which were always accepted after a proper amount of protests and hesitation. But when I exhibited my purchases to my host, he did not compliment me on any great bargains. I am well satisfied, however, provided Uncle Sam is not too hard in the matter of import duties.

At a street corner I noticed a round, dome-shaped pillar, about six feet high and two in diameter. "Here," my guide says, "a little devil is shut up." I am curious to know more about the evil spirit, and make an effort to examine into his abode, but he hurries me forward, as if afraid that the sable gentleman would break out and devour us.

Outside the walls the first mile is across a level, sandy plain. Then we came to cultivated land, slightly undulating, and covered with waving wheat and barley. In another month these fields will be harvested, and during the hot weather they will be parched and dry like a desert, except the few small oases around the wells, where vegetation is kept alive by irrigation.

All the water used in the town is brought from these wells, and we met long processions of women carrying goat skins filled with water, across the plain. They belong to the peasant class, and their life seems a hard one as they toil along in the hot sun, stooping under a burden of sixty or eighty pounds upon their heads, or strapped

WATER CARRIERS IN PERSIA.

to their shoulders. But it is a brighter side to the picture, when we pass others returning to the wells with empty goat skins, laughing and chattering among themselves, quite indifferent to the presence of strangers. They are mostly young, but hard toil and coarse living have left no traces of beauty in their forms or faces.

Though ice, as an article of domestic use, is unknown in this country, there is plenty of snow within sight, a tantalizing view in a climate as hot as this. On our left is a range of very lofty mountains. The highest peaks are from thirty to forty miles distant, and their snow-covered caps loom up nearly ten thousand feet above the level of the sea. No vegetation can be seen upon their bare and deeply furrowed sides. They are separated by deep valleys, which are very fertile, and there is a belt of low land of varying width between these mountain ranges and the sea, which is called by the Persians the hot district. Situated at the southern foot of these hills, watered by no river, and its summer heat tempered by no rain, this district in which Bushire is the principal city, well merits the reputation of being one of the hottest places in the world.

There are many stories current among Europeans here, which illustrate the inefficiency of the Shah and his government. I cannot vouch for their truth, and this may be a good place to quote the adage, " believe nothing that you hear and but half you see." They are, however, so characteristic of these Eastern princes, that I give them for what they are worth.

During the recent visit of the Shah to Europe, where the crowned heads were so delighted to do him honor, he saw postage stamps for the first time, and their use was explained to him. The bright idea struck him that here was an opportunity to benefit his own people, and what was of more importance, make some money for himself. So he ordered a large quantity of postage stamps, which he had printed in Paris, and forwarded to Teheran. As there are no post-offices in Persia, it cannot be expected that he will realize a very large sum from the sale of stamps.

The coinage of Persia is principally silver *kerans*, value about one franc. They are made by hand, of unalloyed silver. Of course, a mint would be a convenient institution. So one was ordered, with all its expensive machinery, six years ago, from Europe. It came by sea as far as Bushire, and after much delay and difficulty, the heavy and cumbrous machine was started by caravan towards the capital. It got stuck fast in a mountain pass about one hundred miles from here, and there it has remained ever since. An elegant English carriage designed for the use of the Shah's harem, is said to have met the same fate.

About thirty miles from Bushire is the island of Karrack, the most important strategic point in the Persian Gulf. This island is ten miles long by three in width. It has about three thousand inhabitants, and a considerable portion of the land is under cultivation. The highest point is nearly three hundred feet above the sea, and it is quite healthy for Europeans, with an abundance of good water. In event of the opening of a new route to India, by the Euphrates Valley Railway, which, if ever constructed, must be built by British capital, this island will be seized and fortified by the English like another Aden. It is perhaps the only spot in the Persian Gulf which is in every way suitable for permanent military occupation. It commands on the one hand the largest sea-port of Persia, and on the other, the mouth of the Euphrates, and through it, the immense territories of Turkish Arabia and Mesopotamia. Karrack was occupied temporarily by British troops during the Persian war in 1856. As we steamed past the island we could see the remains of a fort built in 1754 by the Dutch, who then had a flourishing settlement here. Upon the rising ground west of the fort, is a tomb with a mosque attached. It is the shrine of Mir Mahomet, the son of Ali, the conqueror of Persia. An inscription states that it was rebuilt five hundred and fifty years ago. There are several other shrines on the island, in one of which is the impression of the foot of the prophet Al Khizir, who, according to Mahometan tradition, is still alive and on his travels over the world, like the wandering Jew.

# CHAPTER XV.

Approach to the Euphrates—The Invisible Banks—Mesopotamia—Fäu—
Mahomrah—Sheik Jarbah—The Young Sheik—A Boat Excursion—The
"Bellum"—An Unwelcome Guest—Bassorah—Running the Quarantine—
English Merchants—Captain Carter, the English Sheik—A Warm Wel-
come to Marghil—A Pet Lion—Musselman and Infidel—Exports from
the Euphrates—The Garden of Eden—River Scenes on the Tigris and the
Euphrates—The Bedouin's Tent—An Arabian Horse—Ezra's Tomb—
The Sportsman's Paradise—We cannot Bag a Lion—Ctesiphon and Seleu-
cia—The Barber and the Mule Driver of the Prophet—The City of the
Caliphs in Sight.

OR more than thirty miles
from its mouth, the yellow
waters of the Euphrates
pouring into the Gulf, give
notice of our approach to a
great river. I am reminded
of the *Yangt-si*, in China,
whose muddy waters have
given its name to the Yellow
Sea. But the river we are
now approaching is associated with the earliest recorded
history of the human race.
On its banks was located, ac-
cording to tradition, the Garden of Eden. Here, too, can
still be seen, rising one hundred and fifty feet above the
sandy plain, an immense mass of masonry, supposed to be
the remains of the Tower of Babel—its top fused as if by

lightning, into rock-like masses, where the impious attempt
of the first descendants of Noah was arrested by fire from
heaven. On the banks of the river are the half explored
ruins of Nineveh and Babylon, those mighty cities whose
magnificence and extent were the wonder of the ancient
world.

The two great rivers, the Tigris and the Euphrates, rising among the mountains far away in the north, and flowing southward for more than a thousand miles, unite about
one hundred miles from the Gulf, in one broad stream
called by the Arabs, the *Shat-al-Arab*, or river of the
Arabs. The immense fertile plains of alluvial soil em-
braced between these two rivers, have been known from
the earliest times as " Mesopotamia"—once cultivated like
a garden, and supporting a very large population.

There is as yet no land in sight, but the Arab pilot
says we are within the banks of the river. This sounds
rather paradoxical. But presently I am convinced of its
truth, as the steamer runs into the invisible bank, and
is there stuck hard and fast for five hours, until a rise in
the tide floats her off. Again we steam slowly and carefully on, and soon the low coast dotted with palm trees
comes in sight. At its mouth the river is more than a
mile in width and flows with a rapid muddy current. It
is said that the upper end of the Persian Gulf is gradually
filling up. But as this process has been going on from the
foundation of the world, it is not a very alarming matter
to the present generation. The delta of the Euphrates,
like those of the Nile and the Mississippi, is the gradual
formation of ages, and the soil formed from the deposits of
these mighty rivers, is exceedingly fertile. On the right
bank at the mouth of the river, is a small village called
Fāu. Here we see the low mud walls of a fort, above
which from a tall flag-staff the " Crescent and Star " is

flying, and a small Turkish gunboat is moored near the shore. A long wooden building, with side verandahs, is the English telegraph station. The engines stop, and a boat is sent on shore with our bill of health, for the quarantine officers. It returns with a young Englishman of the telegraph corps, who has a week's leave of absence to recruit his health up the river. The town of Bassorah is situated sixty miles from the Gulf on the western bank, to which point there is sufficient depth of water for the largest ships. The river, up as far as Bassorah, is the boundary between Persia and Arabia. The inhabitants on the western side thoroughly hate their masters, the Turks, and with no fear of extradition treaties, cross the river into Persian territory to avoid conscription or punishment for offenses.

Before dark we came to anchor, and the next morning soon after sunrise are off the Persian town of Mahomrah at the mouth of the Kairoon, a large river which has its rise in the interior of Persia. This place and all the territory from Bassorah to the Gulf, is ruled by Sheik Jarbah, in true patriarchal style. His power is absolute over life and property, and so long as he promptly pays over to the Persian Government the required amount of taxes, they do not interfere. In the war of 1856 the Persian fort at Mahomrah was bombarded and captured by the English, and the Persian soldiers, headed by the Sheik, skedaddled into the interior. He is an old man of seventy, but very energetic and enterprising, and the wealthiest man in this part of the country. From where we are anchored we can see the large white buildings of the Sheik's residence, one of which is evidently the harem, as on its broad piazza there is a great fluttering of female figures in bright colored drapery. We are warned not to direct our glasses in that direction, as it would be a breach of etiquette, and give offense to the

old Sheik. There are several Europeans here in the service of the Sheik, or connected with him in mercantile enterprises, who come on board, and with them the old
man's son, a fine looking young fellow of about twenty-five,
to whom we are introduced. He is richly dressed, rather
reserved in manner, and treated with great respect by all
about him. He is very fond of hunting, a capital shot,
and in feats of horsemanship would rival a Comanche on
our plains. In matters of business he is sharp and enterprising—" a chip of the old block."

We have on board a small iron steamer, built for Sheik
Jarbah in England, and sent out in pieces. It is one hundred
feet long and intended for the navigation of the Kairoon.
To discharge this, the " Gunga " will be detained here two
days, and as Bassorah is but twenty-five miles further up the
river, we decided to take a small boat called a *bellum* and
push on to our destination. These boats with a name so
suggestive of war, are very long and narrow, and usually
painted on the outside in alternate black and white squares
that look like ports. Declining an invitation to breakfast
on shore, we pack our satchels, leaving our heavy luggage
to go up on the steamer, spread our soft Persian rugs in
the bottom of the boat, put in a gun and a brace of revolvers, some umbrellas, and a basket well stocked with provisions for our lunch. Before nine o'clock we are off, hoping to make the distance in about six hours. The *bellum*
is propelled by two men in the bows with long bamboo
poles, assisted by a third man, who sits aft, and steers with
a paddle. We keep close to the banks to avoid the swift
current in the middle of the stream, and for the first two
or three hours find it very pleasant. Groves of date palms
line the shore on both sides all the way to Bassorah, and
are said to produce the finest dates in the world. Behind
this fringe of palms we can see broad, fertile meadows, on

which are grazing large herds of cattle and buffaloes. The
river is very high, and in many places overflowing its
banks. There are frequent canals leading out from the
river for irrigation, and close to the banks are many small
weirs, made of date sticks, for trapping fish. The tide is
now running up, and we push along at quite a rapid rate.
We get an occasional shot from our " Wesley-Richards" at
ducks and pelicans. Of inhabitants we see but few, and
they are not prepossessing in appearance. Some swarthy,
half-naked Arabs crawl out of their mud huts to gaze at us,
while children entirely nude, run along the shore, screaming and holding out their hands for *baksheesh*.

Soon after noon we stopped for half an hour to lunch,
and give our boatmen a rest. We found a pleasant, grassy
bank, unpacked our basket of provisions, put our bottled
ale in the river to cool, and were congratulating each
other upon our grand picnic, when a new comer, in the
shape of a venomous spotted snake, proposed to join our
party. The unwelcome visitor was despatched by the boatmen, but we concluded to adjourn to the boat to finish our
meal. As the day advanced, the hot sun began to tell
upon ourselves as well as our men. The tide had turned
and was now running against us, giving increased velocity
to the current. At every bend of the river we looked anx-
iously ahead for some appearance of a town.

Our men could not speak a word except in Arabic or
Persian, and were evidently slackening in their exertions.
We were scarcely making two miles an hour, and would
have jumped ashore and walked, but the ground was so
swampy, and intersected by so many canals and ditches, as
to render that impracticable. But the application of coin
has sometimes a marvelous effect in reviving the flagging
energies. We gave to each of our men a rupee as extra
*baksheesh,* and by pantomime urged them forward.

It acted like a charm, and before long the tall masts of a Turkish guard ship were discerned above the date trees round a bend of the river. She was anchored near a large fort at the mouth of a creek, a mile up which is situated the town of Bassorah. Near the guard ship were two foreign steamers and several *marhalahs*, or river boats, with large lateen sails. The custom house and the yellow flag of a quarantine station came next in view.

But now a new difficulty arose. Our ship had not received *pratique*, and we had no right to land. If the health officers should see us we would be arrested for violating the quarantine regulations. There is no other country in the world where quarantine laws are so stringent as in Turkey. In this matter even money is useless. This country has suffered so often from the frightful ravages of the plague and cholera, that a most vigorous system is enforced with all ships coming into Turkish ports.

Our destination was not the town of Bassorah, but a place two miles higher up the river, called Marghil, where the docks and warehouses of Lynch & Co., are located. We replaced our India pith hats, which are only worn by Europeans, with the red Turkish fez, and directed our boatmen to keep close to the opposite shore. We took down our sun umbrellas and put out of sight everything that would mark us as strangers. As we passed the guard ship, the officer on deck directed his glass towards our boat, but seeing nothing suspicious allowed us to pass.

Before we reached Marghil, one of our men, overcome by the heat and nine hours' incessant labor, sank down exhausted; but he speedily revived with the application of cold water, to which we added a few drops of brandy.

We reached Marghil before sunset and were warmly welcomed by Captain Carter, the manager of Lynch & Co's business in Bassorah. This is the only firm of

12

English merchants in Turkish Arabia. It was established forty years ago, and has agencies in Bassorah, and Bagdad, which is about five hundred miles up the river. For many years one of the partners resided at Bagdad, but their headquarters are in London. A few years ago they obtained, after much difficulty, a *firman* from the Turkish government permitting them to establish a line of steamers between Bassorah and Bagdad, under the name of the " Tigris and Euphrates Navigation Company." This line receives a liberal subsidy for carrying the English mail between these two points, and has developed a large and constantly increasing traffic. The shipments by this firm to England were last year over one thousand tons of dates, two thousand five hundred bales of wool, and large quantities of gall-nuts and gums.

At Bagdad, the British government has a diplomatic representative, who is also Consul General, under the name of " Resident." It is a very important position, and it is now worthily filled by Colonel Herbert, a veteran English officer and a most accomplished gentleman, who has seen twenty-five years service in India.

My friend Finnis, who has been so long my *compagnon de voyage*, is a junior member of the firm of Lynch & Co., and now visits for the first time their establishments in the East.

Bassorah is the port of Mesopotamia, and contains about fifteen thousand inhabitants, a mixture of Turks, Arabs, Persians, Armenians, and Jews. Most of the buildings within the walls, which are of great extent, are in ruins. The houses are of sun-dried bricks, and the streets very filthy. The governor is a Turkish officer, appointed by the Pasha of Bagdad. The summer heat is intense and the situation very unhealthy, the adjacent country being frequently flooded by water from the overflow of the

THE TOMB OF EZRA, ON THE TIGRIS.

*From a photograph in possession of the Author.*

river. It is hard to realize that this was once one of the
richest and most populous of all the commercial cities of
the East. When Babylon was in its glory, long before
Bagdad was founded, Bassorah was the *entrepot* of the
rich fabrics of India, and the Euphrates the great artery of
commerce between Europe and the East. It has suffered
terribly from the plague. In 1773, it is said that two
hundred thousand of its inhabitants perished. At the last
visitation of this fearful pestilence, in 1831, it was almost
depopulated. Whole families became extinct, and many
valuable estates, including houses and date groves, were
left without owners.

Returning from my one short visit to the town, Marghil
seemed like a paradise. Here, enclosed within the walls
of the *compound*, are the work houses, coal depots, machine
shops, and wool presses of the firm. The bales of wool
are submitted to hydraulic pressure and reduced to the
smallest possible compass before shipment. Outside the
walls there has grown up quite a village of native em-
ployees, of whom Captain Carter is the Sheik. To them his
word is law. He decides their disputes, dispenses medi-
cines to the sick, is quite skillful as a surgeon, and, as he
speaks Arabic like a native, and has that manner of command acquired as a sea captain, his influence is unbounded.
Of his social accomplishments, his generous hospitality,
and the comforts, and even elegance, of his bachelor
quarters, I shall ever retain the pleasantest memories.

There are many pets about the premises that are curious
and amusing—birds and monkeys of various kinds, and a
young lion about half grown, as large as a Newfoundland
dog. He had been permitted to run loose, but was now
chained up, as he could no longer get along amicably with
his former playmate, a large English dog, called "Paul."
In fact, Paul's mate, "Virginia," had come to grief in a

little trial of strength about the possession of a bone.   He
is soon to take a sea voyage for his health, and will have
his permanent residence at the " Zoo " in Regent's Park.
During the last trip of the steamer up the Euphrates, four
lions were shot from the deck of the boat.   They were on

SHOOTING LIONS FROM THE BOAT.

a small island, and a sudden rise in the river had cut off
their retreat to the main land.   The largest weighed three
hundred and fifty pounds, and the skin, one of the finest I
ever saw, was presented to my friend.   The Mesopotamia
lion is usually without the dark and shaggy mane of the
African species, but some have been found on the Kairoon
river with a long, black mane.   The people of the country
make a distinction between these, the former being Mus-
sulmen and the latter *Kaffirs*, or infidels.   By a proper
remonstrance, and at the same time pronouncing the profession of faith, the former may be induced to spare one's
life, but the unbelieving lion is inexorable.

The time here has passed like a dream. While my friends during the day have been engaged in matters of business, I have lounged on the grass in the garden, where the orange and citron are mingled with the date and mulberry trees, the faithful Mahomet always within call to bring coffee or make a *chibouk*. This life has been the more enjoyable after the confinement and monotony of our long sea voyage. But now we must say good bye to Marghil and its genial host, and go on board the steamer for the last stage of our journey.

The "London" and the "Dijleh" or "Tigris" are two iron sidewheel steamers, built expressly for the river service, with powerful engines to stem the rapid current. They are one hundred and seventy-five feet long, flat bottomed, the plates of the hull being of steel, and draw, when loaded down to the guards, but three and a half feet of water.

Forty miles above Bassorah we reach Kernah, the junction of the Tigris and Euphrates. Our course is to the right, up the Tigris upon which Bagdad is situated. According to tradition, Kernah is the site of the original garden of Eden. But alas for these degenerate days! we look in vain for any relic of paradise, for the "tree of knowledge," or any other tree, among the mud huts of the miserable Arab town. Can these swarthy, half-grown children that swarm on the banks, be descendants from our first parents? If so, the "*descent* of man" is here practically demonstrated. Near Kernah, on the Tigris, there was sunk about ten years ago, a vessel laden with interesting relics excavated by the French Government at Nineveh. They were mostly slabs of marble of great beauty, and the loss to antiquarians is irreparable.

The river is very crooked, and to avoid the force of the current the "London" keeps near the shore. As we swing round the sharp bends, we can almost jump from her deck on to the bank. The water is very high, and in many places has overflowed the banks and formed broad lagoons over which are hovering flocks of ducks, herons, and other wild fowls. Laborers are strengthening the dykes with mud mixed with coarse grass and reeds to save their crops of wheat and barley from destruction. The fringe of date palms, so attractive a feature of the Euphrates from the Gulf to Kernah, is no longer seen, only broad, fertile, alluvial plains, over which, when uncultivated, there waves a strong, coarse grass that reminds one óf our great western prairies. Here are immense herds of cattle, and flocks of coarse-wool sheep, buffaloes, whose black smooth hides and humped shoulders seem to indicate a cross with the hippopotamus, wallowing in the mud and water close to the shore, sometimes with only their heads or nostrils above the surface. Mud villages, where the whole population, men, women, children, and dogs turn out and line the shore to gaze at the passing steamer ; black Bedouin tents, always at a little distance from the river's bank, and around them horses grazing ; these are some of the characteristic scenes of our first two days.

At one place we landed and visited the encampment of a Bedouin Sheik. The tents of black goat's hair were pitched promiscuously, large and small, one, two, and three poles in length. Carefully picking our way to avoid stumbling over the tent poles, we entered the lodge of the head man, who welcomed us at the entrance, and invited us to be seated on a carpet and regaled us with black coffee, goat's milk, cheese, and other Arab delicacies, followed by the inevitable *chibouk*. The tent looked more comfortable and much better furnished than I expected. The upper end was hung with striped cloth and the ground covered with carpets and mats, while saddle bags, copper utensils, and arms were hung on pegs, or scattered on the floor near the entrance. Our call was short, and the conversation, entirely by pantomine, could not be very animated. The chief was courteous and polite, frequently bowing and *salaaming*, to which we responded after the same fashion.

As we passed out we stopped to admire a beautiful fullblooded, iron-grey Arab mare, tethered to a long spear stuck in the ground. Her arched neck, fine delicate nostrils, intelligent eyes, and smooth limbs would have turned the heads of many an enthusiastic horse fancier. A Bedouin never parts with such an animal as this, and if she dies the whole tribe goes into mourning.

The second day after leaving Marghil, we passed Ezra's Tomb, a large picturesque building, with an immense green dome in the center. Near it are groves of date and willow trees, and it is a conspicuous object for many miles over the level plain. It is a sacred shrine to the Jews, who come here in great numbers from Bagdad, at certain seasons of the year, to celebrate their feasts.

For three days we pass through a country that is almost destitute of cultivation or inhabitants. Sometimes we see large mounds, once the site of populous towns and cities, but now only the jackals and the wild beasts of the desert prowl among these deserted places. A perfect network of canals and water courses, now choked up with sand, in ancient times rendered this country most fertile and productive.

But game is plenty, and there is an almost constant fusilade of guns and rifles from the deck of the "London." Besides waterfowl, such as pelicans, herons, cranes, and ducks, which are always in sight, we have wild boars, jackals, and antelopes.

In winter the wild boar is hunted on horseback with spears, a most exciting and dangerous sport. My friend is a keen sportsman, and with his long range "Henry Martinez" rifle, is a dead shot at a wild boar at five hundred yards. We are especially on the lookout for lions, but see none during our trip. The officers of the steamer, all English, join in the sport. Captain Cowley, elated by his recent experience, says laughingly that he is above all such small game as wild boars and antelopes, and will not stop his boat to bag anything short of a lion.

The day before reaching Bagdad we arrived at Ctesi-phon, where there is one of the most remarkable ruins on the Tigris. On the opposite bank a long line of mounds mark the site of Seleucia, which like Ctesiphon was built almost entirely from materials brought from Babylon. All that remains of Ctesiphon, once the proud capital of the Parthian empire, is an immense archway one hundred and six feet high, being the entrance to a vaulted hall about one hundred and fifty feet in depth. The front of the building, of which this arch is the center, is over three hundred feet long and ornamented with four tiers of pilas-ters and small arches like corridors. What a magnificent palace the whole structure must have been, with an arch-way over a hundred feet in height for an entrance. Mounds surround the building for many acres, made up of broken bricks, and fragments of pottery and glass.

About half a mile from the arch are two mosques to which, as sacred shrines, the Mahometans make pilgrim-ages. One is the burial place of the *barber* of the Prophet, the other of his *mule-driver*. Though bearing evidence of great age, for if genuine they must date back nearly thirteen hundred years ago, these tombs seemed almost modern compared with the relic at least five hundred years older, which we had just visited.

At length on the sixth day after leaving Bassorah, just as the sun was rising, the morning air heavy with the odor

THE ARCH OF CTESIPHON.

*From a photograph in possession of the Author.*

of orange blossoms, we entered the long reach of the
Tigris, on both sides of which Bagdad is built, and the
" City of the Caliphs," with its vaulted domes and lofty
minarets, is before us.

# CHAPTER XVI.

## THE CALIPHS OF BAGDAD.

O most people the very name
of Bagdad is suggestive of
Oriental magnificence.
There is a *glamour* of romance about this city, that
was once the glory and pride
of Islam. The glowing de-
scriptions in the Arabian
Nights, of the splendors of
the court of Haroun-al-
Raschid and his beautiful
queen, Zobeide, though
doubtless exaggerated, and
embellished by all the hyper-
bole of Eastern imagery, had a substantial foundation in
historical facts. About the eighth century, under the
reigns of the Caliphs, Bagdad attained its greatest splen-

dor, and here the wealth of the world at that time appears to have centered. Manufactures, commerce, science, and the arts all flourished under their fostering care. Colleges and schools were founded and liberally endowed, and the abstruse sciences were cultivated with enthusiasm and success. The artisans of Bagdad were famous for their ingenuity and skill; and we read of a Clepsydra, or water-clock, originally devised in Greece, issuing from its work-shops and being deemed a present worthy of acceptance from one of the Caliphs to a king of France. At that time it was doubtless the most brilliant and wealthy city of the world.

The annals of an Arabian writer (Abulfeda) give an account of the magnificence at the reception by one of the Caliphs of an ambassador from Greece. " The army was drawn up to the number of one hundred and sixty thousand men. The Caliph himself, surrounded by his chief ministers and favorite slaves covered with gold and jewels, resembled a planet amid a galaxy of stars. Eunuchs, black and white, with inferior officers to the number of eight thousand, served as a foil to these gems. Silk and gold-embroidered tapestry, numbering thirty-eight thousand pieces, ornamented the palace walls, and on a curious tree of gold and silver were perched a variety of birds, whose movements and notes were regulated by machinery. Twenty-two thousand carpets covered the floors, and there floated on the broad stream of the Tigris, before the windows of the palace, thousands of vessels, each splendidly decorated; while a hundred lions, in charge of their keepers, lent a contrast to the glittering scene."

Such are the brilliant pictures painted by the early chroniclers of the glories of this famous city. But the wealth and prosperity of its people, and its abundance of riches acquired by the strong arm and abstemious habits of its early Arab conquerors, led to luxury and effeminacy.

The last of its Caliphs passed away, and the succeeding dynasty quarreling among themselves, Bagdad became an easy prey to the Persians, the Tartars, and the Turks, each in succession capturing and sacking the city. In the time of its prosperity its population must have been immense. When captured by the Tartar Chief, *Halaku*, in the thirteenth century, it is said that three hundred thousand of its defenders were massacred in cold blood, and two hundred years later, when sacked by the conquering hordes of Tamerlane, he erected beyond the gates two pyramids, as the trophies of his prowess, constructed of the heads of ninety thousand of its most influential people. By some singular incongruity, in view of its bloody history, this city originally received and still retains the Arab name, signifying the " Abode of Peace."

But before I attempt to picture the Bagdad of to-day, it may not be out of place to devote one chapter to a historical sketch of the Caliphs, whose reign extended from the death of the founder of Islam down to the middle of the thirteenth century.

From the glowing pages of Gibbon later historians have drawn the stern but truthful pictures of the degeneracy of Christianity, at the period when the " False Prophet of Mecca " promulgated his new religion of the Unity of God, and his followers, raising the battle-cry of " victory or paradise," swept with resistless fury over the plains of Asia and Egypt.

Mahomet's immediate successor had been one of his earliest and most devoted converts. Abu-Beker, on whom the mantle of the Prophet fell, despising the pompous epithets of royalty, adopted the simple and unpretentious titles of " Caliph," and " Commander of the Faithful." The term " Saracen " is probably derived from the Arabic word *Sharack*, meaning " Eastern People," which the Mahometans were called in reference to the European nations. The short reign of Abu-Beker was followed by that of Omar, the second Caliph, whose generals led the fanatical hosts of Islam across the desert to Damascus, captured Jerusalem, overran all Syria, and extended the rule of the Saracens throughout Egypt and Persia. Historians record the visit made by the Caliph Omar to Jerusalem, where his victorious generals had compelled the imperial city of David and Solomon to surrender after a fierce and bloody defense.

On this occasion the Emperor of the Faithful, the conqueror of the East, courted no distinction in attire or retinue above the meanest of his followers. His dress was a coarse woolen garment, with a scimitar hung from one shoulder, and a bow from the other. He rode on a red camel, carrying in two sacks the provisions for his journey ; before him was a leathern bottle of water, and behind was suspended a large wooden platter. When he halted on the way, the company was uniformly invited to share his homely fare, and the humblest of his retinue dipped their fingers in the same dish with the mighty successor of the Prophet. The spot where he reposed for the night was never abandoned in the morning without the regular performance of prayers.

The abstemiousness and frugality of Omar is in strong contrast with the extravagance and luxury of some of his successors, into whose coffers the wealth of the East was poured, and by whom it was spent in most lavish profusion.

By order of the Caliph, the ground on which stood the temple of Solomon was cleared of rubbish, and the foundations laid for the splendid mosque which still bears his name. For over twelve centuries the Holy City has remained in the possession of the Mahometans, except during an interval of ninety years, when the valor of the crusaders restored it to Christian rule.

The conquest of Antioch, the seat of the Greek Emperors, soon followed, and Heraclius escaped with a few followers to the Mediterranean, where he embarked for Constantinople.

The attention of Omar was called, early in his reign, to the " golden soil of Chaldea," so famed for its fertility, the magnificence of its cities, the extent and variety of its manufactures, and the multitude of its flocks and herds. The hosts of Persia were as feeble as in the days of Darius ; the power and resources of that empire melted away before the impetuous assaults of the Arabs, and the splendor of the conquest and spoliation of Mesopotamia and Persia filled the conquerors with surprise and delight.    After ten years reign and a most brilliant career of conquest, Caliph Omar fell under the dagger of an assassin.    His piety, justice, abstinence, and simplicity procured for his memory more reverence than any of his successors ; and Arabic historians relate many stories illustrative of his virtues. A conversation is recorded between the Greek Emperor and some of his Moslem captives as to the person and dignity of their sovereign.    " What sort of a palace," said Heraclius, " has your Caliph ?"    " Of mud."    " And who are his attendants ?"    " Beggars and poor people." " What tapestry does he sit upon ?"    " Justice and uprightness."    " And what is his throne ?"    " Abstinence and wisdom."    " And what is his treasure ?"    " Trust in God."    " And who are his guards ?"    " The bravest of the Unitarians."

Othman, the successor of Omar, extended the conquests of the Saracens far into Africa, and by the subjection of the tribes westward of Egypt, prepared the way for the future invasion of Europe across the Straits of Gibraltar.

The third Caliph, like his predecessor, perished by assassination.

Ali, the son-in-law of Mahomet, and one of his bravest and most devoted followers, succeeded to the Caliphate, twenty-four years after the death of the Prophet. On assuming the regal and sacerdotal duties, he retained the accustomed simplicity of his attire. On the day of his inauguration, he went to the mosque dressed in a thin cotton gown, tied around him with a girdle, a coarse turban on his head, his slippers in one hand and his bow in the other for a walking staff. This Prince was not only a brave soldier, but a poet and scholar, and his partisans are fulsome and extravagant in his praise. A volume of maxims and poems, ascribed by Arabic scholars to the Caliph Ali, still remains as a monument of his wisdom and learning.

His reign was disastrous in insurrections and political convulsions. For the first time, the arms of the Moslems were turned against each other, and stained with civil blood. They now became divided into two bitter and irreconcilable sects, the *Sonnites* and the *Sheahs*, which remain to this day. At first the difference was rather one of political parties than of religious tenets. The *Sonnites* which still prevail throughout Arabia and Egypt call themselves Orthodox, and profess a belief in the "traditions" which are not directly embodied in the Koran, but have come down mostly through the authority of the first Caliph. The latter sect, or *Sheahs*, claim that Ali, himself the cousin, and his wife the daughter, of Mahomet, should have been, by divine right, his immediate successor; and maintain that the first three Caliphs and all their descendants who afterwards occupied the throne, were usurpers. The Persians, and the Mahometans of India and other more Eastern lands, are *Sheahs*, and the hostility between these rival sects is still very bitter. During the *Ramidan*, or holy month, great numbers of both *Sonnites* and *Sheahs* from the furthermost limits of the Mahometan world meet at Mecca, but unlike the rival sects of Christian pilgrims in Jerusalem, they never openly come to blows while visiting the sacred places of their religion.

The virtues and accomplishments of Ali could not save him from a violent death, and his son Hassan, though inheriting his father's piety, was deficient in the courage and energy necessary to rule a turbulent people. He soon resigned the Caliphate, and retired to Medina, devoting his life to deeds of charity and benevolence.

His successor, Moawiyah, the sixth Caliph, was the first of the dynasty of the Ommiades, who are generally styled the " Caliphs of Syria," their capital being at Damascus. During the period that this dynasty remained in power— scarcely one hundred years—sixteen Caliphs in succession ascended the throne, of whom seven perished by the hands of assassins. In the meantime Akbah, the conqueror of Egypt, had crossed the great desert and the Atlas range of mountains, and traversed the wilderness in which the Moslems afterwards erected the splendid capitals of Fez and Morocco. His career, though not his zeal, was checked by the prospect of a boundless ocean. Spurring his horse into the waves, and raising his eyes to heaven, he exclaimed : " Great God ! if my course were not stopped by this sea, I would still go on to the unknown regions of the West, preaching the unity of thy holy name, and putting to the sword the rebellious nations who worship any other gods but thee !" Before the close of the reign of the Ommiades the Mahometan empire had extended from the Indus to the Pillars of Hercules. Nor did the banner of the Crescent stop here. The Moors from Africa had overrun the most fertile provinces of the Spanish Peninsula, and laid the foundations of a State which was to make the name of Grenada famous in history. Their victorious generals had already formed the bold design of making themselves masters of all Europe. With a vast armament, by sea and land, they were preparing to invade Europe, to cross the Pyrenees, and subvert the Kingdom of the Franks in Gaul then distracted by the wars of two contending dynasties; to extinguish the power of the Lombards in Italy, and place an Arabian *Imaum* in the chair of St. Peter.

Hence, after subduing the barbarous hordes of Germany, they proposed to follow the course of the Danube, from its source to the Euxine Sea, where they would have joined their countrymen under the wall of Constantinople.*

From these impending calamities was Christendom delivered by the genius and fortune of one man, Charles Martel. His huge mace, which he wielded with resistless force, gave him the epithet of Martel, or the Hammer.

At the head of his troops he stayed the advance of the victorious Saracens, and rolled back the tide of battle. For the first time in Europe the Crescent met with a serious repulse. The Arabs turned their arms towards the East, pressing the siege of Constantinople, and hoping to strike Europe over the ruins of the Byzantine Empire.

The dynasty that succeeded the Ommiades, about the middle of the eighth century, was that of Abbas, the uncle of Mahomet. The Abbassides, as they are called, are known in history as the "Caliphs of Bagdad," the city to which they transferred their court. For more than five hundred years, from the eighth to the thirteenth century, they ruled the Eastern world with various degrees of authority. During this period, thirty-two Caliphs ascended the throne. In the height of their power, these Ma-

---

* Crichton's History of Arabia.

13

hometan Princes were the most powerful and absolute rulers on earth. They united in one person all regal and sacerdotal authority, and though the Koran was nominally their rule of action, they claimed to be the infallible judges and interpreters of that book most sacred to Mahometans.

Bagdad was founded by the Caliph Almansor, in the 145th year of the Hegira (A. D. 763). On the long roll of his successors there are but few names familiar even to the student of history. But so long as the fascination of that wonderful book, " The Tales of the Arabian Nights," shall endure, the name of the fifth Caliph of Bagdad, Haroun-al-Raschid, will remain a household word in both Christian and heathen lands. During his reign of nineteen years, Bagdad reached the height of its glory. Beautifully situated on the banks of the Tigris, a splendid metropolis, the seat of imperial power and luxury, it seemed to merit the titles of the " City of the Enchantress" —the " Abode of Peace."

This Caliph, whose name Eastern romance has made so familiar to us, was eminently a liberal and humane ruler. He excelled as a warrior, a statesman, and a scholar. He conversed familiarly with all classes of his subjects, and from his personal adventures in wandering through the streets of his capital, many anecdotes have been derived, which historians have been careful to preserve. To the attractions of these adventures there is added the romance associated with the name of his beautiful and virtuous Queen Zobeide. The author of the Arabian Nights may never be surely known, but I remember with what feelings of reverence I looked upon the marble tomb of the Persian poet Chusero, near Delhi, in Northern India, from which I brought away a few rose leaves as mementoes of one who is the reputed author of the " Thousand and One Stories." And now, as I wander through the streets of Bagdad, and

see reproduced many of the identical scenes that so delighted my youthful imagination, the most marvelous of these
stories assume an air of probability.

BAGDAD IN ITS GLORY.

Almamoun, the son and successor of Haroun-al-Raschid,
(or " Aaron, the Just,") is generally regarded as the most
profuse and generous of all the Caliphs of Bagdad. At
his nuptials a thousand pearls of the largest size were
showered on the head of the bride, gifts in lands and
houses were scattered in lottery tickets among the populace,
and before drawing his foot from the stirrup, he gave away
2,400,000 gold *dinars* ($5,000,000), being three-fourths of
the income of a province.

He was called the *Mœcenas* of the East, and learned
men from all parts of the world were invited to visit Bagdad, where they were treated with great honor. In return
for such marks of imperial favor, these happy scholars

were expected, of course, to extol, in prose and verse, the glory of their generous patron.

The history of the Caliphs, from the time of their greatest prosperity down to the capture of Bagdad by the Tartar hordes in 1258, is a succession of pictures showing the increasing corruption and degeneracy of the people, and the effeminacy and weakness of the rulers. During the later reigns, insurrections broke out in almost every province. Usurpers arose, who succeeded in making themselves independent sovereigns. Corruption and venality crept into every department of the State. Bitter religious feuds broke out, and rival sects hated each other worse than infidels. Vice and licentiousness everywhere prevailed. Like other great nations of antiquity, the policy of the Saracens seemed better adapted for the acquisition of an empire than for its preservation.

The wild tribes of Tartary poured down over the fertile plains of Mesopotamia, and with the capture of Bagdad, the history of the Saracens, both as a military and political nation, may be said to have expired. The second dynasty of the Caliphs of the House of Abbas, held a nominal supremacy in matters of religion for two hundred and fifty years after. But Bagdad was no longer the seat of a mighty empire, and gradually sunk to be the capital of a province. The Sultans of Turkey who acquired supremacy over Arabia in the sixteenth century did not, like the Caliphs, style themselves the descendants and successors of the Apostle of God.

A stray scion of the race of the Caliphs, whose ancestor had fled from Bagdad to Cairo when that city was sacked by the Moguls, was yet living in Egypt. The Sultan Selim invited this last remnant of a sacred race to Constantinople, where he was treated with every mark of honor and respect. Before his death he made to the Sultan a formal

renunciation and transfer of the Caliphate. By this empty
title the Turkish Sovereigns have secured a distinction of
great service to them in maintaining authority over the
Arab tribes, as well as pious Musselmen throughout the
world. The Sultan of Turkey is now saluted as " Commander of the Faithful."

# CHAPTER XVII.

## THE CITY OF THE ENCHANTRESS.

TO receive a favorable impression of Bagdad, one should approach it, as it was my good fortune to do, in an early morning in Spring. For miles below we had been passing through groves of date palms and orange trees, and the fragrance of their blossoms was almost oppressive. The Tigris is here nearly half a mile wide, and flows in a broad, full stream, washing the buildings and gardens on either side. The city seems half buried in palm trees, which rise above the buildings in every direction, but far above the palms tower the cupolas and minarets, ornamented with colored glazed tiles, arranged in arabesque designs. The houses facing the river are

VIEW ON THE TIGRIS AT BAGDAD.    *From a photograph in possession of the Author.*

not imposing in height or style of architecture. They are evidently dwellings and not places of business. The numerous lattices, projecting windows, and verandas looking out upon the stream, give them a picturesque and agreeable appearance. Many houses have small gardens facing the river, where one can see the bright spring flowers, and latticed awnings of wood or canvas, under which are seats and divans, suggestive of the coolness and comfort of an out-door lounge.

We steam slowly up the stream, past the Residency, with its beautiful garden, in which we see the uniform of Sepoy soldiers from India. In the river opposite the British Residency, is moored an English gunboat, the "Comet." Thus Great Britain everywhere in the East, leaves with her diplomatic representatives the emblems of her power by land and sea. The impression is a salutary one on both the people and the government. A short distance above we drop anchor near the custom house, where a floating bridge, resting on boats, spans the river. We are quickly surrounded by the most curious of boats, called *goophas*, which have been used on those rivers from the earliest times. Not even the original Noah's Ark would attract so much attention on the Thames or the Hudson as a Bagdad *goopha*. It is made of light wicker work and covered on the outside with a thick coating of black bitumen, and ornamented sometimes with cowrie shells. It is *perfectly round*, being slightly drawn in at the top, and from eight to ten feet in diameter. It suggested to me at once the nursery story about the " three wise men of Gotham who went to sea in a bowl." To an inexperienced eye it seems the most unmanageable of all boats,—but two men with short paddles propel it quite rapidly across the swift stream, and being light, its carrying capacity is very great. As many men as can stand upright, or twenty sheep, and sometimes horses, are thus ferried across.

Near us there is moored to the bank another transport which is peculiar to the rivers of Mesopotamia. It is a raft of skins called a *kallek*, which has floated down the Tigris five hundred miles from Mosul. The timber and inflated goat skins of which it is composed, as well as the produce which forms its freight, all find a market in Bagdad.

Above the floating bridge, on the eastern bank, extend for a long distance the gardens and low buildings attached to the Pasha's palace. There one can see, scattered in groups over the grounds, or reclining on divans under the broad verandas, amidst wreaths of smoke, the officers and soldiers attached to the Governor's household. On the opposite shore is a large building with a tall smoke stack, the only un-Oriental object within sight. This is the government arsenal and machine shops, where they are constructing under the supervision of English engineers, a small iron war steamer. Still further up on the same side at the bend of the river, a singular object attracts our attention. It is a mosque cut in two by the undermining of the rapid current. One half its lofty dome still remains, leaving the innermost recesses of its places of prayer exposed to view.

This is the only interior of a temple sacred to Moslem worship which an unbeliever can see in Bagdad. The people here are not especially fanatics. The largest liberty in the exercise of their religion is granted to Jew and Christian, and this has been characteristic of Bagdad from the earliest times. It is rather pleasant to feel that I am outside and beyond the great stream of European travel. But when the enterprising Cook shall extend his " tours " in this direction, and the crowd of London cock-

neys, who follow in the wake of "Gaze & Co.," shall fill
the streets, the power of *baksheesh* will probably open to
the *Giaours* the most sacred precincts of the holy places.

To the stranger who arrives here by the river, the first
impressions of Bagdad are curious sights, even if he has
seen Cairo, Damascus, and Constantinople,—so that the
charm of novelty lasts longer than in any other city in
the East, and to describe a few of these is all that I shall
attempt to do.

And first let me take the reader to the highest attaina-
ble point from whence the city can be viewed. It is the
top of a half ruined minaret which overlooks the " cotton-
thread market." The mosque to which it was once attached has all crumbled away and disappeared. The sa-
credness of the place being gone, we are permitted to climb
its broken stairway to the gallery, about ninety feet from
the ground, where six hundred years ago the *Muezzin*
called the faithful to prayer.

From this point, we command a fine view of the whole
city and surrounding country for miles in every direction.
We trace the line of the crumbling walls which enclose an
area of about six hundred and fifty acres, not over one-
third of which is covered with buildings. Groves of
palms and other trees fill large areas in the south-eastern
part of the city, through which we can see the ruins of a
once densely populated tract, as if nature was trying to
cover from sight these sad relics of former grandeur. To
the north and south as far as the eye can reach, the river,
glistening in the morning sun, winds through dense groves
of palm and orange trees, but in every other direction the
desert sands come up to the very walls of the city. Six
miles up the river the double gilded domes and four elegant minarets of *Kathmain*, rise high above the sombre
foliage of the trees. This is the burial place of two

*Imaums*, direct descendants of Mahomet, and is visited every year by thousands of pilgrims, especially from Persia and India. A short distance from this shrine we see a pine-shaped cone of snowy whiteness which covers the tomb of Zobeide the lovely queen of Haroun-al-Raschid. Ten miles away, standing alone in the desert, is a tower one hundred and fifty feet in height called *Akker-goof*. A spiral way ascends on the outside, like the common ideal pictures of the tower of Babel. It is of great antiquity, and early travelers supposed it to be the work of the immediate descendants of Noah.

But while we have been scanning these interesting objects in the far distance, a scene is passing at our feet too characteristic of Bagdad to escape notice. The houses here are usually built two stories in height, with ranges of apartments opening into a square or inner court. Subterranean rooms called *serdaubs*, are occupied during the day for the shelter they afford from the intense heat, but the flat roofs are used for the evening meal and for sleeping on at night. From this lofty station hundreds of these bedrooms are exposed to view, and domestic scenes, illustrative of the habits and manners of the Bagdadees—such as we read of in Madrid, when " Le Diable Boiteux " unroofed the houses—are open before us. These people are early risers, and in most cases, it being now a few minutes after sunrise, the servants have rolled up the beds and carried them to the rooms below, to which the occupants have retired for the bath and to commence the occupations of the day. But a few late sleepers still linger on the terraces, and little suspect that the stranger is taking note of their movements.

The English traveler, Buckingham, who stood on this spot nearly fifty years ago, thus describes the scene in which half a century has produced no change. " Among the more wealthy, the husband sleeps on a raised bedstead, made of light wicker work, called a *doeshick*. It has a mattress and cushions of silk or cotton, and covered by a thick quilt, but is without curtains or mosquito net. The night air is always dry, and towards morning there usually springs up a cool breeze that dies away soon after sunrise. The wife occupies a similar bed but always on the ground —that is, without a bedstead, and at a respectful distance from her husband. The children are scattered about on mattresses, and the slaves or servants sleep on mats, but all within sight of each other. In a few houses there are low parapets dividing off the sleeping apartments, but these are rare and probably occupied by Europeans. On retiring the natives do not divest themselves of the clothing worn during the day, except to lay aside the outer robes."

" After rising the husband performs his devotions, and then seats himself on his carpet, where his wife serves him with a *chibouk* and coffee with her own hands, retiring at a respectful distance to wait for the cup, and sometimes with hands crossed, and even kissing his hand on receiving the cup from it—a mark of respect very common in the East. While the husband is lounging on the carpet or cushions enjoying his morning pipe the women of the family generally pray, going through the same forms and prostrations as the men, but the children under twelve years of age never join their devotions."

But while we are lingering in our lofty perch the sun is getting uncomfortably hot, and we descend, groping our way down the dark stairway, and emerge into the narrow and crooked streets, as yet cool and shady. The walls on either side look solid and substantial. The building material is hard kilnburned bricks of a light dun color. Their rounded corners show that they have been used over and over again, taken from the ruins of one edifice to construct another. New bricks are very rarely seen, and can readily be detected. The streets are narrow and unpaved and in wet weather are very muddy and disagreeable. There are few windows or other openings except heavy iron-clamped doors on the first stories, but *oriels*, or projecting windows, frequently overhang the street, and you may chance to see a pair of bright eyes peering through the half closed lattice. Sometimes the projections cross the street and unite two houses on opposite sides.

As you glance within the open doors you frequently see the square court yard shaded by orange and lemon trees; or the leaning date palm overhangs the wall and its long pendant leaves droop down in the street. These date palms seem to spring up singly from the most crowded parts of the city, and must have a remarkable tenacity of life to flourish in such locations. They do not afford much shade, but their graceful forms and feathery leaves are a great relief to the eye.

On our way back to the *Khan* of Lynch & Co., we pass a tall minaret attached to a ruined mosque, called the " Minar of the Storks." On its summit these birds have built an enormous nest, and hold undisputed possession of the place. They are never molested, but held as sacred by all Moslems. During the winter months they migrate to some warmer clime, but it is firmly believed that at this time every year they make a pilgrimage to Mecca. These birds are so pious and reverent that if a number of persons cry out, " Allah!" " Allah!" as they fly overhead, they will drop to the ground and bury their heads in the earth. If once touched by human hands they never rise again but droop and die. I will not vouch for the truth of this, but the Mahometans all believe it most sincerely, and I have met Europeans of undoubted credibility, who assert that they have witnessed such a feat.

Shortly after my arrival, on the evening of the first of
May, as we were dining at eight o'clock on the terrace, we
were startled by a terrific din.   We then noticed that there
was a nearly total eclipse of the moon, and on consulting

THE ECLIPSE.—FRIGHTENING AWAY THE JIN.

an English almanac, we found that " it would be invisible
at Greenwich, but a total eclipse in Australia and some
parts of Asia."   The tumult increased, and soon the whole
population of Bagdad seemed to have assembled on the
housetops, armed with pots, pans, and kitchen utensils,
which they beat with a tremendous clatter, at the same
time screaming and howling at the top of their voices.
Frequent explosions of guns and pistols added to the tur-
moil, and it was kept up for nearly an hour, until they had
succeeded in frightening away the *Jin*, or evil spirit, who
had caught hold of the planet.   It was a most amusing
scene.   Our own servants caught the excitement, and our
host told us the next day that they well nigh knocked out

the bottoms of all his cooking utensils. It was a dozen New Years Eves, Fourth of Julys, and wedding serenades rolled into one, and the noise was sufficient to drive away a whole army of evil spirits, even at so great a distance.

The ignorant Mahometan population of Bagdad are exceedingly superstitious, and the Fakeers, Dervishes, and other mendicant orders, contrive to make a very comfortable living out of the charity of the faithful. The members of these societies do not openly or clamorously beg, although they do not refuse the gifts of the charitably disposed, but they elicit money by the performance of pretended miracles, giving charms against illness, wounds and evils of all kinds. One sect assert they are invulnerable to steel, and incapable of being burned by fire.

The Arabs are implicit believers in the efficacy of charms and other mystic arts. No species of knowledge is more venerated than that of the occult sciences, which afford maintenance to a vast number of quacks and ignorant pretenders. Some of the professors of the " black art " pretend to know what is passing in their absence, to expel evil spirits, cure diseases by laying on of hands, calm tempests at sea, and to be able to say their noon-day prayers at Mecca without stirring from their houses in Bagdad. A still lower class of mendicant *dervishes* and *mollahs* practice the art of jugglery, in which they are adepts. To the astonished spectators, they seem to pierce their bodies with spears, strike sharp pointed lances into their eyes, or leap from the roofs of houses upon poles shod with iron, which appear to run through their bodies, after which they are carried like spitted victims about the streets.

I have before described the weekly exhibitions of the dancing *dervishes* in Cairo, but their *howling* brethren in Bagdad far surpass these in wildness and frenzy. Educated and intelligent Mahometans repudiate these sects, but their hold on the ignorant and superstitious masses is so strong that not even the government dares interfere, except in extreme cases to preserve the public peace.

# CHAPTER XVIII.

## STREET SCENES IN BAGDAD.

THE street scenes in Bagdad,
the bazaars, market places,
and coffee houses, are more
unique and curious than any
I have ever before seen.
They deserve a more minute
description than space will
allow me to give. I have
strolled through all parts of
the city, at first accompanied
by my servant, Yusef, but
latterly alone, as I have become more familiar with the
streets and localities. Every
where I have been treated with civility, without the scowls
that I have sometimes detected on the faces of the Chinese,
when the "foreign barbarian" invades their seclusion. I

have picked up a few words of Arabic, but of course I cannot understand any comments or remarks that may be made by the people about me. It is a national trait of these Arabs and Turks, never to show any surprise or curiosity.

The bazaars in every Eastern town are interesting, and especially so here, where they are very extensive, and seem crowded at all hours of the day with the most varied and heterogeneous mass of humanity that the sun shines on. It can best be likened to the constantly changing views of a kaleidoscope.

Everywhere, in streets and bazaars, you meet trains of donkeys laden with water-skins. Many hundreds must be employed in this business, as all water used in the city is brought from the river in this manner.

The attractions of bright colors and gaudy costumes all belong to the male sex. The street dress of the women is the extreme of ugliness, being the same hideous wrapper of black or white cotton, enveloping them from head to foot. Sometimes a dainty little yellow boot peeps out from under this disguise, and one is tempted with sacrilegious hand to lift the veil that *perhaps* conceals a face of ravishing beauty, such as romance associates with the ladies of Bagdad.

The females here wear in the street a peculiar black mask of thinly woven horse hair. It effectually conceals the face, but allows the free circulation of air, and through it they can see all that passes before them. Behind this friendly screen, youth and age, deformity and beauty, are alike safe from prying curiosity or insulting stare. I have sometimes laughed, when an accident has deranged one of these veils, to see behind it a face blacker than the mask itself.

The lower class of Arab women go abroad unveiled.

14

They are very ugly, their arms being tattooed with blue marks, and the married ones wearing on the side of one nostril a gold or silver ornament like an immense filigree-work button, and large anklets and bracelets of silver or brass, according to their means.

The indoor dress of the wealthy ladies of Bagdad is spoken of as singularly rich and beautiful in color and material, but as I have never had the good fortune to see the *penetralia* of a Turkish house, I shall not attempt to describe it.

These Eastern people are fond of any shade of red and other bright colors, and there is always a glittering stir, in which gay-colored flowing robes, shawled turbans, silver-hilted daggers, swords, and pistols, make up a lively picture. The Persian, the Bedouin, the Arab, the Turk, the Jew, and the Christian, each has his characteristic dress, and to describe all the different costumes that pass me every half hour, would fill a small volume.

The principal bazaars are in a triple range, and are shaded from the sun by a lofty, arched roof of brick and mortar. Each kind of merchandise and branch of trade has its own section. Here can be seen the beautiful fabrics of Persia and Cashmere, the jewels of India, the spices and perfumes of Arabia, and the more familiar manufactures of Europe. The languages spoken are as various as the costumes of the people.

In the center of a stall sits a bearded Turkish merchant, with his legs crossed under him, as stately and motionless as a statue, waiting with true Oriental resignation, while he slowly puffs his *chibouk*, for Providence to send him a customer. If you stop to look at his wares he silently displays the goods required, and names the price with seeming indifference whether you purchase or not. If you pass on without buying, he quietly resumes his pipe, and without showing the least disappointment, he smokes on until another customer calls his attention.

The bazaars are none of them over twelve feet wide, and while we are gazing about, half bewildered at the curious scenes, we are in danger of being trampled on by a train of loaded camels, mules, or donkeys, or from the heels of a mettled Arab horse, whose rider, a Bedouin from the desert, looks neither to the right nor the left, but goes his way with an air of fierce independence, as if lord of the soil.

A long procession of donkeys loaded with wood, remind me of the lady in the "Arabian Nights," who by falsely attributing the wound in her cheek to a blow from the pannier of that animal, endangered the lives of the whole respectable community of wood drivers.

The coffee shops are very numerous, and on the large benches, covered with straw matting, there is always a crowd of loungers. I am told that wine, forbidden by the Koran, and *arrack*, a fiery spirit distilled from dates, are sold in many of these places, but I have never seen a person here who seemed intoxicated.

I have often stopped when alone, at one of these shops, where room would be made for me on one of the divans, and an attendant would bring a little egg cup, holding not over a tablespoonful of strong, black coffee of most delicious flavor. Then a *narghileh*—a supply of which is always kept ready for use. This pipe, which in India is called a *hookah*, and in Persia a *killion*, is made here in the form of a letter V without the long flexible tube common in Damascus and Constantinople. The mouth-piece is a reed, and the water through which the smoke passes is held in a large cocoanut shell. The tobacco used for the *narghileh* is of a peculiar kind, and is wet before being lighted, in doing which they always use a piece of live charcoal. The smoke is deliciously cooled and purified by passing through scented rose water. For this entertainment, I pay at the coffee shops two *comrais*—about five cents.

The *narghileh* is as universally used among Europeans residing here, as by the natives. It is brought in after every meal, among the wealthy people being richly ornamented with silver, and placed upon a little stand by your side.

These two articles, coffee and tobacco, are so intimately associated with life in the East, that they may be called the habitual refreshment, and only want of a Turk or an Arab. They are the chief mediums of social communication and hospitality, being offered as a matter of course, to every visitor and stranger on his arrival.

The tobacco of Arabia and Persia is lighter colored and milder than that grown in Syria and Egypt. The soothing weed of Persia does not satisfy the craving of English residents here, accustomed to the use of wines and strong stimulants. They use *narghilehs* and *chibouks* only as preliminary to the more rank and powerful narcotic that has come across the Atlantic from Virginia.

The story of the wandering Arab who built his fire beneath a wild shrub on the edge of the desert, and thus first inhaled the delicious fragrance of the roasted berry, is probably as authentic as that told by the " gentle Elia " of the accidental burning of a Chinaman's house, by which " roast pig " came to the knowledge of mankind.

The reader may be curious to hear a little about Arabian coffee, and how it is prepared, although it may be tantalizing to a devoted lover of the fragrant berry. Palgrave, in his " Travels in Arabia," says that the *only real coffee* is that grown in the Arabian province of Yemen, and commonly called " Mocha," from its main port of exportation. Of this but a small proportion ever reaches the Mediterranean. It is picked over and over by hand, sifted and resifted, the hard, rounded, half-transparent, greenish-brown berries being selected, grain by grain, for home consumption. It is only the flattened, opaque and whitish berries that find their way to Europe. According to this authority, the list of coffees begins and ends with " Mocha," and the produce of India, Java, and South America should be classified as *beans.* It is well in these days of rye and chicory that all of us have not so refined and delicate a taste as Palgrave.

In an Arab house, to prepare and pour the coffee is the special duty of a favorite servant, as it forms so important a part of the domestic economy of the household. A large coffee pot about two-thirds full of water is placed close to the fire and becomes gradually warm, while the other operations are in progress. Two or three handfuls of un-roasted coffee are in the meantime taken from a niche in the wall close by, carefully picked over, and being poured into a large open iron ladle, are placed over the glowing charcoal. They crackle, redden, and smoke a little, but are withdrawn long before they turn black or become charred. They are then pounded in a mortar till they are coarsely broken, but not reduced to powder. A smaller coffee pot is then half filled with boiling water from the larger one, and the coffee poured into it. A few aromatic seeds or saffron are added, and the boiling process is not allowed to be long or vehement. Last of all the liquid is strained off through some fibres of the inner palm-bark, placed for that purpose in the spout. It is served very hot, in this country without sugar, in small cups which are never more than half filled. In Egypt and Syria it is made very sweet by adding sugar while boiling. It is considered etiquette to sip but a single mouthful, and return the cup to be frequently refilled. In the coffee shops the preparation is not so elaborate as here described, but the flavor always seemed to me more delicate than any I ever tasted in Europe or America. Whether this is to be attributed to the mode of preparation or to the quality of the berry, I am unable to say.

The social amusements of the people, both here and in other Oriental cities, are very few and simple. Cards are unknown, but chess, draughts, and a game called *mangala*, are frequently played in the coffee houses, and in the open air around the market places. The latter game is by far the most common, and it consists of a table or board, with about a dozen holes, into which the players drop cowrie shells or small pebbles. The more domestic amusements are singing, dancing, and story telling. Of the latter they are excessively fond, and the professional reader, or teller of stories located in the golden age of the Caliphs, is sure of a circle of eager and attentive listeners.

Some years ago when in Damascus, which next to Bagdad is the most thoroughly Oriental city of the world, I strolled out one day alone, and entered a large public garden, where several hundred people of the better class were seated under the trees, enjoying the delicious coolness and shade. The waters of the Abana and the Pharpar, the beautiful rivers of Damascus flowed through the garden, and sparkled in many a fountain, as beautiful now as in the time of Naaman, the Syrian. I wore a *fez* and no one stared at me, although I was known, of course, to be a *Frank*, or European.

I stopped for a moment to watch a game being played by two well dressed Arabian gentlemen, which seemed identical with our common game of back-gammon, except that no boxes were used, the dice being thrown by the hand. Presently one of the players rose, and the other with a courteous salaam motioned me to the vacant seat. I accepted the invitation and played nine games, winning four of them, but losing the others. In the meantime I ordered *narghilehs* and coffee for both of us. My opponent was very polite, and at the end of every game with its varying result, his pleasant nod and smile were as full of meaning as any words could possibly be. My knowledge of Arabic was very limited, and my companion could speak no French or English ; but whatever our conversation may have lacked in brilliancy was amply made up by the most ex-

DAMASCUS.

pressive pantomime. At the close of the play, the major-ity of the games being against me, I called the attendant, and being the losing party, I proposed according to West-ern customs, to pay the score. This my Arabian friend at first strenuously opposed, but I insisted, and holding out to the servant a dozen or more silver coins of various denominations from a *piaster* (five cents) to a *mejeide* (about a dollar) I pointed to the *narghilehs* and coffee, and by pantomime, told him to take his pay.   Having no definite idea of the proper charge, I should have been entirely satisfied if he had chosen the largest coin in my hand.   To my surprise he selected a two-piaster piece.   Thinking that he had made a mistake, I again pointed to the table, *narghilehs* and coffee, and held out my hand for him to take the proper sum.   But he only made a low salaam, and held up the trifling coin as all right.

TEST OF MAHOMETAN HONESTY.

The result of such a trial to the honesty of a waiter in Europe or America can readily be imagined.   In the one case he would certainly have selected the largest piece offered him—but in an American restaurant I fear the waiter would have shown his advance in knowledge since he landed on our shores, by taking all the coins in my hand, and perhaps asking for more.

Some whole streets in Bagdad are devoted to provisions and fruits. Rice, barley, and wheat are stored in great quantities in a quarter of the city called the " Corn Market." Oranges, melons, and cucumbers are very abundant, and many kinds of fruit of which I do not know even the names. But no one fruit as an article of food or commerce, compares in importance with the product of the date palm. It is sometimes called " the bread of the land, the staff of life, and the staple of commerce." Mahomet said to his followers, " Honor the palm tree for she is your mother." There are more than a dozen varieties of dates, the choicest being of a rich amber color and semi-transparent. The yearly product of a date tree is from one hundred to three hundred pounds, worth from four to ten dollars. Some of the date groves number thousands of trees, growing quite closely together, and requiring very little care or attention. The dates exported from Bassorah, near the mouth of the Euphrates, are very large and of fine quality. I am told that no Bassorah dates are sent to America. Our supply comes entirely from Muscat, which produces a smaller and inferior variety. This fruit, which when fresh is about the size of a large plum, is juicy and of delicious flavor. During the date season, August and September, it forms the staple article of food for all classes of people.

It bears no more resemblance in looks or taste to the mashed and sticky mass sewed up in matting, that is familiar to us under that name, than a bunch of fresh grapes to a box of raisins.

# CHAPTER XIX.

## THE PASHA OF BAGDAD.

HE Pasha of Bagdad is Governor of a Province three times as large as the State of New York, and containing a population of about two millions. He is an absolute and despotic ruler, subject only to his master, the Sultan of Turkey. He has the command of a large army stationed in Bagdad and other large towns within the Pashalic, which is bounded on the east and south by the Persian frontier and the Gulf. More than once, ambitious men holding this position so remote from Constantinople, have been suspected of designs to render themselves independent sovereigns, as was successfully accomplished by Mohamet Ali, Pasha of Egypt. The present governor is Redif Pasha, who has occupied this post for about a year. He was a successful general in the late campaign of the Turkish army against the revolting Arab tribes in Yemen, and is a man of unquestioned energy and ability. As he is supposed to be hostile to foreign influence and projects within his province, he is not popular with the foreign residents and officials.

Since I have been here, he has had an opportunity to show his power as a despotic ruler, and has acted with a nerve and energy worthy of all praise. About two weeks ago the Tigris, which has been on the rampage for the past two months, reached a point unprecedented within ten years, and the city was threatened with inundation. The water broke through the dikes ten miles up the river, and the torrent swept down with irresistible force, doing great damage to crops, and in a single day turning the broad plain back of the city, into an immense lake. Since then Bagdad has been an island, having no communication with the country, except by boats. The water was only kept from flowing into the city by a broad embankment, or *sud*, just outside the walls, which in many places is out of repair. Great alarm was felt of such an inundation as occurred in 1831—the year of the plague—when seven thousand houses were undermined and fell in a single day.

Here was an emergency for prompt action. The Pasha issued an order closing all the bazaars and shops, and for four days impressed the whole male population (foreigners excepted) to work on the dikes. Half the force was sent up the river, and the balance set to work under the direction of the officials to repair the embankments around the city. I rode out in that direction one morning, and the scene was a lively one. Several thousand men were at work, and the Pasha himself was on the spot, surrounded by a brilliantly uniformed staff, superintending the operations. These energetic measures saved the city. The break in the dike up the river was stopped and the water gradually subsided. But much sickness is sure to follow, as the lake outside evaporates under the scorching heat of the sun.

Before I left Cairo, at the suggestion of Mr. Beardsley, our Consul General to Egypt, who informed me that there were no American officials, ministers or consuls, in the countries I was about to visit, I enclosed a letter of introduction kindly given me by Hon. John M. Francis, late United States Minister to Greece, to the United States Minister at Constantinople, with the request that he would forward to me at Bagdad such credentials to the Pasha as would be of service in any excursions I might desire to make to Babylon or other places of interest in Mesopotamia. I found awaiting me at Bagdad an envelope of portentous size, containing a very polite note from Mr. Boker, and a *firman* from the Turkish Government. This document was addressed to the Pasha of Bagdad, and written in Turkish characters, on a large sheet of heavy official paper. The translation reads in English as follows :

"To Redif Pasha, Governor General of Bagdad :
    "Excellency :—
            "The bearer, an American Citizen of distinction, intends to resort to Bagdad in order to visit the country round that city. The American Legation has consequently requested me to address a letter of recommendation to your Excellency.
    "The voyage of foreigners having always been considered as an object of protection and special deference, I request you to treat the said traveler with all honors on his arrival at Bagdad, and to afford him all possible facilities, under any circumstances, which may be in conformity with existing treaties ; and to extend to him your protection and hospitality.
            "I am, Sir, etc., etc."
                            *Seal of the Grand Vizier.*
"Ministry of Foreign Affairs, Constantinople, Feb'y 19th, 1289." *

---

* (The date, 1289, being of the Hegira.)

THE WALLS AND MOAT OF BAGDAD.    *From a photograph in possession of the Author.*

About a week after my arrival, armed with this formidable document, and escorted by two *Cawasses* from the Residency in showy uniforms, I started to pay my official visit to the Pasha.

Declining the offer of a horse, as the narrow streets and bazaars can be threaded with more convenience, if less ostentation, on foot, I proceeded to the *Serai*, or palace, accompanied by my armed escort, who cleared the way through the crowded streets with, as it seemed to me, unnecessary rudeness. But the officials strutted on, regardless of remarks, not complimentary, I fancy, hurled at them by persons whom they jostled out of the way. As a compliment to the official I was about to visit, I wore my Turkish *fez*—a plain red cap with long black tassel—such as are frequently worn by travelers in Egypt and Syria. In Cairo the *fez* is worn by every officer and soldier, from the Khedive down to the drummer boy. It is considered a matter of etiquette never to remove it at dinner, ball or opera, neither in the presence of the highest officials, nor in the mosque. Even the Sultan, when I saw him going from his palace on the Bosphorus to the mosque, wore a *fez*, in appearance the same, though perhaps of finer texture than that on the head of his meanest subject. But here in Bagdad the *fez* is considered the distinctive mark of a Turk, and it is seldom worn by foreigners, and never by a native Arab, unless he is in some way connected with the government. While wearing my *fez* in the streets of Bagdad, I have sometimes noticed a scowl as an Arab glanced towards me, such as I never saw when I had on my much more comfortable Indian *pith* hat, and was taken for an Englishman.

The Palace is not an imposing building, but its situation on the river's bank is very pleasant. Adjoining it are the barracks and arsenal, built a few years ago by a former

pasha,—large and handsome structures in modern style of
architecture. The *Serai* is only occupied by the Pasha
during the day for the transaction of business. An elegant palace two miles up the river, surrounded by gardens,
is his private residence. Passing through the guards at
the gate and an outer court, where several horses saddled
and bridled were held by grooms, past more guards, we
entered a large court-yard, filled with groups of soldiers
and surrounded by long two-storied buildings, with verandas facing the court, occupied by officers and clerks. I
sent in my credentials and card by one of the *cawasses* and
requested an audience with his Excellency. He quickly

THE PASHA OF BAGDAD.

returned, accompanied by a handsome young Turkish
officer, *aid-de-camp* to the Pasha, who ushered me through
an ante-chamber where several officers were waiting, the
doors guarded by soldiers with fixed bayonets, into a large

and handsomely furnished audience room overlooking the river. Wide divans covered with silk ran around the lofty room, and the hangings over the doors and windows were heavy and of rich materials. The Pasha was seated at the further end of the apartment, and near him was a large table, on which were writing materials and piles of papers. As I advanced down the long room he rose to receive me, shook hands, and courteously motioned me to a seat beside him. He is a large man, tall and quite portly, perhaps forty-five years old, with a brown beard, full face, and eyes sharp and piercing. His dress was entirely European, except the *fez*, without even a button to indicate his rank. His countenance indicates energy and firmness, and his manners are very courteous and pleasant. Several officers of rank standing near were presented to me, but none were seated except the Pasha and myself.

As he spoke only Turkish and Arabic, Mr. Stanno, a Levantine in the service of the government, was summoned to act as interpreter. Our conversation was necessarily slow, but the questions and replies were very readily translated, and I felt quite at my ease. The Pasha enquired by what route I had come, how long I intended to stay, etc., and seemed gratified when I told him that I was better pleased with Bagdad than with Cairo or Constantinople. I took occasion to compliment him on the energy and efficiency of the measures he had taken to prevent an inundation. Taking up my credentials, which mentioned me in complimentary terms as a traveler, he made very intelligent enquiries regarding the countries I had visited, and seemed fully to comprehend that England and America are two distinct and separate countries. He kindly offered me every facility for seeing Bagdad, and said that, as I was the only American who had visited him, he hoped I should receive a favorable impression. When I mentioned my plans for visiting the ruins of Babylon, he offered me an escort of soldiers, and letters to the governors of the different towns on the route. I accepted with thanks his offer of letters, but said that a guard of soldiers was quite unnecessary, as under his efficient rule the country was everywhere safe to a peaceful traveler.

In the meantime, a servant had brought in coffee and sherbet on a silver tray, and long, jasmine-stemmed *chibouks*. My audience lasted about an hour, and as I rose to take leave he again shook hands with me and renewed his offers of anything in his power to render my visit to Bagdad pleasant.

I left with a very agreeable impression of the courtesy and politeness of a Turkish Pasha. The next day Mr. Stanno brought me a document in Turkish, similar in appearance to the one before given, addressed to the governors and other officials on the route to Hillah and Babylon, and commending the "American Traveler" in the strongest terms to their attentions and protection. How this *firman*, which I still retain as a souvenir of my journey, saved my life, perhaps, in a position of great difficulty and danger, will be told hereafter.

The traveler in the East often hears the most extravagant statements as to the venality and corruption of officials—that they are open to bribery from the highest to the lowest,—that foreign goods are admitted without paying duties,—that fraudulent contracts are made in behalf of the government, etc. I have heard of a former Pasha of Bagdad who paid off his soldiers in tobacco and soap at exorbitant prices, which the poor fellows were obliged to dispose of in the bazaars at half their cost. A story was once told me with a sober face, that a Persian governor of Bushire once cleared off the arrears due his

men with *bricks*, a species of " hard currency " not convenient to handle, but easy to obtain in a town where half
the buildings are in ruins. I cannot put faith in such
stories. An Englishman's standard of official integrity is
very high, and I honor them for it. But it is hardly fair
to judge an Oriental people by their ideal. Government
officers are nowhere in this country held to such strict
accountability as in Europe.

The rulers of provinces distant from the home government, and with difficult means of communication, are
especially liable to temptation, with no fear of " Investi-
gating Committees " before their eyes. And yet I believe
that dishonesty is the exception, not the rule.

Corrupt officials are not the exclusive outgrowth of
Oriental barbarism. As extremes sometimes meet, the
" far East " and the " far West " may have much in common. Pashas as well as Members of Congress sometimes
get rich during their terms of office. The Turk feels jus-
tified in pocketing a " retainer," and so does the M. C.
But it is neither charitable nor just to infer that all officials
on either continent are equally corrupt.

The person who is always on the lookout for a rogue is
apt to overlook an honest man when he meets him. It has
been my good fortune to meet a large proportion of honest
and conscientious people of every nationality, in different
parts of the world. A far pleasanter retrospect this will
ever be to me, than a long row of thieves and rascals, whom I
might perhaps have detected, had my attention been specially directed to the dark side of human nature.

Every Sunday morning the English Episcopal service is
read by Colonel Herbert at the Residency, to a congrega-
tion of about twenty persons, which comprises nearly the
whole Protestant population at Bagdad. I visited the different Christian places of worship one Sunday afternoon
15

with Doctor Colvill, who has resided here for a long time, and speaks Arabic and Persian like a native. In the East no class of foreigners have so much influence as physicians. The doctor is welcome alike in the *Khan* of the wealthy merchant and the tent of the Bedouin Sheik.

We first called at the Latin (Catholic) church, attached to which is a school for children. The entrance is through a heavy iron-studded door in a blank wall, then a narrow passage leads to a court, in which are the church and school buildings. The priests are French and their flock is composed of the few residents in Bagdad from the Catholic countries of Europe, some of whom are married to native women. The church is neatly fitted up, with the usual tinsel decorations on the altar, and there are several paintings on the walls, none of any especial merit, except one of the Virgin and child, of which the priests are very proud.

From here we went to the Chaldean and Armenian Churches, of which there are two distinct sects. The orthodox Armenians comprise many of the oldest and wealthiest Christian families.

The other Church of this ancient race acknowledges the Pope as its spiritual head, and includes within its fold a large population of Chaldeans and Copts. This church is large and handsome. Adjoining is the residence of the Bishop upon whom we called, and Dr. C. being his special friend, we were received and entertained with much honor. The Bishop is a fine looking man, wearing a full black beard, with a bright intelligent face and courteous manners. He was dressed in a robe of purple silk, with cap and shoes of the same color. He visited Rome at the time of the Ecumenical Council five years ago, and was invested with the rank of a Cardinal. He is the head of all the churches of his denominations in Arabia. Coffee and cigarettes were brought according to the universal custom, and the Doctor acting as interpreter, a very interesting conversation followed. I was introduced as an American, and the Bishop expressed a great desire to visit that country, and was only prevented from fear of the stormy Atlantic. During the interview I detected the word "Yankeedonia," and my friend, being a native of the "land o' cakes," I supposed it was of his own invention to signify America. But I learned that this is a proper Arabic word and means the " New World."

Leaving the Christian prelate, we next called at the house of a wealthy Jew, and were presented to the whole family, from the aged patriarchal grandfather, down to the youngest children, with each of whom we in turn shook hands. They were very hospitable and polite, the ladies were quite good looking, and the children handsome and well bred. One of the ladies was disfigured by the " date mark," a scar the size and shape of a date, resulting from a boil, to which all the people of this country are subject once in their lifetime. Every European who remains here any length of time has to pass through this ordeal. When it appears on the face the scar it leaves is especially unfortunate.

The Jewish population of Bagdad is about twenty thousand. Here as elsewhere, they are the principal *serafs*, or money changers, and brokers, and are confidentially employed by all classes in the money transactions of the place. Their great wealth, which in former times was a temptation to rob and oppress them, now commands the respect even of the most bigoted Turk and Mohametan.

Our last call was on the ex-King of Oude, who is called here *The Nawab*. He is very rich, and besides his private fortune, receives a pension of $60,000 a year from the English Government. His name is *Akbar-ood-Dowlah*, and he is addressed officially as " His Royal Highness." His house and grounds are on the banks of the Tigris and very beautiful. He fortunately yielded his royal dignities and palaces in Lucknow to the English, before the breaking out of the Sepoy rebellion, and has ever since resided here, enjoying the protection of a British subject. The *Nawab* entertained us with coffee, sherbet and *narghilehs.* He understands English and has traveled all over Europe. In England he was received by the Queen with the honors due to his former rank. He is an old man of about sixty-five, but still active and vigorous, and has the courteous manners of a cultivated gentleman.

# CHAPTER XX.

## HABITS AND CUSTOMS OF THE ARABS.

Their Courtesy and Politeness—Morning Salutations—Scurrilous Language
Very Rare—The Beard Always Worn—Hardy Children—Rite of Cir-
cumcision—Hospitality, an Ancient and Hereditary Virtue—Under no
Circumstances to be Violated—Robbery no Crime—An Arab's Property—
Courtship, and Marriage Ceremonies—The Bride Sometimes to be Caught
—She Scratches and Bites like a Vixen—But only for Show—The Husband
Pays for the Wife—Widows and Divorced Women Half Price—Song of
the Lover, Rather Rough on the Father—Divorce Made Easy—Funeral
Ceremonies—Arabian Horses—Their Beauty, Intelligence, and Speed—
Description of a Famous Breed—Their Wonderful Endurance—National
Dress of the Arabs—Picture of a Bedouin—Characteristics of the Race—
Customs Unchanged for a Thousand Years.

HE Arabs who dwell outside
the towns, though rude in
manners and fierce in general character, are not without civility and politeness.
Their usual salutation is,
"Peace be with you."
When friends meet after a
long absence, shaking hands
and kissing are the usual
custom, and sometimes a
passage, returning thanks
to Allah, is repeated from
the Koran. On entering a
house or tent, the pious exclamation, "Bismillah," is
rarely omitted. In the towns, where more ceremonious

phrases are current, the morning salutation to an acquaintance is, " May your day be white "—and the reply, " May
yours be like milk." I have sometimes seen gray-bearded
old patriarchs, meeting in the street, stop and embrace
each other, kissing the beard, or if there is much difference
in rank, the hand, with every indication of kindness and
respect. The women salute each other by kissing the
forehead, the chin, and both cheeks. Even in quarreling,
the Arabs rarely use the ill names and scurrilous language
so often heard among more polished nations. In some
interior provinces, and during the pilgrimage to Mecca, the
head is closely shaved, but the beard is invariably worn its
natural length, and is considered a mark of dignity and
honor. In some parts of Arabia it is the fashion to dye
the beards a bright red, but this practice is not common.

Among the Arabs the children are brought up in the
most hardy manner. The name is given them immedi-
ately on their birth, and at the age of six or seven the
boys undergo the ceremony of circumcision. This is an
occasion of great feasting and rejoicing. The boys are
dressed in the richest stuffs, put upon fine horses, highly
adorned with trappings, and carried in public procession
through the streets with drums and rude music. These
celebrations are kept up far into the night at the houses of
their parents, but in the absence of all intoxicating drinks,
the wild music, and shrill discordant singing are not associated with a disturbance of the peace. Though the
revelers may awake the next morning with splitting head-
aches, they never find themselves in the police station.

Hospitality, the ancient and hereditary virtue of the
Arabs, is strictly enforced by the Koran, and one of the
most prominent traits of their social life. The tent of the
Sheik is always located at the point where the stranger
will be most likely to approach, and if seen coming from

afar he is reckoned the guest of the person who first des-
cries him. So long as he remains a guest his life and
property is perfectly secure. Should any robbery occur,
his host is bound in honor to indemnify him for any loss he
may sustain while under his protection. No emergency
can be so urgent as to palliate, much less excuse, any violation of the sacred rights of hospitality, after the stranger,
whether friend or foe, has put his hand upon the tent pole
of a Bedouin, or tasted his bread and salt.

An Arab has been heard to say that if his bitterest
enemy should present himself at the door of his tent, carrying the head of his own son, he would still be entitled
to a hospitable reception. No greater insult can be offered
to an Arab than to tell him that he has not treated his
guests with proper civility and attention.

The force of custom and tradition leads to such in-
congruities, that the defenceless traveler, who is sure to
receive every kindness as a guest, is liable a few days
after, to be waylaid, seized, and stripped of everything he
may possess by his former host. His life is rarely taken,
unless he resists to the shedding of the blood of his assail-
ants. With the wild tribes of the desert, robbery is a
science, and in their predatory raids it is reduced to a
regular system, in which they display great skill and
audacity. If detected and captured, the robber is kept in
close confinement until ransomed by his relatives and
friends. They attach no disgrace or criminality     to
theft, but if the attempt at robbery proves a failure through
bungling or bad management, it reflects discredit upon
the whole tribe.

An Arab's property consists in his flocks and herds.
No family can subsist without a least one camel; the man
who has ten is reckoned poor; thirty or forty place him in
easy circumstances; and sixty make him a rich man.

Marriages are generally solemnized on Friday. After the preliminary negotiation with the father, for the Arab husband pays for his wife instead of receiving a marriage portion, the contract is drawn up by the Cadi. The father usually consults the wishes of his daughter, but in some tribes the girl is only made acquainted with the proposed change in her condition, by being waylaid at a short distance from the camp by her future spouse, who seizes her and carries her by force to her father's tent. Though she

BEDOUIN STEALING A BRIDE.

may entertain no dislike to her lover, she defends herself to the best of her ability, and the more she struggles, bites, kicks, and cries, the more she is applauded ever after by her companions.

She is conducted to the women's apartment in her father's tent, where she is decked out in all her finery, the wedding suit being provided by the bridegroom, then mounted on a camel and escorted by her female relations, she is conducted to the camp of her husband. During these preceedings, etiquette requires that she should sob and cry most bitterly; but as her face is covered with a veil, it is not supposed that her weeping is more than empty sound.

The sum paid to the father depends upon the rank and circumstances of the parties; but if the bride be a widow, or a divorced woman, the price paid is never more than half what is expected for a maiden. These marriages are always reckoned ill-omened, and an occasion of very little ceremony or rejoicing.

Under the Mahometan law divorce is easy, and reflects no discredit or dishonor on the woman or her relatives. If she is turned away without any valid reason, she is entitled to a small sum of money, or some articles of household property. The process of divorce is simple, and cases of this description never cumber the dockets of the courts. The husband has only to pronounce the words, " Thou art divorced," in the presence of a witness, and the deed is done, and cannot be revoked.

But this does not prevent the man from again marrying the same woman, if both parties get over their pet, and consent to be once more united. The wife, too, has a kind of divorce. If ill-used or unhappy, she may fly to her father's house, and her husband has no right to reclaim her against her will.

In courtship the Arab often displays a good deal of gallantry, but owing to the constraint to which the women are subjected, the opportunities of the lover's meeting or seeing the face of the object of his affections are rare. While Europeans merely languish and sigh, and town Arabs compose amorous verses, the Bedouins have been known to cut and slash themselves to show the violence of their affections. In their amatory songs the lover sometimes expresses his passion in language that sounds oddly to western ears:—" O, Ghalia! if my father were a jack-ass I would sell him to purchase thee, my darling Ghalia!"

Funerals in Arabia are attended with some peculiar ceremonies. They usually take place at sunset, and the *Mollahs*, or priests, read passages from the Koran over the grave. Some tribes bury with the dead man his sword, turban and girdle. Women, but not men, wear mourning, and at the houses of the dead and in the processions to the burial place, there are females, hired for the occasion, who howl in the most heart-rending manner, beating their arms, tearing their hair, and behaving like furies.

In saying their prayers for the dead, Mahometans make no prostrations. This omission is considered significant of the coming resurrection. A man expecting shortly to meet a violent death will sometimes recite these same prayers by way of preparation, in anticipation of the event. They always lay the dead body on its side, with its face towards Mecca.

It is an authentic saying of Mahomet that " ghosts, ap-paritions, and the like, have nothing to do with Islamism." But it is well known that the Prophet himself was not free from superstition, and was especially credulous in regard to omens.

To most people of the West the name of Arabia is associated with the idea of horses of most wonderful beauty, intelligence, and speed. We have all read how they play with the children, eat and drink with their mas-ters, and sleep alongside them on the desert. All the pretty anecdotes of their docility and gentleness may be authentic, but even Palgrave, who is most enthusiastic in praise of Arab horseflesh, thinks that a Bedouin would be quite likely to rap his mare over the nose if she thrust it into his porridge. He describes the famous Nejdean breed which he saw in the royal stables at Raid, the capital of Wahābees, as the loveliest collection of horses, about three hundred in number, that he had ever seen or imagined. " Their average height was only about fourteen hands, but they were so exquisitely well shaped that want of greater size seemed hardly a defect. They were remarkably full in the haunches, having a shoulder shaped with exquisite elegance, a little saddle-backed, 'just the curve which indicates springiness without any weakness,' a head broad at the top and tapering down to the finest nose, a most intelligent and yet a singularly gentle look, full eye, sharp thorn-like ear, legs fore and hind that seemed as if made of hammered iron, so clean and yet so well twisted with sinew; a neat round hoof, just the requisite for hard ground ; the tail set, or rather thrown out at a perfect arch ; coat smooth, shining, and light ; the mane long, but not overgrown nor heavy ; the prevailing color chestnut or gray. Horses of this description are never sold—they only pass by war, legacy, or by free gift. When policy requires a present to Egypt, Persia, or Constantinople, mares are never sent, but the poorest stallions, though deserving to pass elsewhere for real beauties, are picked out for that purpose."

No Arab ever dreams of tying up a horse by the neck ; a tether replaces the halter. In Arabia, horses are much less vicious and refractory than in Europe or America. They are brought up in close contact with men, and having the free use of their senses and limbs, the Arab quadruped naturally developes more intelligence and gentleness than the closely stabled, blinkered, harnessed animal of western countries. Of the wonderful endurance of these choicest Arab horses the stories told are most marvelous. Twenty-four hours on the road, without drink and without flagging, under the burning Arabian sky, seems almost in-

credible, but when that period is doubled under the same
conditions at a single stretch, no one can be expected to
believe it, though vouched for by an authority as good as
Palgrave.   The exportation of horses is strictly forbidden,
both from Egypt and all parts of Arabia.

The peculiar national dress of the Arabs is well worth
description.   A coarse shirt, on which is a close fitting
tunic of silk or cotton, generally striped, and closely
belted around the waist,—over this is worn the *abba*, or
cloak of camel's hair, black, or with broad white bars,
through which the arms are thrust.   On their feet are red
shoes, pointed and turned up at the toes.   The head dress
is neither a turban nor a *fez*, but a square, thick handkerchief of silk or part cotton, in yellow or red stripes, the
woof of the ends being twisted in cords like a long fringe.
This is doubled triangularly, and thrown over the head so
that the two long ends hang down before the shoulders
and the third hangs down the back.   Around the crown
of the head is wound a double wisp of brown camel's
hair, partially twisted.   With this strange head gear and
their long, coarse cloaks, they rather resemble witch-like
women than men.   In very cold weather, they wind the
long ends of the *kaffeah* around their chins, leaving only
their eyes visible.   Silk being a non-conductor, this head
dress forms an excellent protection against both heat and
cold.

The Bedouins are tanned to an almost sooty blackness,
and with this wild head dress, and their black, piercing
eyes looking out from under elf-like locks, as they scour
along on their blooded horses, their clothes flying wide in
the wind, their long spears shaking over their shoulders,
they form a picture which must be seen to realize in full
its wild effect.

The basis of the Arab character is frank and manly :

the intellect active, the perceptive faculties acute, the judgment sound. Good qualities, but stunted, and often blighted, by the mere savageness of their life : good materials, spoilt or wasted in the using. The cool nights are often spent outside their tents in story telling and poetical recitations. Frequent sleep during the day renders them independent of the prolonged night rest usual among inhabitants of towns and villages.

Away from the large cities, the wild Bedouin tribes are essentially the same now as they were a thousand years ago. Their manners are patriarchal, and their virtues, as well as their vices, are such as naturally result from a nomadic life. Their natural jealousy and fiery temperament have always been the source of implacable enmities and feuds among themselves. Quick to resent an injury and sensitive to the slightest violation of etiquette, quarrels frequently arise which result in bloodshed. These wild tribes would long ago have exterminated each other, but for that provision in the Arab code which permits the shedding of blood to be atoned for, by payment of money or property. Their laws are very full and explicit, regulating the revenge for blood and the right and privilege of asylum.

There are many very curious social customs and traditions which retain their hold with wonderful tenacity among these people, despite their constantly increasing intercourse with foreigners, resulting from more intimate commercial relations, and easier communications with Europe. To my own experience and observation, I have added in the short account above given the results of other writers, whose more extensive travels in the interior and longer residence in the country, render them good authority as to the social manners and habits of the people.

# CHAPTER XXI.

## EXCURSION TO BABYLON.

THE site of ancient Babylon is on the Euphrates, about sixty miles southwest from Bagdad. The ruins cover a large tract on both sides of the river, and near them is built the modern town of Hillah. The country lying between the Tigris and the Euphrates, except a narrow belt bordering on each stream, is now a sandy desert. In ancient times this great plain was most populous and fertile, covered with groves of palm trees and beautiful gardens. A complete network of canals and water courses spread over the plain carrying fertility to hundreds of towns and villages, which are now heaps of rubbish. These canals were neglected and became gradually choked up, vegetation ceased, and a vast arid desert, parched by the burning sun, in time replaced the fertile gardens and teeming population of this part of Mesopotamia

But Babylon, though in ruins, is classic, indeed sacred ground. Here was the resting place of the first families of our race. Here Nimrod built his tower to Belus, and called down upon himself the wrath of the Almighty. In these deserted halls Nebuchadnezzar boasted of the glories of his capital, and was punished for his pride. Here Belshazzar feasted and beheld the writing on the wall, while the victorious Persian was thundering at his gates.

My excursion to these great ruins was undertaken under difficulties, and had nearly ended in disaster to myself. In some villages a few miles below Hillah, a disease, rapid and fatal in its effects, had lately made its appearance, which had been pronounced to be *the plague*, and the panic had spread even to Bagdad. It was rumored that a quarantine would soon be declared, cutting off communication with all that neighborhood, to prevent the spread of this terrible disease. It was now the second week in May, and the weather would soon be too hot to make such an excursion possible. My friend, Mr. Finnis, could not accompany me, and I must either give up my project, or go alone. But to visit this country without seeing Babylon would be leaving the part of Hamlet out of the play, and after considerable hesitation, I decided to go, trusting to my uniform good fortune to see me safely through.

My friends were by no means agreed as to the prudence of this decision, some predicting difficulty from the flood as well as the threatened pestilence. The unprecedented high water in both rivers had flooded some portions of the plains, and I must be prepared to wade, or perhaps to swim. This, however, did not frighten me, but what was more to be dreaded, was being caught within the *cordon* of the quarantine, in case one should suddenly be declared.

This matter of quarantine is one of the things most to be dreaded in Turkey. Once on the wrong side of the line, and not even all the power of the Pasha could save me until I had served out the forty days.

On the other hand it was not fully decided that the disease was the plague, and a commission of medical men were to start in a few days for the infected district. It did not seem probable that any quarantine would be established until their report was received, and this was the impression in official circles when I called at the palace to make inquiries. The Pasha's Secretary assured me that I should have a week before the commission returned, which was all the time I required.

My preparations being made, and armed with credentials from the Pasha and letters to the Nāwāb, Agha-Dowlah, a wealthy Indian nabob residing at Kerbella, I found myself on Tuesday morning before sunrise, in a *goopha* with my servant and guide, Yusef, and all my baggage, to cross the Tigris to the west side where our horses had been taken the day before. As I gaily said *au revoir* to the friends who had come down to see me start, I had for a moment the feeling that I was taking too much risk. But it was now too late to turn back, nor was I inclined to show the *white feather*. We were quickly paddled across the rapid stream, and found Hassan, our Arab muleteer, waiting with two horses and a pack mule on the opposite bank. I had left preparation of the outfit to Yusef, whose experience in such matters rendered him thoroughly competent to manage my small caravan. He is a Mosulie Christian, from near Mosul, far up the Tigris, a man of energy and resource equal to any emergency, well acquainted with all the places on our route, and speaks Arabic, Persian, and Turkish, as well as sufficient English to make himself understood. As the "traps" are being landed from the *goopha*, under his direction, let us take an inventory of the outfit: An English saddle, bridle, riding whip, and sun umbrella; a thin cotton mattress, quilt and pillow, rolled up tightly in a Persian carpet and around it a waterproof blanket; a small satchel containing a change of clothing and a few toilet articles of the simplest campaign character. Next come large Arab saddle-bags, well stuffed with the commissary stores, tea, sugar, coffee, salt, knife, fork and spoon, cold chicken and sandwiches, half a dozen bottles Bass' ale, one ditto brandy, a tin tea-pot, and a supply of Persian tobacco for my *chibouk*; then two unglazed water jars, called *cudjees*. My kind and hospitable friends seem determined that I shall be neither hungry or thirsty on the desert. The last articles are a large clumsy Arab saddle for Yusef, and a roll containing his bed clothing. My own kit is all white, an Indian pith hat, and high riding boots.

My horse was first saddled, and mounting my "Arab steed," I watched with curiosity the operation of packing these various sized bundles upon the mule. The art seems to be to arrange all into pairs as nearly equal as possible in weight, so as to balance each other on the animal, then tie them on so securely that if he should take a notion to lie down in the road, or bolt off at a tangent with heels in the air, he cannot get rid of his load. All being secured Hassan climbs up from the rear, perches himself on the top, guiding the mule with a halter decorated with cowrie shells, and in his hand a persuasive argument in the shape of a stout, sharp-pointed stick.

We thread the narrow streets single file, Yusef leading the way, and the sun is just rising as we pass through a gateway in the half ruined wall, and emerge upon the open

16

plain.   These Eastern people are early risers, and the road is already alive with caravans—camels, horses, mules and donkeys by the hundred—Arabs on foot, leading pack animals with enormous loads of fresh cut grass or faggots towards the city—Bedouin horsemen scouring along the road, armed with guns, swords, or long, quivering spears. They pass us at full speed without deigning a glance, their long, dark *abbas*, or cloaks, and the ends of bright *kaffeahs* tied round their heads, streaming out behind like banners.

Our course for the first hour is along the river's bank, among date groves and through fields of waving corn. Then diverging to the right, leaving behind the strip of cultivated land, all vegetation disappears, and we are fairly launched upon the desert.   It rained last night and there is no dust, the road is a mere track across the sandy plain, and, exhilarated by the pure, clear air and the novelty of the situation, I touch my horse with the spur and he darts ahead at a fast gallop, leaving my little caravan far behind.   A caravanserai is within sight four or five miles ahead, a conspicuous object standing alone in the desert, and here in the shade of its low walls I wait for them to come up.

These *Khans* are built at intervals of six or eight miles along all the main roads throughout Arabia and Persia for the free accommodation of travelers.   They are usually of brick, one story in height, with an open court in the centre.   The gates are very heavy and strongly barred, and the outer walls are loopholed.   The arrangements inside are most primitive.   Stone or brick platforms about five feet from the ground, covered with an arched roof for protection from the sun and rain, and open to the courtyard, where the animals are secured, are the only apartments they furnish.   On these the traveler spreads his carpet and makes himself at home.   On his arrival here, no dashing hotel clerk holds out a pen for him to register his name, nor scans with lordly disdain his dusty and travel-stained garments, while the poor fellow submissively waits to be shown to the meanest room in the topmost story.

THE HOTEL OF THE DESERT.

As I ride through the arched gateway of the *Khan-a-Zaad* an Arab holds the stirrup for me to dismount, loosens the saddle girth and walks my horse slowly up and down in the shade. Another piles some fresh cut grass on the stone platform, on which I sit while he brings me a small cup of strong black coffee. Then he offers me a bowl of fresh water or sweet milk, and brings a live coal to light my *chibouk*. Not a word is said except the first respectful salutation of " *Salaamar.*"

Soon after Yusef and Hassan came up, took their coffee, and in half an hour we were again on the road. As Yusef paid the bill I noticed how pitiful a sum it was, and told

him to give them as much more for *baksheesh*. A short
distance beyond this *Khan* we came to a *wallah*, or hollow
place, nearly a hundred yards in width, which the Tigris,
overflowing its banks, had filled with water. This, and
several others in the course of the day, we were obliged to
ford, but in no case was the water above our horses'
girths, so that they were not considered a serious obstacle.

Our first day's journey was to Moseyib, a town on the
Euphrates, forty very long miles from Bagdad. The sun
was now getting hot, and I began to feel its influence in
spite of pith hat and umbrella. Leaving Yusef as a guard
to the pack mule, I pushed on towards the Khan Mohammedeah, half way to Moseyib, which I reached about noon.
On the road I met many parties on horse-back, most of
whom I recognized by their dress as Persians returning
from a pilgrimage to the shrines at Kerbella and Kifil.
Just before reaching the half-way *Khan* I discovered
ahead a large cavalcade, and as it approached I saw it was
no ordinary caravan. My servants were a long distance
behind, and my only weapon being a small " Smith &
Wesson " I felt a little nervous. Most of the party were
armed, and at the head rode a fine looking man of about
thirty, mounted on a beautiful full-blood Arab horse. As
he came up I touched my hat with a courteous *salaam*,
and was startled at his suddenly reining up, and saluting
me in English with " Good morning, sir ; are you going
to Hillah ?" We exchanged a few words and rode on. In
the center of his armed band, and surrounded by black servants, was a large *howdah*, covered with bright scarlet cloth
and carried on four mules. Through the partly open curtains I could see that it contained his wife, and as I passed
I caught just a glimpse of a pair of flashing black eyes peeping curiously out from beneath a veil that covered her face.
I knew it would be resented as an insult to stare in that

direction, or to turn in my saddle and look back. Behind the *howdah* were several females, probably servants, riding on mules, and seated on double panniers of light wickerwork. A dozen or more well-armed horsemen brought up the rear. It was the Nāwāb Agha-Dowlah, to whom I had letters, coming from Kerbella to Bagdad. When the Nāwāb met Yusef and ascertained who I was, he sent a man back with his compliments and regrets that he should be absent, and said that so soon as he reached Bagdad he should telegraph to his steward to place his house at Kerbella at my service.

We stopped but a short time at the Khan Mohammedeah, as we had the hardest and hottest six hours ride yet before us, and it was necessary to reach Moseyib before dark, so as to secure a boat for the night to go through the Kerbella canal. The sun was pouring down its fiercest rays and the air seemed stifling. I stopped at two other *Khans* only long enough to secure a cup of coffee, while I waited in the shade for Yusef and Hassan to come up.

During this afternoon's ride I saw for the first time the wonderful effects of a *mirage on a desert*. Far away across the sandy plain, under the quivering rays of the sun, was a *Khan*, but between me and it was a river, which receded as I approached, and then suddenly disappeared, as if by magic. The deception was so complete that I thought several times that the Euphrates was in sight. Then the exhibition took another form. Clumps of palm trees and long processions of camels could be seen raised several degrees above the horizon. These objects were usually reversed, the trees upside down, and the camels standing upon their heads. I can realize now what I have often read of the poor weary and thirsty traveler on the desert, who sees before him the green oasis and sparkling water, enticing him on with tantalizing mockery, then suddenly vanish, leaving him to drop down exhausted and perish.

It was after sunset when we reached Moseyib, a large town surrounded by palm trees and gardens. Riding through the narrow streets and bazaars, down to the banks of the river, we stopped at the guard-house, where a crazy bridge of boats crossed the Euphrates to the house of the governor on the opposite shore. I sent Yusef with my letter from the Pasha of Bagdad, and requested the governor to furnish me a boat for the canal. Yusef speedily returned with the message—"The governor send plenty salaams, and says you have boat in half an hour." A large *mar-hallah*, or river boat, of eighteen or twenty tons, was promptly forthcoming. My carpet and mattress were spread upon her deck, and I threw myself down completely exhausted with my twelve hours' ride. Yusef prepared for me a cup of tea, but I was too tired to eat.

My plans were to go that night to Kerbella, where I should spend the next day, and thence by the Hindeah canal the next night to Kufil, the ancient capital of the Kufic Empire, and to Kifil, where there is a shrine very sacred to Mahometans, being the burial place of Ali, the son-in-law of the Prophet. Our horses, under the care of Hassan, were to meet us at a place called Nejif, whence we could ride to Hillah and the ruins of Babylon.

But now Hassan comes in a fright, having been told that the Turkish soldiers are seizing all the horses in the neighborhood. So I again dispatch Yusef to the governor with my compliments, and a request for a protection for my animals as far as Nejif. He returns with the startling news that the governor has just received a telegram from Bagdad, declaring Hillah in quarantine, as the plague has broken out in that town; but I might go as far as Kerbella, that place being outside the *cordon sanitaire*. Here was a dilemma. Prudence dictated an immediate return to Bagdad, but pride and a desire and hope to yet see Babylon opposed that course. I appealed to my man Friday. "Now Yusef, what shall we do?" "Whatever you please, Sahib," was his reply. "Are you not afraid of the plague?" "No, Sahib, no fear it, no catch it." I commended Yusef's philosophy, and determined to push on that night for Kerbella, a very interesting place, almost within sight of the Birs Nimroud, or the tower of Babel, see what I could the next day, and return the night after to the horses. Our luggage was all on board, and in five minutes more we were off toward the "infected district."

The boatmen hoist the large lateen sail, and we cross the rapid stream diagonally towards the mouth of the Kerbella canal. I can just discern in the dim twilight, the plain where more than twenty centuries ago the battle of Cunaxa was fought, which proved so disastrous to the younger Cyrus, as minutely described by Xenophon in the Anabasis. Visions of that text book, whose smooth and elegant Greek was never a hard task in my younger days, rise before me, and I wonder whether the unfortunate expedition against Babylon in which the 'ten thousand' took part is not an unlucky omen for my present raid in that direction. And shall I be as fortunate in my retreat as were the Greeks under the wise leadership of Xenophon.

Once under weigh I half repented my decision, but it was now too late to turn back. Yusef filled and lit my *chibouk*, and I made myself as comfortable as circumstances would permit. The *marhallah* was drawn by four Arab trackers, who walked along the bank pulling the heavy boat by a long rope attached to the mast.

The *Reis*, or captain, was close behind me steering the boat, and continually shouting to the trackers on the bank, whose monotonous chanting was by no means soothing to the weary traveler.

As we passed through the mud villages hundreds of dogs took part in the concert, which was varied on the open plains by the howling of jackals, whose cries at times were a perfect imitation of the wailing of infant children. Add to all these, the blood-thirsty *zip* of mosquitoes by the million, and it can easily be seen that in spite of fatigue, sleep was impossible.

The night was warm and clear, and for hours I gazed up at the bright stars overhead, my only coverlid, and re-called the incidents, as related to me by an old resident, almost the only European survivor, of the plague of 1831, which in two months carried off one hundred thousand of the inhabitants of Bágdad.

The people of the West have no conception of the horror which the very name of the *plague* suggests to Oriental nations. We think of it only as a disease which in remote ages afflicted humanity—or possibly we may remember reading of the "great fire" and the plague, which within the same century ravaged London, over two hundred years ago. But in several countries of the East the plague is endemic, and the dread of it is ever present. Scarcely a year passes that some alarm or rumors of this frightful disease do not spread through Persia and Arabia, or the Turkish ports of the Mediterranean. It is strictly conta-gious, very rapid in its progress, and fatal with two-thirds of the persons attacked. Complete isolation is the only preventive, and upon its appearance the people shut them-selves up in their houses, provisioned as for a siege, and hold no communication with friends or neighbors until the "Angel of death" has passed by.

In the Spring of 1831, when the plague broke out in Bagdad, the city contained about one hundred and fifty thousand inhabitants. The ruling governor, Daoud-Pasha, had largely increased his army, and being ambitious and very popular, he was suspected of an intention to throw off the yoke of the Sultan, and follow the successful example of Mohamet Ali in Egypt. He kept up a brilliant court, encouraged commerce, and the city was rapidly increasing in population and wealth.

The terrible disease was brought by Persian pilgrims to Kerbella, and a more frightful detail of human suffering can hardly be found on the page of history. The Pasha, by a mistaken policy, to prevent undue alarm, prevented the egress of those who would have fled, so that the disease had full scope within the city walls. The daily mortality rapidly increased to five thousand; many houses were emptied, and no one was to be met, except the persons employed to drag to the river's bank the dead bodies thrown over the walls of the dwellings into the streets. Many dying parents exposed their young children in the streets, hoping to attract the sympathy of the charitable; but at such a time all feelings of humanity seemed deadened, and the helpless little creatures were left to perish.

When the mortality was at its height, the misery of the wretched inhabitants was increased by the river overflowing its banks, bursting through the walls and undermining the mud-built foundations of the houses, of which seven thousand fell in a single day, burying in their ruins many of the sick, the dying and the dead.

Nor was the Pasha better off than his subjects. His palace was in ruins; his guards were dead, or had fled, and he was indebted to the bounty of a poor fisherman for a little food to save him from starvation. The British Minister and his family escaped down the river. Of the eighteen Sepoys and servants left at the Residency, but two survived, and some whole sections of the city were left without a single inhabitant. Other towns in the neighborhood suffered frightfully. Hillah, which contained ten thousand people, was entirely depopulated. Some, no doubt, had fled, but the greater number fell victims to the disease.

Such are some of the horrible details of the pestilence in 1831, within the memory of many of the inhabitants of Bagdad now living. In 1772 the plague was still more destructive of human life. At that time it is supposed that over a million people perished in this section of Arabia and Persia.

Revolving such pleasant fancies in mind, I lay awake until long past midnight. But tired nature at last triumphed, and I fell into a sound sleep. I awoke with a start to find the bright sun shining in my eyes, and Yusef standing by with a cup of coffee in one hand, and my lighted *chibouk* in the other.

# CHAPTER XXII.

## HOSPITALITIES IN BABYLON.

O my great surprise I found that we had already reached Kerbella. My *marhallah* was moored alongside many other boats of various kinds, and all around us were the bustle and activity of a large town. After a simple "canal boat toilet" I followed Yusef to the r e s i d e n c e of the Nāwāb, where I found every preparation had been made for my comfort by Mirzah, the head steward, to whom the hospitable proprietor had sent a telegram the night before.

Refreshed by a bath and two hours sleep in a cool, darkened room, I was invited to a breakfast of coffee, sweets, and a great variety of curious dishes. Then Mirzah showed me through the different apartments of the house, which is the finest in Kerbella. That portion occupied by the ladies, called the *harem,* was separated by a wall from the reception rooms for male visitors, and was built round an open court, paved with marble, in the center of which was a beautiful fountain. We passed through these elegantly furnished rooms, now unoccupied, to the top of the house, from which we had a fine view of the city.

Kerbella is a great resort of pilgrims from Persia and India. These Mahometans are all of the *Sheah* sect, who revere the memory of Ali almost as much as the Prophet himself. In this place are two very sacred shrines of Abbas and of Hassein, grandsons of Mahomet, who are buried here and worshiped as saints. Thousands of the devout come here to die, as the Hindoos resort to Benares, their sacred city, to drown themselves in the Ganges. The two mosques containing the ashes of these saints are very beautiful. I could only see the outside, as no " dog of an unbeliever " is ever permitted to enter the sacred precincts. The mosque of Abbas has an immense dome and one of its minarets is entirely covered with plates of burnished gold. The dome and minarets of the other mosque are beautifully ornamented with glazed tiles of various colors arranged in arabesque designs, and with passages from the Koran. No mosque in Cairo, Damascus, or Constantinople will compare with these in richness of exterior decoration. From the number of devotees buried at Kerbella, the soil is full of human bones. Pilgrims carry away as relics small pieces of the " clay of the saints," upon which they rest their foreheads in saying their prayers.

Here is the residence of several hundred nabobs from India, some of whom are very wealthy. Many of these are from Lucknow the capital of Oude and were relatives of the former ruling princes of that province. When the English seized that most important kingdom in India, they granted liberal pensions to all connected with the royal family. They reside here, protected as British subjects, and are all Mohametans of the same sect as the Persians.

After breakfast I was called upon by another Nāwāb, who proposed to show me through the bazaars. Our procession as we passed along the crowded streets was decidedly showy. My ideas of republican simplicity were rather shocked at the unceremonious manner in which the *Cawasses*, who marched ahead, armed with swords and in showy uniform, pushed aside the people. Next came the stranger with a dignitary on either side, and a dozen or more servants and *Cawasses* brought up the rear. The bazaars were very interesting, but I was myself too much an object of curiosity to make it comfortable to stop and examine the shops. I presume at that time there was not another European or foreigner nearer than Bagdad.

On our way back, we stopped to call on the widow of one of the ex-kings of India—an old lady over eighty years of age. She receives a pension of six thousand rupees (three thousand dollars) a month from the English government, and maintains a large establishment. Of course, I did not see the ex-queen herself—that would not be according to etiquette—but as I was being conducted through a long passage towards the reception room, I caught a glimpse of a very old and wrinkled face peering through a half opened door, and am inclined to think that she saw *me*. I was received by her brother and cousins, and seated myself on a cushion placed upon a large Persian carpet. Five or six officers of high rank were located around me on the carpet, while those of lower grade sat upon the marble floor farther down the room.

After exchanging elaborate salaams, coffee was brought

in and offered to me on a silver tray, then a dish of preserved fruit.  A *narghileh* came next, richly decorated
with gold and silver filagree work, and prepared with rose-
scented water.  Supposing this to be the end of the entertainment, I now made a movement toward my hat—but
my conductors politely intimated that more was yet to
come, so I resigned myself to see the end of the play.

A large tray was brought in, on which was a bowl of
pink-colored sherbet, from which the servant filled a glass
with a curiously carved ladle of sandal wood ; and some
very sweet cakes were a part of this course.  Again came
the " hubble-bubble " pipe, but this time of a different
pattern.  The last course consisted of four dishes of sweetmeats, which were urged upon me by my hosts, as especially
*Indian* preparations; so as a matter of courtesy I had to
taste of each.  It is impossible to describe them, or to tell
of what they were made, but they certainly were very delicious.  Another bowl of sherbet of a different color and
flavor, and then a *chibouk* with amber mouthpiece and
long jasmine stem closed the entertainment.

We took leave of the ex-royal family with the usual
amount of bowing and *salaaming,* and returned to the
Nāwāb's, where I found a lunch spread, consisting of tea,
coffee, and more sweetmeats.  Now, I have confessed a
weakness for this sort of condiments, but here I began to
feel a surfeit.  As an article of exclusive diet I would
prefer something else to sugar.

It was now past noon, and I began to feel anxious to
get started towards Moseyib.  From what I had heard
that morning about the plague being in the immediate
neighborhood of Kerbella, and the evident panic among
the people there, I was not inclined to waste any time
after I had seen everything of interest in that place.  So
I took leave of my kind hosts, who insisted upon accom-

panying me through the hot sun down to my boat. Here
I was surprised to find, as a present from the ex-queen,
a neat willow basket containing the last four dishes of
sweetmeats which I had tasted and praised at her house.
The *Reis* and his men were fast asleep, but Yusef roused
them without ceremony, and urged an immediate departure.

But before we leave this, the nearest point I shall attain
to ancient Babylon, and within sight of the loftiest tower
that marks these ruins, I must give the reader a brief
description, gathered from eye witnesses and the records
of other travelers.

According to Herodotus, the only ancient writer who
has left a description of Babylon from personal observation, the city formed a square of which each side was
twelve miles long. It was built on both sides of the
Euphrates, which was spanned by a bridge of stone, and
the banks of the river were lined with bricks. In the
midst of one quarter stood the royal palace and hanging
gardens, in the other the temple of Belus. The city was
surrounded by a double wall of hard-burnt bricks, and
between them was a wide and deep moat. The streets were
all straight and at right angles; those toward the river
had gates of brass. The houses were three and four
stories in height, and Babylon was the most richly adorned
city the historian had ever seen.

Benjamin of Tudela, a learned Hebrew traveler, visited
Babylon in the twelfth century, and states that in his
time no less than twenty thousand Jews resided near the
ancient city, and worshiped in a synagogue built, according to tradition, by the prophet Daniel himself. These
Hebrew families claimed to be descended from the Jews
of the Captivity, and traced their lineage from the princes
and prophets of Judah. Their chief, who lived at Bagdad,

was called the " Lord Prince of the Captivity," and traced
his descent from King David.

Let us take a rapid survey of the ruins as they appear
to-day, which in extent seem to warrant the most extravagant descriptions of the glories of Babylon under the
successive dynasties of the Assyrians, the Chaldeans, and
the Persians.

Coming from Bagdad, which in a direct line is fifty
miles distant, three immense mounds appear in succession, which have the appearance of natural hills. But
close examination shows that they are composed of bricks,
and are the remains of large buildings. These are on the
eastern side of the Euphrates, and the largest is about
one hundred and fifty feet in height. They are supposed
to be an ancient citadel that defended this part of the
town, the royal palace, and a temple. How immense
must the original buildings have been, when it is considered that these mounds have been the storehouses from
which for twenty centuries bricks of the finest description
have been taken to build the great cities of Ctesiphon,
Selucia, and Bagdad. Fragments of alabaster vessels and

ANCIENT LAMPS FROM BABYLON.

images, fine earthenware, marble, and great quantities of
enameled tiles, the glazing and coloring of which are still
surprisingly fresh, can yet be found in these mounds. On
the face of every brick is stamped in cuneiform characters

the name and titles of Nebuchadnezzer. They are all laid
face downward, and the cement in which they are im-
bedded is so hard that they can only be detached with the
greatest difficulty. Near these ruins are the remains of

ANTIQUE VASES AND FIGURES.

pillars and buttresses that supported the celebrated hanging gardens and terraces which were numbered among the
wonders of the world.

Among these ruins stands a solitary tamarisk tree, a
species strange to this country. It bears every mark of
great antiquity, its originally enormous trunk being worn
away and shattered by time. Travelers early in the
present century have described its spreading evergreen
branches, adorned with tress-like tendrils, as very beautiful. This is perhaps the last descendant of the trees that
decorated the hanging gardens of the Chaldean monarch.

The Arabs have a tradition that this tree was saved by
God at the general destruction of the city, that Ali might
rest beneath its shade after the defeat of the enemies of
the prophet at the great battle of Hillah.

The enormous stone lion, described by Rich, still lies
half buried in the ruins. Some imaginative travelers see

17

in the group a representation of Daniel in the lion's den, as it stands over a man with outstretched arms.

DANIEL'S LION.

On the western bank of the river, and several miles below the ruins above described, is the largest monument that yet remains of ancient Babylon. It has the appearance of an immense oblong hill. It is nearly half a mile in circumference at the base, and rises about one hundred and seventy feet above the plain. Upon its summit is a tower forty feet high, of beautiful masonry. The whole mound is composed of kiln-burnt bricks, and the ruin upon the top appears to have formed the angle of some square building, originally of much greater height. This ruin is rent nearly from top to bottom, as if struck by lightning.

This great mound is called the Birs Nimroud, " palace of Nimrod," by the Arabs. By the Jews it is called the " Prison of Nebuchadnezzar." But most Christian travelers recognize this as the veritable remains of the Tower

BIRS NIMROUD.

*From a photograph in possession of the Author.*

of Babel. It can be seen many miles away across the plain, and was pointed out to me while it seemed but a speck upon the horizon. Fragments of stone, marble, and basalt are scattered among the rubbish at its base, and show that it was adorned by other materials besides the kiln-burnt bricks of which it was composed. The cement which connects the bricks is so hard that it is impossible to detach one entire from the mass, and shows the perfection of Babylonian masonry.

An early traveler says: " The Tower of Nimrod is sublime even in its ruins. Clouds play about its summits. Its recesses are inhabited by lions." Thus the words of the prophet are fulfilled. "Wild beasts of the desert shall lie there. Jackals shall feed in their palaces, and the wild beasts in their pleasant places."

Within sight from the top of Birs Nimroud is the shrine of Nejif, sacred to the Jews as the tomb Ezekiel, and a few miles beyond in the same direction is Kifil, where Ali was buried. After his death, in accordance with the orders he had given, his devoted followers placed his body upon his favorite mare, and buried it on the spot where she laid down to rest. A splendid mosque covers his remains, and a large town, half buried in date trees, is the resort of thousands of pilgrims. After Mecca and Medina it is the most sacred shrine to the Sheah Mahometans.

And now leaving behind us these grand ruins of ancient Babylon, which from the Mosaic records and the accounts that have come down to us from later historians, must have been for many centuries the most magnificent city in the world, we will return to the *marhallah*, on which I was slowly retreating towards Moseyib.

An awning had been spread over the deck and I was fast asleep. In my dreams *hubble-bubbles* and sweet-meats, *narghilehs*, and *chibouks* were mixed up with nabobs and Nāwābs in inextricable confusion.

I was suddenly awakened by Yusef, who pointed to a large boat, rowed by six men, on which I could see officers and soldiers in uniform, coming rapidly down towards us. In the stern was the Turkish flag, and Yusef, in evident alarm, told me it was the Governor of Moseyib. I quickly roused myself as the boat came alongside, and the Governor stepped on board my *marhallah*. He was a tall, fine looking man of about forty, with full black beard, and wearing the dark, gold-laced uniform of a Turkish officer. He said a few words to the *Reis*, who salaamed very low, and then courteously, but with rather a haughty air, saluted me. He held in his hand a dispatch which he read and Yusef translated. It was from Bagdad, and contained the alarming intelligence that Kerbella had been placed in quarantine, directing him to turn back all boats coming from that place, and to stop all communication between Moseyib and the capital. This announcement was indeed astonishing, and I felt that my affairs had now reached a crisis. Inside the quarantine—shut up for an indefinite period, with no countryman or European near, but the terrible pestilence all around me—the weather every day growing hotter, and no communication with my friends in Bagdad or at home.

# CHAPTER XXIII.

## THE RETURN FROM BABYLON.

HE captain of my boat, in obedience to the Governor's orders, was detaching the tow rope, and I began to feel desperate. But I could not give up without an effort. I showed him my letter from the Pasha of Bagdad, and he then recognized me as the traveler who had applied to him for a boat. He could speak only Turkish, so that all our conversation had to be interpreted by Yusef.

I would have given all I know of other tongues (except the vernacular) if I could only talk with the Turk in his own language, and try my powers of persuasion and eloquence.

We had been standing in the hot sun, and I invited him

to a seat beneath my awning. Then, with the instinct of hospitality, I asked him if he would drink some English beer. The Governor shrugged his shoulders and nodded assent. A bottle had been towing astern to cool, which Yusef quickly opened, and filled a large glass with foam‑ing Bass' ale. The Governor took it down at a gulp, and held out the glass for more. Now, theoretically, at least, no Mussulman can drink wine, beer, or spirits; but the Turks are not very strict observers of the Koran in this re‑spect. It was plain that my guest was no ascetic. In re‑ply to his inquiry I told him I had two more bottles of beer and one of brandy, "all of which were at his service."

A happy thought seemed to strike him. He called his secretary, and after a short consultation announced that he would return to Moseyib in my *marhallah*, and send his own boat on to Kerbella, which was but a few miles dis‑tant, with letters and dispatches. His soldiers and ser‑vants, carpet, cushions, *chibouk*, etc., were transferred to my boat, and four Arab idlers, who had collected on the bank, were impressed, in Turkish style, to man an extra tow rope. We were soon spinning along towards Moseyib at a rapid rate, with the prospect of reaching that place before dark, instead of at midnight, as I had ex‑pected.

The Turk now made himself comfortable. It was aw‑fully hot, so he doffed his heavy military coat, rolled up shirt sleeves, kicked off his patent leather gaiters, called for his *chibouk*, and squatted on his carpet and cushions which had been spread under the awning. I did the hos‑pitalities to the best of my ability. Perhaps never before did I exert myself so much to please a guest.

I made Yusef spread out the remains of yesterday's lunch, to which I added the basket of sweetmeats sent me by the ex-queen, and another bottle of ale. With the second bottle, the Governor began to melt, and asking to see again the Pasha's letter, he apologized for not calling upon me when I was in Moseyib, and invited me to dine with him that evening. The third bottle made him quite sociable. He repeated his apologies, renewed his invitation to dinner, and said he would manage some way to get me through the quarantine.

I exerted all my powers to please and entertain him. I showed him my pictures, my little revolver, which he admired very much, and I thought seriously of presenting it to him on the spot. But we were getting on swimmingly now, and I held it back in reserve for an emergency.

Having finished the ale he signified a wish to taste the English *arrack*, which I told Yusef to administer in very small doses, as I was fearful of its effects. But my fears were groundless, for he proved to be thoroughly *seasoned*, and never got beyond the point of feeling social and good humored.

When I told him that I had been in Constantinople and had seen the Sultan, his respect for me was immensely increased. He was lamentably ignorant about America—did not know whether we were ruled by an Emperor, King or President—and I gave him the first lesson he ever had in the geography of the New World. He did not even know our flag, so I drew the " Stars and Stripes" on paper, but he would not admit that any flag was handsomer than the " Star and Crescent."

As all this had to be done through an interpreter, or by pantomime, it was no easy task, but I saw that by winning his good will I had a chance of escape, and I succeeded even beyond my expectations. Only once, when the Governor proposed that I should sing, I felt that he had me at disadvantage. Now, my talents as a vocalist had never been developed, and I needed as much urging as if I had

really been a first-rate tenor.   But the Turk insisted, and
by way of an encouragement volunteered to hum an air he
had heard in a *café chantant* at Pera.   This was so hor-
ribly discordant that I yielded at once, and gave him the
" Star spangled Banner," mixed up with " The beautiful
star."   As my audience understood neither the words nor
the tune, it is not surprising that I achieved a wonderful
success, and elicited great applause.   The version was so
entirely original, that if my audience had understood English, it would perhaps have been encored.   Elated at this unexpected success, I tried "Rally round the flag," "Old John
Brown," and " Marching through Georgia."   Then a
medley of negro songs closed the entertainment.   The
whole performance was so comically absurd, that I laughed
as heartily as the Governor himself.   He slapped me on
the shoulder and said :   " You are a good fellow ; I like
you.   Come and dine at my house—then we drink *arrack*
and have more songs.   When the moon rises I let you go
to Bagdad."   I saw a twinkle in Yusef's eyes as he translated this speech, and he said to me in English :  " We are
all right now, Sahib."

Before dark we reached Moseyib.   I at once sent Yusef
across the river to look up Hassan, and bring the horses
to the palace, so as to be in readiness for a moonlight flitting, as soon as it should be light enough to see the road.
I followed the Governor through the gateway, where the
guard presented arms, and up to the reception room, where,
motioning me to a seat on the divan, he excused himself
and retired to the harem, when I presume he dipped his
head into cold water, for he soon returned looking as fresh
as if Bass's ale and English arrack were his daily bever-
ages.   He had exchanged his uniform for a striped silk
robe, a Cashmere shawl tied round the waist, the inevitable
red *fez*, and loose white trowsers.   Calling for his *narghi-*

*leh*, he tucked his bare feet under him on the divan, and looked every inch a Turk.

A servant had drawn off my boots and replaced them with a pair of embroidered slippers, and I was curled up at the other end of the divan, puffing away at a long-stemmed *chibouk*. Quite a large crowd was waiting for an audience with the governor, and I was an amused spectator of the way business is dispatched by a Turkish official.

I could not understand a word that was said, but heard " *quarantina* " often repeated, and as each one in turn was admitted and stated his business, 1 inferred that they were soliciting permits for themselves or their goods to pass the lines. The Governor seemed to generally deny their requests, but several times there was a little by-play. The applicant would whisper a few words to the secretary ; then there would be a private confab with his Excellency, and the man would go away apparently satisfied.

It is the common impression that all Turkish officials, from the highest to the lowest, are open to bribes. I can only say that what I saw looked suspicious. The Turks have a horror of the plague, and the quarantine is their only method of checking its ravages. Remissness of duty on the part of any subordinate would be fatal—while in the matter of customs and taxes all such *peccadillos* as bribes are considered pardonable. So strong is this impression, even among those who denounce all the officials as a set of " blackmailing scoundrels," that I was warned before leaving Bagdad that once within the quarantine, neither money nor influence could relieve me. But perhaps the force of habit is strong with my friend the Governor, and he presumes that the quarantine regulations are not yet firmly established.

It was nine o'clock before the last applicant was dismissed, and in the meantime Yusef had returned and

whispered to me that Hassan and the horses were in the
court-yard below.   Dinner was now announced, and was as
unique an entertainment as my breakfast at the Nāwāb's,
or my *tiffin* at the house of the ex-Queen of Oude.

A servant brought in a large round tray, which he
placed on the divan between the governor and myself.   In
the center was a dish of stewed chicken, and on each side
a napkin, fork, and spoon.   My host, inviting me to follow
his example, tucked the napkin under his chin, seized
spoon and fork, and went in with a good relish.   Thinking
of the old adage, which will suggest itself to the reader, I
followed suit.   This dish was removed, and others followed
in quick succession, but whether fish, flesh, or fowl I could
not always tell.   I dipped into each as a matter of courtesy, although the flavor was sometimes far from agreeable
to my taste.   The last course was boiled rice and curry,
then came small cups of coffee, and the tray being removed, two servants came in, one holding a towel and a
large basin, while the other poured water from a ewer over
our hands.

The dinner was now over, and the Governor, who had
evidently enjoyed the repast, fell back into his corner of
the divan.   *Narghilehs* of the Turkish pattern, with long,
flexible tubes, were brought in, and *arrack* in small wine-
glasses passed round.   My host again urged me to sing,
but I had made reputation enough in that line for one day,
and excused myself on the ground of fatigue.   It was now
getting late, and the governor seemed tired and sleepy.
So I told him, through Yusef, not to sit up on my account,
as I would rest on the divan until it was time for me to
leave.   He called an officer of the guard, gave some directions about allowing me to pass, then cordially shook hands
and pointing through the window in the direction where

the moon would rise, by pantomime wished me a good nap, and retired to his own apartments.

I tried in vain to sleep. The exciting events of the day, my narrow escape, the uncertainty of reaching Bagdad, for there was a possibility of being quarantined at its very gates, the breakfast *a la Indienne*, the dinner *a la Turque*, all passed in review before me. The divan was in the projection of a large open window, and beneath it the wide, swiftly-flowing river. It was yet dark, but I could hear the ripple of the water against the boats of the floating bridge, and across the broad stream I could discern the outline of the higher buildings of the town, and the masts of vessels moored along the banks. At last the moon rose from behind the city, deepening the shadows and forming a weird-like picture, bringing out dome and minaret, palm-tree and mast, in bold relief, and sparkling brightly, like silver, as its rays touched the rippling water.

I awoke Yusef, who was asleep in the outer room, and in half an hour he came up to tell me that all was ready. We quietly descended, mounted our horses, rode through the gate past the sleepy sentinel, filed across the bridge, and turning to the left, so as to avoid the town, soon struck the road leading out on the plain.

Once more fairly on the desert track, I cared nothing for the long, weary ride before us. I was free from the horrors of quarantine and plague, and felt elated like a Bedouin escaping from the restraints of city walls, to whom the " desert is liberty." Then came drowsiness. For three nights I had slept scarcely as many hours. We could only ride at a foot pace in single file. For the four hours until sunrise it was with the greatest difficulty that I could prevent myself from falling asleep in the saddle. At length the sun appeared, slowly rising above the horizon of sand, and I struck out at a faster pace towards a *Khan* two or three miles away.  Here I got a cup of Arab coffee and a draught of fresh new milk, and as it was advisable to reach the half way station as early as possible, I pushed on towards the *Khan Mohammedeah.*  The Arabs recognized me, and spreading an *abba* on one of the stone platforms, I was asleep long before my caravan came up.  Yusef very considerately did not disturb me, and after two hours refreshing sleep I awoke to find a breakfast prepared, that tasted infinitely better than the Indian sweetmeats, or the most elaborate products of the Turkish cuisine.  Arab bread, unleavened, and baked in thin, wafer-like cakes, new sweet butter, white cheese from goats' milk, a bowl of roasted wheat coarsely ground, and plenty of fresh new milk.  This was a regular Arab meal, and I did it full justice.

Before noon we were again in the saddle, with the hardest and hottest part of our journey yet before us.  The quarantine had put an embargo on travel, and the road, on which a few days before we had met an almost constant stream of caravans, was now deserted.  With the increasing heat the same wonderful exhibition of *mirage* appeared which I have before described.

When we reached the *wallah,* which we had forded on our way out with no difficulty, we found that another rise in the river had caused the water to flow back on the plain, and it was now fully five feet in depth.  I sent Yusef in to explore, and the water in the deepest part came up to his neck.  Here was a fix ; but there was no way getting round it, and it must be bravely met.

While we were deliberating a small caravan of Arabs, in which there were four women carried on mules in wicker panniers, came up the opposite bank, and we watched their proceedings before making the attempt ourselves.  The men stripped off their clothes, rolled them into bundles which they carried upon their heads, and boldly dashed in, leading the horses by the bridles. Then they returned and carried the women over, holding the panniers above the water.

Following their example, I first sent the animals across, where they were left in charge of Hassan, who spread out the wet packs to dry in the sun. Then Yusef came back for me, and I took to the water, Arab fashion. He carried over my clothes rolled up in a bundle, and with the umbrella to keep off the sun I went in. It was rather embarrassing, as the Arabs delayed starting. We heard them laughing, and Yusef said they were chaffing the

FORDING THE STREAM.

*Sahib*, and calling out " good," " good." I thought I detected in the sound more *silvery* tones than the hoarse voices of men, but my umbrella answered a double purpose, and I rather enjoyed the bath, as the water was refreshingly cool. After an hour's delay, we are again on

the road.    Before sunset the welcome date-groves and
above them the domes and minarets of Bagdad came
within sight.

Passing through the gates without question as to whence
we had come, we hurried down to the river banks, where
our horses were left, and our baggage transferred to a
*goopha.* Crossing the river I jumped on shore and hastened
to the *Khan.* My friends received me with open arms,
and welcomed me almost as one risen from the dead.

The unexpected declaration of quarantine on the same
day that I left Bagdad had taken everybody by surprise,
and they had given me up, and were even consulting as to
what message should be sent to my friends at home by the
next mail.    As I glanced into a mirror for the first time
since I left, I scarcely recognized my own face, so black
and sunburnt had it become.    Thoroughly exhausted by
my sixteen hours in the saddle, I threw myself down on
a divan and drank cup after cup of tea, the best thing to
quench one's thirst.

A bath, clean clothes, a good dinner, a most sincere
welcome from my friends, followed by a sound night's
sleep in a clean bed, and the next day I was as well as
ever.    But not the sight of all the ruins in the world, present or prospective, from the tower of Babel to the time
when the New Zealander shall sit upon the ruined arch of
London bridge, would tempt me again to repeat my adventures in search of Babylon.

# CHAPTER XXIV.

### NINEVEH AND ITS REMAINS.

Difficulties in the Way of my Visiting Nineveh—The Site of that Ancient
City—*Savans* disagree as to its Size—Sketch of Modern Explorations—
Inscriptions upon the Walls of its Palaces—The Cuneiform Language—
An Unknown Character of an Unknown Tongue—Significance of the
Word "Cuneiform"—Ancient Civilization of Assyria and Egypt—Biblical
Accounts confirmed by Modern Discoveries—The Behistun Rocks—Rec-
ords of Darius, "the Great King"—Peculiarities of Cuneiform Writing—
Bricks of Babylon and Nineveh—Translation of a Babylonian Cylinder—
George Smith, the Discoverer of the "Deluge-Tablets"—His own Account of
this Remarkable Discovery—His recent Book of "Assyrian Explorations"
—Extracts from the Flood Series of Legends—The Chaldean Account of
the Deluge.

O visit the site of Ancient
Nineveh, before leaving this
country, had been my earnest
desire. But as my journey
was not one of exploration
or scientific discovery, I was
obliged to forego the satisfaction of standing upon the
spot identified with so many
historical associations, which
could only be enjoyed at the
expense of much personal
discomfort and loss of time.

The modern town of Mo-
sul is situated upon the western bank of the Tigris, nearly

opposite the ruins which mark the site of Nineveh, and about three hundred miles north of Bagdad. The rapid current of the river makes its upward navigation impracticable, and Mosul can only be reached from Bagdad by a horseback journey of ten days, which, during the hot season, with recent Babylonian experiences fresh in my mind, is not an attractive excursion. Add to this the probability that the plague, if it spreads to Bagdad, will cut off my retreat down the river to the Persian Gulf, and I think the most enthusiastic antiquarian would come to the conclusion that in this case, " discretion is the better part of valor."

But as I am here in Babylonia, with the atmosphere of *the antique* all around me, I shall venture to give a short and necessarily imperfect sketch of the explorations and discoveries, which within the last thirty years have attracted the attention of the civilized world, and opened a new chapter to the student of ancient history.

Although the site and identity of these ruins with ancient Nineveh is unquestioned, yet *savans* differ as to the extent and size of the city when visited by the prophet Jonah, and described by him as "an exceeding great city of three days' journey."

Rawlinson maintains that "a city of three days' journey may be one which it requires three days to traverse from end to end, or one which is three days' journey in circumference, or, lastly, one which cannot be thoroughly visited and explored by a prophet commissioned to warn its inhabitants of a coming danger, in less than three days time." And he adds, that if Nineveh was in Jonah's time a city of even one hundred and twenty thousand people, it would deserve the title of " an exceeding great city," and the prophet might well be occupied three days in traversing its squares and streets. His theory is that the walls which can now be traced on the plain, and are only eight miles in circuit, once enclosed the whole of that great capital of the Ninevite kings. This would give much more limited dimensions to the city than would seem consistent with the Biblical account, unless one adopts the ingenious explanation above given.

Layard maintains that three other great palace-mounds lying on the east bank of the Tigris, which, if connected, would have required walls over fifty miles in circuit, should, also, be included as portions of the site of a city so grand and populous as Nineveh is represented to have been by both sacred and profane historians.

Heaps of earth, and grass-grown mounds, with no signs of habitation, and no indications that they cover the ruined palaces of great kings

SENNACHERIB.

whose empire extended for a thousand years over the larger portion of the then known world, can now be seen scattered over this great area. There are immense trenches and excavations in these mounds, through which, under the direction of Layard and other explorers, hundreds of Arabs dragged with ropes the colossal winged bulls that guarded the entrances of these grand palaces. The British Museum and the Louvre at Paris are enriched with splendid collections of Assyrian marbles, and although but a small fraction of these long-buried antiquities have as yet seen the light,

18

after nearly thirty centuries of entombment, it would almost seem as if the proud capital of the Chaldean monarchs had been transferred to the banks of the Thames and the Seine.

The first explorations at Nineveh were made by M. Botta, the eminent French *savant*, who was appointed French consul at Mosul in 1842. Mr. Layard commenced operations in 1845, and the interesting account of his explorations has made the subject familiar wherever the English language is spoken. Then came Colonel, (now Sir Henry) Rawlinson; and more recently the "Assyrian Discoveries" of Mr. George Smith, of the British Museum, in 1873–4, have thrown much additional light upon the history, language, manners, and customs of ancient Assyria and Babylonia.

But, although the walls of these palaces were covered with inscriptions, they were in an unknown tongue, and as mysterious and unintelligible as was the handwriting on the wall to the priests of Belshazzar. To decipher the unknown characters of an unknown language is no easy task, and Prof. Grotefend was the first to find a clue to the mysteries of the *Cuneiform*, or *Arrow-head* language.

The word *cuneiform* is derived from the Latin *cuneus*—a wedge—and in this style of letter are all the monumental records of the ancient empires of Assyria, Babylonia, and Persia. The accidental discovery of the famous Rosetta Stone, (now in the British Museum) furnished the key to decipher the hieroglyphics of Ancient Egypt, by means of which a flood of light has been thrown upon the history and civilization of the Pharaohs. The patience and perseverance of Rawlinson, Layard, and others have rescued the *Cuneiform* from the position of a " dead language," and have made it one full of life and interest to the antiquarian student.

Pliny declares that it is to the Assyrians we owe the

invention of letters; and it would seem probable that simple perpendicular and horizontal lines, of which the *Cuneiform* is composed, preceded the rounded or cursive forms, being better suited to letters carved by a primitive people on stone tablets, or the smoothed faces of rocks. The great antiquity of carved documents on stone is shown by the Bible. The Divine commands were first given to mankind on stone tablets, and in early ages this was considered the most appropriate and durable method of perpetuating records. The *cuneiform* inscriptions on most of the monuments of Assyria and Persia were formed with great neatness and care. The letters were evidently cut with sharp implements of iron or copper, and on the seals, gems, and small cylinders of stone the characters were so elaborately made and so accurately minute, that only an instrument of the most delicate construction could have produced them. It is said that no implements or tools of iron or steel, but only those of copper have been discovered among the ruins of ancient Egypt. But the cutting-tools of the Egyptians, as well as of the early Asiatic nations, were not of pure copper, nor were they of *bronze*, according to the modern acceptation of that term. They were made of copper with an alloy of about five per cent. of tin, which gave them the requisite hardness for use.

We know little of the civilization of the Assyrians, except what can be gathered from the casual notices scattered through the works of the Greeks. It is evident that they attained a high degree of culture at a very remote period. The testimony of the Bible, and the monuments of the Egyptians, on which the conquests of that people over the Asiatic nations are recorded, lead to this conclusion. There is a great discrepancy in the date assigned by *savans* to the earlier monuments of Egypt, but very few ascribe

them to an epoch later than that of the foundation of Nineveh, about 2,000 years B. C.  It is probable that the Assyrians at that time shared in the arts and sciences which
had already reached so high a degree of perfection in
Egypt.  They copied nature carefully, and gave more scope
to taste and invention than their Egyptian rivals, who were
restricted by certain prejudices and superstitions to a conventional style, from which it was not lawful to depart.

The exact date of the destruction of Nineveh, the proud
capital of the Eastern world, by Cyaxares, king of the
Medes and Persians, as fixed by the concurrent testimony
of Scripture and Herodotus, was about 608 years B. C.  It
did not occur before the death of Josiah, King of Judah B. C.
609, because a " King of Assyria" is mentioned at that time ;
and Zephaniah in a prophecy delivered in the reign of Josiah predicts the destruction of Nineveh as a future event.
But the prophecy of Jeremiah, written in the first year of
the captivity of the Jews, B. C. 605, enumerates all the
" Kings of the North," far and wide, and " all the Kingdoms
of the World," and among these Nineveh is not named.  The
statement of Herodotus that in the year 608 B. C. Cyaxares conquered Assyria to revenge his father's death is remarkably consistent with the accounts of Scripture.  The
destruction of Nineveh was so complete that when Xenophon passed over the remains of that city in his retreat,
some centuries later, with the " Ten Thousand Greeks," its
very name had been forgotten, and he describes it as a vast
uninhabited city, called Narissa, anciently inhabited by the
Medes.  Lucian speaks of it as so completely laid waste,
that not an inhabitant nor scarcely a vestige remained of the
magnificent palaces, once the dwelling-place of the Assyrian Monarchs ; and in modern times, so utterly was it forgotten, that skeptics of the last century even denied its
very existence.

Mr. Layard, speaking of the results of his own important discoveries, and of the utter destruction which had visited this once magnificent city, wrote:

" The ruins of Nimroud had been again covered up, and its palaces were once more hidden from the eye. The sculptures taken from them had been safely removed to Busrah, and were now awaiting their final transport to England. The inscriptions, which promise to instruct us in the history and civilization of one of the most ancient and illustrious nations of the earth, had been carefully copied.

" On looking back upon the few months that I had passed in Assyria, I could not but feel some satisfaction at the result of my labors. Scarcely a year before, with the exception of the ruins of Khorsabad, not one Assyrian monument was known ; almost sufficient materials had now been obtained to enable us to restore much of the lost history of the country, and to confirm the vague traditions of the learning and civilization of its people, hitherto treated as fabulous.

" It had often occurred to me, during my labors, that the time of the discovery of these remains was so opportune, that a person inclined to be superstitious might look upon it as something more than accidental. Had these palaces been by chance exposed to view some years before, no one could have been ready to take advantage of the circumstance, and they would have been completely destroyed by the inhabitants of the country. Had they been discovered a little later, it is highly probable that there would have been insurmountable objections to their removal. It was, consequently, just at the right moment that they were disinterred ; and we have been fortunate enough to discover the most convincing and lasting evidence of that magnificence and power which made Nineveh the wonder of the ancient world, and her fall the theme of the prophets, as the most signal instance of divine vengeance.

" Without the evidence that these monuments afford, we might almost have doubted that the great Nineveh ever existed, so completely ' has she become a desolation and a waste.' "

The earliest records of the Assyrians, like those of most other ancient nations, were probably monumental, and these are all in the arrow-head, or *cuneiform* character. There are three dialects or forms of these letters—the Assyrian or Babylonian, the Median, and the Persian, and to one of these may be referred all the *cuneiform* inscriptions that are known to exist. The Babylo-Assyrian alphabet contains about three hundred letters, while the Persian *cuneiform* has but forty. The former is supposed to be of much more ancient date, as in this dialect are all the inscriptions found in Nimroud and Nineveh, belonging to a period preceding the Persian domination.

The element of all the characters in the three different dialects of the *cuneiform* is the *wedge* ; and they differ only in the combination of wedges to form the letters. In many of the records of the Persian monarchs the three dialects occur in parallel columns, representing three languages.

The most remarkable inscription in this tri-lingual *cuneiform* character is that on the sacred rocks at a place called Behistun (" God's Place") on the western frontiers of Persia. Here Darius, " the Great King," inscribed his conquests and the most important events of his reign. Until within a few years this immense tablet has been a wonder and a puzzle to the most learned antiquaries, and to the few European travelers who have visited these remote regions. The labor of deciphering an unknown character, probably representing an extinct dialect, if not an extinct language,

must be very great. To Sir Henry Rawlinson, whose ingenuity and perseverance have given an accurate translation of the inscription at Behistun, we are indebted for this
valuable addition to the written records of the ancient
world.

Here upon the main road between Assyria and Persia,
the rocks rise abruptly from the plain to the height of
nearly seventeen hundred feet. The inscription covers several hundred square feet. It is unrivalled in extent, beauty
of execution, and correctness, especially the Persian, which
is said to be superior to any engraving of the kind, even
that on the tomb of Darius, at Persepolis, the ancient capital of Persia. It is about three hundred feet above the
base of the rock, and its inaccessibility has preserved it
from the iconoclastic fury of the Mahometans. It is probable that after the inscription was completed the rock beneath was cut away, so that the whole immense face is
nearly vertical. The rock is limestone, and a coat of sili-
cious varnish is yet visible on the tablet, which was designed to protect it from the atmosphere.

Darius begins by proclaiming his genealogy and titles,
tracing his descent from Adam. He then enumerates the
provinces of his empire, which in extent would seem to entitle him to the name of " the great King." After these
follow the great events of his reign, the reform of the national faith, his victories over the rebels in Assyria and
Babylon, and the suppression of insurrections in other
parts of his vast empire. He also engraves his thanksgiv-
ing to Ormuzd on this sacred spot, and in many particulars
this record corroborates the Mosaic accounts as well as the
writings of Herodotus.

There is one peculiarity of all *cuneiform* writing, that it
reads from left to right; while the ancient languages composed of rounded forms of letters (the Arabic, Hebrew,

and Persian), read from right to left. These characters are stamped or engraved, according to the nature of the material, on all the ruins of the great cities of Assyria and Babylonia—on the bricks of all the public buildings— on the walls of the temples, palaces, and other edifices, on stone slabs and bas-reliefs, on vases, gems, seals, and small cylinders, some being so minute as to require a microscope to decipher them.

I have before mentioned that the bricks of Babylon are uniform in size, and that all have stamped upon them the standard inscription of Nebuchadnezzar. It gives his name and titles, describes the wonders of the great city, and invokes the gods to grant duration to the temples and other great edifices which he had built. The inscriptions on the Babylonian bricks are always enclosed in a small square, and are formed with considerable care and nicety. They appear to have been impressed with a stamp upon which the entire inscription, not isolated letters, was cut in

BABYLONIAN BRICK.

relief. This art, so nearly approaching the modern invention of printing, is proved to have been known to the Egyptians and Chinese at a very remote period. The Pharaohs stamped their names on bricks, the stamps used being of wood, and several are preserved in European collections. But all the impressions on Egyptian bricks, unlike those of Assyria are in relief. The Babylonian bricks are about fifteen inches by three inches thick. They are made of a very tenacious clay, mixed with chopped straw and burnt hard in a kiln. They were always laid face downward in a cement of bitumen so hard as to make it almost impossible to remove one entire.

The bricks from Nineveh are also rectangular, but somewhat thicker than the Babylonian. The inscriptions on these Assyrian bricks appear to have been made in single *cuneiform* letters, and sometimes the workmen seem to have been careless in stamping them.

Among other antiques from Babylon which I was fortunate enough to secure is a small black cylinder of very hard stone with an exceedingly fine grain. It is an inch long by about three-eighths of an inch in diameter, and was picked up in the sand among the mounds of the ancient city. The surface of the cylinder is completely covered with an inscription in minute *cuneiform* letters very finely cut. A copy is given below, the letters being considerably magnified. For the translation I am indebted to the kindness of Mr. Smith, of the British Museum.

[" *The seal, or amulet, of a man named Kizirtu, son of the woman Satumani, servant (or priest) of Ishtar and Nana.*"]

Mr. George Smith, in his recently published work entitled " Assyrian Discoveries," gives an interesting account of the progress made by himself during the eight years that he has been engaged in the study and translation of the *cuneiform* inscriptions. He says, " Everyone has some bent or inclination which, if fostered by favorable circumstances, will color the rest of his life. My own taste has always been for Oriental studies, and from my youth I have taken a great interest in Eastern explorations and discoveries, particularly in the great work in which Layard and Rawlinson were engaged." " In 1866, seeing the unsatisfactory state of our knowledge of those parts of Assyrian history which bore upon the history of the Bible, I felt anxious to do something towards settling a few of the questions involved." Through the kindness of Sir Henry Rawlinson he was granted permission to examine the large collection of paper casts of *cuneiform* inscriptions in his workroom at the British Museum.

For several years Mr. Smith devoted himself to this study with an assiduity and perseverance that evinced his eminent fitness for this class of scientific investigation, and was rewarded with discoveries that attracted much attention from *savans* both in Europe and America. " In 1869," he says, " I discovered, among other things, a curious religious calendar of the Assyrians, in which every month was divided into four weeks, and the seventh days or ' Sabbaths' were marked out as days on which no work should be undertaken." But the discovery which has especially made him famous, and which has linked his name with the men most eminent in *cuneiform* research, is that of the celebrated " Deluge Tablets." I give his account of this fortunate discovery in his own words.

" In 1872 I had the good fortune to make a far more interesting discovery, namely, that of the tablets containing the Chaldean account of the deluge. The first fragment I discovered contained about half of the account ; it was the largest single fragment of these legends.

"As soon as I recognized this, I began a search among the fragments of the Assyrian library to find the remainder of the story.

" This library was first discovered by Mr. Layard, who sent home many boxes full of fragments of terra-cotta tablets, and after the close of Mr. Layard's work Mr.Rassam and Mr. Loftus recovered much more of this collection. These fragments of clay tablets were of all sizes, from half an inch to a foot long, and were thickly coated with dirt, so that they had to be cleaned before anything could be seen on the surface. Whenever I found anything of interest, it was my practice to examine the most likely parts of this collection, and pick out all the fragments that would give, or throw light on the new subject. My search for fragments of the ' Deluge Story' was soon rewarded by some good ' finds,' and I then ascertained that this tablet, of which I obtained three copies, was the eleventh in a series of tablets giving the history of an unknown hero, named Izdubar; and I subsequently ascertained that the series contained in all twelve tablets. These tablets were of remarkable interest, and a notice of them being published, they at once attracted a considerable amount of attention, both in England and abroad."

In consequence of the wide interest taken in these discoveries, the proprietors of the " *Daily Telegraph*" newspaper came forward and offered to advance the sum of one thousand guineas for fresh researches at Nineveh, in order to recover more of these interesting inscriptions.

This liberal offer was accepted, and Mr. Smith, having obtained six months leave of absence from the trustees of the British Museum, started for the East in January, 1873.

The records of this journey and of the subsequent expedition in 1874, are given to the public in the book already referred to. Mr. Smith encountered much difficulty, and had every possible obstacle thrown in his way by the local Turkish officials, but he persevered, and ultimately succeeded in excavating at Kouyunjik, near Nineveh, many additional portions of these inscriptions, which he calls the " Flood series of Legends."

I was shown by him one of these terra-cotta fragments of the " Deluge Tablets." It was about a foot long by eight inches in width, and completely covered with *cuneiform* characters. The initial design at the head of this chapter is a *fac-simile* copy of a fragment of one of these " Deluge-Tablets."

Beside giving the Chaldean account of the deluge, they form one of the most remarkable series of inscriptions yet discovered. These tablets record the adventures of a hero whose name is given as Izdubar, who has given no inconsiderable amount of employment to the learned. Mr. Smith is of opinion that this fabulous personage is the same as the Nimrod of the Bible, and that these legends were composed more than 2,000 years B. C. The translations of these Izdubar legends seem to be literal, but they are very fragmentary and disconnected in form. So far as they are preserved they represent Izdubar, or Nimrod, as a mighty hunter, or giant, whose mission it was to destroy " the divine bull," and other fabulous monsters and wild animals, and who in the height of his power ruled over all the valley of the Tigris and Euphrates, from the Persian Gulf to the Armenian Mountains. Mr. Smith says, " During the early Babylonian monarchy, from B. C. 2500 to 1500, there are constant allusions to these legends. The destruction of the lion, the divine bull, and other monsters by Izdubar, is often depicted on the cylinders and engraved gems, and Izdubar in his boat is also on some specimens. The legend of the flood is alluded to in inscriptions of the same epoch, and the ' city of the ark' is mentioned in a geographical list, which is one of the oldest *cuneiform* inscriptions we possess."

I give below but a few extracts from the "Flood Legends" to show the outlines of the story :

"And he spake to me . . . Make a ship after this . . . I destroy the sinners and life . . . Cause to go in the seed of life, all of it to the midst of the ship . . . Into the deep launch it . . . I entered to the midst of the ship and shut the door . . . The raging of the storm in the morning . . . The bright earth to a waste was turned . . . The surface of the earth like . . . it swept. It destroyed all life from the face of the earth . . . Six days and nights passed. . . . The wind, deluge, and storm overwhelmed . . . On the seventh day in its course was calmed all the storm and all the deluge . . . The sea he caused to dry, and the wind and deluge ended . . . I sent forth a dove and it left . . . The dove went and turned and a resting place, it did not find and it returned . . . I sent forth a swallow and it left . . . The swallow went and turned, and a resting place it did not find, and it returned . . . I sent forth a raven and it left . . . The raven went, and the corpses on the water it saw, and it did eat, it swam and wandered away, and did not return . . . I sent the animals forth to the four winds . . . I poured forth a libation . . . I built an altar on the peak of the mountain."

The few extracts above given are not consecutive, but they show a remarkable similarity of this traditionary account of the Flood with the Biblical record of that event. The question of *priority*, or which is the *editio princeps*, I will not here discuss. What are traditions but unauthenticated history?

The facility with which Mr. Smith reads the *cuneiform* language is very remarkable. The fine inscriptions upon the cylinder before mentioned, and upon other antiques which I submitted to him, he copied and translated at sight, as readily as a Professor of Greek would read a sentence in that language. A lexicon of the *cuneiform* I presume has yet to be made. For thousands of years these inscriptions were an unknown tongue. An attempt to do justice to the wonders which the key to the *cuneiform* inscriptions has unlocked would occupy volumes. I can only hope in this chapter to call attention to a subject on which very little is known to the mass of the people. This is an age of scientific research, and while our *savans* are opening new fields of knowledge, it seems eminently proper that they should recover from the remote past whatever of value is already recorded upon tables of stone.

# CHAPTER XXV.

## VISIT TO THE PUBLIC INSTITUTIONS.

F E W days after my re-
turn from Babylon I called
at the palace to thank the
Pasha for his kindness and
attention, and to take leave
of his Excellency, as I expected soon to start on my
return to Europe. I was received as before, with much
politeness, and when I told
him of some of my adven-
tures in search of the ruins,
leaving out, of course, all
mention of Bass' ale and
moonlight flitting, he expressed the hope that I should
come again next year and complete my explorations. He
said that the *cordon sanitaire* was now extended entirely
around the city, three miles outside the walls, and orders had

been issued to shoot every man that attempted to cross the line. But the increasing heat of the weather he thought would soon check the spread of the plague, although its effect would be the opposite in case of cholera.

He hoped President Grant would send a diplomatic or consular representative to Bagdad ; but I reminded him of how few Americans had ever found their way to Turkish Arabia, and that at present we have no commercial intercourse with this country. He then unrolled a map and pointed out to me the line of the Euphrates Valley Railway, already commenced, from the port of Alexandretta on the Mediterranean to Aleppo, and thence to a point on the Euphrates eight hundred miles from Bagdad. This road when completed will be about one hundred and fifty miles long, and will open a new route by railway and river from the Mediterranean to the Persian Gulf, and thence to India. The Pasha pointed through the open windows to the government machine shops on the opposite side of the Tigris, where he is building two iron steamers for the navigation of the upper Euphrates, and asked if I would like to inspect them, as well as the Arsenal, Military Hospital, Palace and other public buildings. I was most happy to accept his invitation, and taking my leave, he accompanied me to the door, an especial mark of honor, and told his *aide-de-camp*, the young Turkish officer whom I had before met, to take me round in his own barge. These attentions were quite unexpected by me, and were doubtless the result of the credentials sent to me from Constantinople. They were very gratifying, not so much from the *prestige* they gave me, as from the opportunity they afforded to see everything of interest to a stranger, and to obtain the information I was seeking as to the country, the people, and their institutions.

The Pasha's barge was moored at the garden steps on

the river in front of the palace. It was an elegant affair, manned by eight oarsmen, the cushioned seats protected from the sun by a scarlet awning on which were embroidered the " Star and Crescent."

Mr. Stanno accompanied us as interpreter, and we were first rowed across the river to visit the arsenal, machine-shops and foundry. Here about sixty men are employed under the charge of an English engineer. The machinery is all imported from Europe, but the workmen are natives, and seem skillful and intelligent. Some pieces of work were shown me by the superintendent, which to my inexperienced eye would be creditable to any workshop in Europe. I examined with much interest the two iron steamers pointed out by the Pasha, which were built on the Clyde, sent out in pieces, put together here, and are now nearly ready to launch. They are one hundred and ten feet long, flat-bottomed, covered with thin steel plates, furnished with powerful engines, and are expected to draw when loaded but one foot of water. They are intended to ply on the upper Euphrates, where the river during the dry season is very shallow and rapid.

Being an American I was supposed to know something about river navigation, and both the Englishman and the Turk expressed great astonishment when I told them that we have steamers in America, which, it is said, can go anywhere, if there is *only a heavy dew.* As I was careful to explain that I could not vouch for the literal truth of this statement, I trust they will not repeat it except as one of the " tales of a traveler."

We were then rowed a short distance up the river to the military hospital, a large, handsome building, where I was introduced to the surgeon in charge. He conducted me through the wards, where there are one hundred and eighty patients, all soldiers, in various stages of convales-

19

cence. The rooms are lofty and well ventilated, the cots neat and clean, and the whole management as systematic and well conducted as in any European institution of the kind. I was shown through the dispensary, bath houses, and well shaded grounds, and then to the private offices of the superintendent, where cigarettes, coffee and sherbet awaited us. The Doctor spoke excellent French, but to my surprise informed me that he was a native Turk, born and educated for his profession in Constantinople.

Taking leave of the polite and accomplished surgeon, my conductors next took me to the Pasha's palace, about two miles up the river, on the eastern bank, beyond the city walls. It is an elegant modern villa, surrounded by a garden handsomely laid out in European style. It was built four years ago for the especial use of the Shah of Persia, on the occasion of his visit to Bagdad. It is now unoccupied, but is being put in readiness for the Pasha's family, or harem, who are soon expected from Constantinople. The apartments are furnished with the greatest luxury, and regardless of expense. Elegant crystal chandeliers, French furniture and *bijouterie*, soft Persian carpets and silken hangings seemed to make it a palace worthy of the Caliph Haroun-al-Raschid, in the palmy days of Bagdad. In the garden was the most beautiful tent I ever saw. It was made of alternate stripes of blue and crimson silk, and above it floated the flag of the Pasha. In the stables were a score of the finest Arab horses, several of which were brought out for our inspection. I am not especially a horse fancier, but I thought if the Pasha, with all his kindness, would only ask me to select, as a souvenir of Bagdad, one of those beautiful animals, so intelligent, docile and graceful in every motion, I should be extremely grateful, and fully appreciate the present.

It was very fortunate for me that the harem had not

arrived, for then the palace and grounds will be tabooed to all male visitors.

As we passed out through the gates of the palace the guard presented arms, and entering the boat I was next taken to an institution by far more interesting than any I had visited. It is an "industrial school" for orphan boys. The superintendent, whose benignant face and white beard suggested his fitness for the position, received us with great courtesy, and conducted us through the building. Here are eighty boys from ten to fifteen years old, dressed in a neat gray uniform, and as bright, intelligent looking lads as any country can boast. Some were weaving different fabrics of silk and cotton on hand looms, others making shoes and sewing garments, while about a dozen were setting type in an adjoining building. The manufactured articles were shown me, and they certainly were creditable to the industry and mechanical skill of the boys.

In one of the school-rooms a class was receiving instruction in the elements of geometry from a teacher, formerly one of the pupils, which he illustrated on a blackboard. We were shown through the dining room, dormitories, and hospital, where the clean white cots were without an occupant. Our visit was unexpected, and we saw everything in its ordinary working condition. In reply to my inquiry as to how he enforced discipline, he said that he very rarely was obliged to resort to corporeal punishment, but "boys will be boys" all the world over, and he took me to a cell-like chamber where a bright eyed little fellow was being punished for some breach of discipline, by being made to stand upon a barrel in the middle of the room.

This charitable institution, as well as the hospital which I had before visited, was founded by Midhut Pasha, the predecessor of the present ruler. To this enlightened and intelligent governor, Bagdad is indebted for nearly all the benevolent institutions and public enterprises of which it can boast. He built a tramway, or street railroad, to Kasmaine, six miles up the river, and a great resort of pilgrims, encouraged steam navigation on the Tigris and Euphrates, and built the military barracks, by far the finest buildings in the city. He was very popular with both natives and foreign residents. But the home government was displeased at his spending the money instead of remitting it to Constantinople, and perhaps was alarmed at his increasing popularity. He was superseded, and carried away with him the regrets and good will of all his people ; but was so poor that he was obliged to borrow money to pay his expenses home. This last fact was an evidence of honesty almost without a precedent, for a Pasha is expected to retire immensely rich. On the wall of the superintendent's office, to which I was invited for coffee, etc., was hanging an engraving of Midhut Pasha, and my attention was called to it with every mark of respect.

Before we left, the boys were collected in the large room, and the superintendent introduced me to them as the first American who had ever visited the institution. I was so much gratified at what I had seen that I longed once more to be able to speak Arabic or Turkish, that I might tell the boys something about my own country. I do not suppose that even the teachers had very definite ideas of America ; and the lads before me probably knew less about our land, its institutions and history, than an American school-boy does about the Hottentots. I did not care to make them a speech, or give them a lesson in geography; but it is not often in one's life that he can have an attentive audience of bright, intelligent lads, not one of whom has ever heard of Washington and his little hatchet, or of Franklin munching his roll through the streets of Philadelphia. What an opportunity was lost, to be sure ! But it occurred to me that the present of a gold *lirah*, as a prize for the best boy at the next examination, would be quite as acceptable, and perhaps do more good, than a " story with a moral."

It was no affectation in the superintendent to say that he was " taken by surprise," and he accepted it in behalf of the boys with many thanks. Holding up the coin, he explained the matter to the lads, and the scene that followed I shall not soon forget. Instantly every boy rose to his feet and three ringing cheers for America echoed through

THREE CHEERS FOR AMERICA.

the building. Far more gratifying it was to me than if the cheers had come from a whole regiment of Turkish soldiers. If this little story has a moral, I respectfully commend it to the visitors of similar institutions at home.

Adjoining the industrial school is the government printing office, the next object of our visit. I had never suspected that such an institution existed in Bagdad.

Here I found a steam-power press with the capacity of thirty-five hundred impressions an hour, besides several hand presses and a machine for cutting and folding envelopes. All the type-setting and light work is done by the boys from the industrial school. Everything looked neat and orderly, and it seemed in every respect a well managed establishment. They were working off an edition of a weekly paper, printed on one side in Turkish and on the other in Arabic. Besides the newspaper, which being an official institution, is probably neither republican nor democratic in politics, they execute here all the blanks and forms used by the Pasha's government.

While crossing the river Mr. Stanno mentioned to me that among the projects of the present ruler of Bagdad, is the building of a suspension bridge across the Tigris. They are obliged for two or three months every year to remove the present floating bridges, to prevent their being carried away by the rapid current. I surprised him by saying that the greatest number, as well as longest suspension bridges in the world were in America. He earnestly requested that on my return home I would put the Pasha's government in communication with some of our most eminent engineers. The feeling here is very favorable towards our countrymen, and I have no doubt there is an opening in this matter for American science and skill.

We afterwards visited the barracks, a large and handsome building adjoining the Serai, which can accommodate several thousand troops. The bakery of this establishment is on a most extensive scale, and is fitted up with machinery which to me was quite novel. Bread in this country is a much more important article of diet with all classes than in western lands.

Having finished our tour of inspection, I said good-bye to my polite escort with a much better impression of the

civilization of Bagdad than I had ever before conceived of.
Who will say that there is no hope of future progress
among a people where an hospital, an orphan asylum and
a printing office have been established, and are in successful operation!   And who would expect to find these evi-
dences of refinement and civilization in a city which is
only associated in the minds of Europeans, as well as
Americans with the barbaric splendor of the Caliphs in the
time of the " Arabian Nights!"

# CHAPTER XXVI.

## SOCIAL LIFE OF NATIVES AND FOREIGNERS.

Climate of Bagdad—In Cellars by Day, and on the Roofs at Night—No Ice
—*Cudjees* a Substitute—Population and Currency—Antiques from Baby-
lon and Nineveh—Slavery among the Mahometans—No Colorphobia—
White Donkeys—The Pariah Dogs—Noises of Bagdad—Abdallah Adver-
tising his Band—Municipal Regulations—Social Life among the English
Residents—The English Minister, Colonel Herbert—Dr. Colville—Officers
and Civilians—No Hotel—Americans Rarely Seen—A Dubious Compli-
ment—A Day's Routine—Story by Abbe Huc—" Our American Cousin's"
Experience of Bagdad Hospitality—Routes Home—The Dromedary Mai-
—Foundered in the Desert—The Only Line of Retreat for the Writer.

HE climate of Bagdad, generally speaking, may be
deemed a healthy one. The
great heat is at times almost
insupportable, and yet it is
said that the least sickness
prevails during the hottest
summers. While the air on
the Persian Gulf is very
moist, with heavy dews at
night, and consequently sick-
ly, here the air is remarkably
dry and pure, so that the
whole population sleep in the
open air during the hot months. In winter it is one of the
finest climates in the world, the thermometer standing at
fifty degrees, the air cool, yet mild and invigorating. The
ancient Persian Kings preferred these plains bordering on

the Tigris to any other winter residence. During the hot-test summer months the range of the thermometer is from ninety to one hundred and twenty-five degrees; in the middle of the day usually as high as one hundred and five degrees. When the *shammāl*, or north wind, blows, it is quite cool and comfortable; but during the " date season," or August and September, it is frequently a dead calm, and the heat is suffocating. Sometimes a *sirocco* will blow from the south, and then all business is suspended, the people shutting themselves up in their houses until the " hot blast" is over.

The underground apartments, or *serdābs*, are peculiar to Bagdad. About the first of June the desks and furniture from offices and parlors, are transferred to these unique rooms with high arched ceilings, the *punkahs*, or fans, are suspended from above and kept constantly in motion, and here the hot hours of the day are spent. The dim light streams down through grated windows near the ceiling, the temperature is cool and uniform, and much less humid than in such cellar-like apartments with us. After the sun goes down they ascend to the flat roofs, or terraces, where they have the evening meal and sleep.

People who at home object to city-built houses, where they " eat in the basement and sleep in the attic," would call this living in the cellar and sleeping on the roof. No one goes out of doors, if it can be avoided, during the heat of the day. Business is transacted and exercise taken during the early morning or after sunset.

To those of us who are accustomed to a supply of ice during our comparatively temperate summers, it would seem impossible to live comfortably without a particle of this luxury with the temperature at one hundred and five degrees. But a wise provision of nature comes to the aid of people living in tropical countries. Evaporation

produces cold.   Water is always kept in porous, unglazed
earthen jars, called *cudjees*.   These are made of every
shape and size, and are in universal use.   The evaporation
from the exterior of these *cudjees* keeps the water from ten
to twenty degrees colder than the air, and quite cool enough
to be wholesome to drink.   Milk, butter, wine, and every
article that can be immersed in water is cooled in this way.
It is only when I think of the delights of a *long iced drink*,
or a dish of ice cream, that I miss the article considered so
indispensable to comfort at home.

ANTIQUE COINS.

Bagdad contains a population of about one hundred thousand.   Nowhere, perhaps, in the world, can there be seen an
admixture of so many races, and in no city can be heard such
a diversity of language.   At the table of the English Resident, where the guests sometimes comprise many different

nationalities, a medley of thirteen languages has been counted in one room.

The coins in ordinary circulation are as various as the speech of the people. Very curious Persian, Indian, and Turkish coins are mixed in the change given me in the bazaars, with European, and especially Russian money. I can no more tell whether my change is correct than I could decipher the cuneiform inscription on an antique from Babylon. To the " specimen bricks" from Nineveh and Babylon, and many other interesting antiques which I hope will reach home in safety, I shall be able to add some very curious coins for the collections of any of my friends who are interested in numismatics.

Slavery in the East is quite a different institution from our idea of this " relic of barbarism" as it existed in the Southern States. The Turks are very lenient in their treatment of slaves, and they frequently occupy important positions of honor and trust. Color seems to have very little to do with the matter. By Mahometan law slave families cannot be separated, and all slaves taken to Mecca become free. The slave mother of a child by her master, not only becomes free, but, together with her child, is entitled to a share in his estate. The mothers of all the Sultans of Turkey have been Circassian or Georgian slaves, and some of the most devoted and faithful officers under the Viceroy of Egypt were slave boys whom he has educated. So far from opposing, the laws encourage the education of slaves, and the institution as it has existed here from time immemorial, is free from many of those obnoxious and inhuman features which, under the influence of avarice and *colorphobia*, were developed in America.

In Bagdad the very black slaves are preferred as household servants. We frequently see them very richly dressed in attendance upon their masters and mistresses. The supply of these fashionable black slaves has hitherto come from Zanzibar and Madagascar, but lately the English have in a great measure put a stop to the traffic. They wear no air of abject misery, but strut through the bazaars, better fed, and more insolent and conceited than the free Arabs around them. Their beauty consists in its special and perfect ugliness, and they seem to be valued on the same principle as Isle of Skye terriers.

The white donkeys of Bagdad are famous all through the East, and sell at high prices. Some of them are of considerable size, and fancifully dyed with henna, their tails and ears bright red, and their bodies spotted, like the heraldic talbot, with the same color. As in ancient times, they bear the chief priests and men of the law, and the ladies prefer them to any other animal. They are splendidly caparisoned, and each one has his nostrils slit—a practice prevalent also in Persia—which is supposed to make them *longer winded*. I never hear a donkey bray without thinking this quite unnecessary.

The dogs of Bagdad are so important and prominent a feature in the life of the place, that they almost deserve a chapter by themselves. They are all *pariahs*, that is, they have no especial masters or owners, but here, as in other oriental cities, they are considered a public institution. They number many thousands, and are the scavengers to whom the inhabitants are indebted for keeping the streets clean from offal. You see them basking all day in the sun, stretched in the middle of the thoroughfare, where there is a constant stream of camels, horses, and mules. But they seem to escape all these perils, and if disturbed, they sneak away with a cowed and suspicious look. They are of a light dun color, and their appearance betrays their wolfish descent. These neglected curs have regular quarters to which each one belongs. They are divided into republies, and woe betide a foreign dog who crosses the frontier of his own territory. He is set upon tooth and nail, and is glad to beat an ignominious retreat. It is a curious fact that in this great multitude of half-starved dogs, hydrophobia is unknown. It is said that at night the jackals from the desert come into the city over the ruined walls, and join their brothers hardly more civilized, in doing duty as scavengers. These dogs seem to sleep during the day, but when night comes the howling and barking is incessant. They have no attachment to persons, and nothing amongst the canine tribes of the East is to be heard like the honest bark of the faithful house dog, when he gives a cheerful welcome to his master on his return home.

Bagdad is certainly the most noisy place I was ever in. The only quiet time is at midday. Then for an hour or two everybody and everything, except flies and mosquitoes, seem to be asleep. An Arab never talks except at the top of his voice, and I at first supposed they were quarreling, when in fact, they were only conversing in their ordinary tone. During the day and often until late in the evening, there are constant processions headed by *tom-toms* and *dulcimers*,—an ear piercing wind instrument something like a clarionet. The occasion of these processions I could not always tell. Sometimes they were weddings or betrothals, and sometimes funerals. In the latter case, the body was carried on men's shoulders, and followed by the mourners, some the relations of the deceased, and others professional howlers, who vied with each other in their wailings and mournful cries. Add to these the official town criers, the beggars and *fakeers* soliciting charities "in the name of Allah and the Prophet," the *muezzins* calling the faithful to prayer from the gallery of the minarets, professional singers practicing their voices, and every morning the heavy bass drum of Abdallah, who is the conductor of a band, and goes through the streets to advertise his calling and solicit orders. Many of these sounds, together with the howling

ARAB BEGGAR.

of dogs and braying of donkeys, are kept up half the night. But one gets used to all noises, and after the first night I think they never deprived me of a minute's sleep.

Much of the space within the walls once covered with houses, is now laid out in gardens and date groves. These are surrounded by walls eight or ten feet high, made of tenacious mud mixed with cut straw. In my walks among the gardens, I noticed frequent recesses where the walls were set back about three feet, and in some places where they had fallen, the workmen were rebuilding them that distance back from the street line. This I found to be a municipal regulation. Whenever a man permits his wall to fall he must rebuild it three feet from the street. This regulation is calculated to make land owners keep their walls in repair, and in course of time will widen many of the narrow streets of the city.

Of the social life of the English colony at Bagdad it is pleasant to speak. In so small a circle the distinctions of rank, which would obtain at home, are in a great measure lost sight of, though not entirely ignored. The British Minister Resident and his charming family are, from official position, as well as eminent social accomplish-

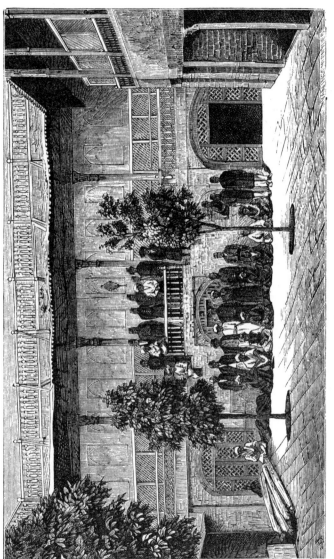

INTERIOR OF ENGLISH RESIDENCY. *From a photograph in possession of the author.*

ments, the head of the English speaking community. That generous hospitality, which in all foreign lands characterizes the representatives of the English government, is here maintained in a style befitting the great power, wealth, and commercial importance of the English nation. The accomplished Surgeon to the Residency, and the officers of the gunboat " Comet," are gentlemen whose genial qualities would be appreciated in any community. Dr. Colville's long residence in the East, his familiarity with the manners and customs of the people, his knowledge of the many languages spoken in Bagdad, as well as his eminent skill as a physician, give him great influence with the best class of people of all the different nationalities. His official duties are only nominal, but his house is often filled with people who seek his professional advice. I do not know how lucrative his practice may be, but his kindness of heart never permits him to turn away from his door the sick and needy who ask his assistance. Besides these, the manager of the great commercial establishment of Lynch & Co., the only English merchants in Bagdad, and the several young men attached to the house, are important elements in the social life of the place. It is not unlikely that the coming of my friend, Mr. Finnis, as the first visit to Bagdad of a member of the firm since the senior partner returned to London some years ago, is looked upon as an important event in the little community. There are no hotels here, and the few visitors and travelers are the welcome guests of the foreign residents. So rarely does an American find his way here that I have several times been asked, much to my amusement, whether I knew Mr. W——, who, I would be told, was an American from Philadelphia, and spent a few days here some four or five years ago. Of course, I do not know Mr. W——, but I have heard so much about him, that I should almost recognize him were I to meet him in the street or on a train of cars at home.

A few days ago one of my English friends said to me at dinner, intending it doubtless as a compliment: " Why, my dear sir, you don't seem to me like an American." In reply, I said that he must not suppose every American talks through his nose and " guesses " in every sentence like the stage Yankee ; that I am always and everywhere an American, but I trust never offensively so ; that I have too much respect for the prejudices and opinions of others to make my republican ideas unduly prominent, while I am the honored guest of those who conscientiously believe in the " divine right of kings."

It may be interesting to know how the day is spent in this out of the way place, where the mail and the daily newspaper form no part of the routine of life. We sleep upon the terraced roofs in the open air, and half an hour before sunrise it is the duty of our servants to wake us, and bring a *chibouk* of fragrant Persian tobacco and a small cup of tea or coffee. Then we hastily dress and mount our horses, which are ready saddled in the court-yard below. We slowly thread our way, single file, through the narrow streets, already filled with people, towards the half-ruined South gate, leading out upon the open desert. Our horses are restive, and, from a bad habit they have of kicking and biting each other, must be kept well apart. No sooner do we emerge upon the plain than off we dash at full run, our horses wild with delight and excitement, sometimes rearing, and the next moment with their heels in the air. It requires skillful horseman-ship to keep one's seat, and *spills* are by no means infre-quent. But these tough, wiry young Englishmen, accus-tomed to field sports, make light of such accidents. A wild ride of half an hour and we return to the town by the East gate, invigorated in frame and spirits by the pure morning air. Then a bath and a light meal of bread, eggs, and tea. Now we are ready for the day's work, provided we have anything to do. If I have no writing on hand I stroll through the bazaars, or make a morning call. At noon comes the regular breakfast, consisting of several courses of meats and vegetables, washed down by Bass' ale. Then a *siesta* until two o'clock, after which another hour or two is given to business. As the sun gets low and the oppressive heat is no longer felt, the horses are again in readiness, or we take a quiet walk through the " green lanes"—sometimes a game of croquet or quoits in a date garden, or a sailing party on the river is made up, in which the few ladies will join, and occupies the time until dark. At eight we dine on the terrace, never alone, but by previous arrangement, with some of our friends, or on the cool deck of the " Comet." Dinner to an Englishman is always the event of the day, and if at the Residency, it means full dress. At the bachelors' quarters it is not so ceremonious. Dinner over, whist always follows, which lasts until midnight. Each person has his own personal servant, who accompanies his master when he goes out to dinner, waits upon him at table, prepares and lights his *narghileh*, and when the party breaks up, escorts him home through the dark and narrow streets, carrying a lantern.

It is related by the Abbé Huc in his Travels in China, as an instance of the inconvenience of not understanding the habits and customs of a strange people, or the rites and ceremonies of well-bred natives, that a country cousin coming unexpectedly from a great distance, was invited to dine by his city relative. After waiting some hours and seeing no signs of the meal, he ventured to hint that it was getting late and he was very hungry—upon which his relation and host burst into a torrent of abuse. " What ?" said

20

he, " Are you so ignorant and rustic as not to know that it was my duty to ask you, but by the same rites and ceremonies it was your duty to refuse the invitation ?"

The experience of " our American cousin" at Bagdad has been so different from that of the " Heathen Chinee," that had he been of their own flesh and blood, his English friends could not have treated him with more kind and generous hospitality. My best wish to any of my countrymen who may come after me, is that they may meet as cordial a reception. If the railway from Alexandretta to Aleppo shall ever be finished, and the navigation of the

THE DROMEDARY MAIL.

upper Euphrates prove a success, this part of the world will lose the charm of novelty, and be overrun with cockney tourists. But with the present facilities for travel to reach the Mediterranean is almost as difficult as it was to Xenophon and his ten thousand Greeks. The shortest but most dangerous route is to Damascus and Beyrout, via Palmyra—the "city of the desert." The English residents of Bagdad maintain a fortnightly mail with Europe by this route, which is carried on a fast dromedary in eighteen days to Damascus, six or eight of which are without water. Occasionally both mail and rider disappear, never being heard from after they leave port, like a ship foundered at sea.

They are supposed to be gobbled up by the wild Bedouins, who care nothing for the letters nor the Arab rider, but rarely miss a good opportunity to appropriate a fast camel or dromedary.

Another route is up the Tigris three hundred miles to Mosul, near the site of ancient Nineveh, thence via Diabekia and Aleppo to Alexandretta. This involves a fatiguing journey of nine hundred miles on horseback, subject to all the annoyances of stopping at the public *khans* at night, and traveling by day under a burning sun.

The third and most attractive route is eastward through Persia to Teheran, its capital—thence to the Caspian Sea, in all a horseback journey of seven hundred miles—by steamer up the Caspian and the Volga through Russia to eastern Europe. I give these several routes for the benefit of any future wanderer in these strange lands. The season is now so far advanced that they are all impracticable to me on account of the heat. The best line of retreat open to one who has no dread of a sea voyage in the tropics, is the route by which I came, down the Persian and Arabian Gulfs, and up the Red Sea to Egypt, thence across the Mediterranean to Europe.

# CHAPTER XXVII.

## FROM BAGDAD TO BASSORAH.

Farewell to Bagdad—Night Scene—The " City of the Enchanters" Disappears—Seleucia—Ctesiphon—Coal from England—Novel Receipts for Specie—Seals instead of Signatures—A Young Arab Chief—Story of Abdul-Kareem—Betrayed by his Friend—Executed without Trial—Arab Hatred for the Betrayer—Abundance of Game—Shooting Wild Boars—How they are usually Hunted—An Ugly Customer—Lively Sport—My Breech-Loader Ahead of the " Enfield "—Fig Leaves from the Garden of Eden—"A Thousand Welcomes to Marghil "—How I Passed the Time There—The Lonely English Cemetery—Wailing Jackals—Trip in a *Mashoof*—Climate of Bassorah—The Shāmmāl—Arrival of the *Mesopotamia*—The Steamer's Cargo—Through Tropical Seas in Midsummer—A Trying Journey Before Me.

THE " Dijleh " was to leave Bagdad at midnight. My luggage was on board, and the farewells had all been said, except to the half score friends with whom I was to dine that night. Late in the evening a message came from Captain Holland that the boat was only waiting for the passenger. Still we did not hurry ; but when the last rubber was finished, the whole party adjourned to the oanks of the river. As the "Dijleh " swung round with the swift current, the splash of her paddle-wheels mingled with the notes of "Auld Lang Syne," sung by my friends on the bank. To me it seemed more like leaving *home* than any parting I had ever known on a foreign shore.

It had been my good fortune to first approach Bagdad while the early morning sun was gilding dome and minaret, and pouring a flood of brightness through palm and orange groves. Now, as I sadly bade good-bye to the " city of the Caliphs," the moon, just rising in the east, threw far out on the river dark shadows from buildings, trees, and gardens, and there was something weird and unreal in the scene. We dropped rapidly past the custom-house, the Residency garden, the silent " Comet " shrouded in her white awnings, and then suddenly, as if under the wave of a magic wand, the "City of the Enchantress" disappeared from view, to be hereafter to me but a memory and a dream.

Early the next day we passed the sandy mounds where the successors of Alexander built the great city of Seleucia, floating through the canals between the Euphrates and the Tigris the building materials for their new capital from the inexhaustible mounds of Babylon. A short distance below, on the opposite shore, stands the magnificent arch of Ctesiphon, a solitary monument to mark the spot where a few centuries later the Parthian monarchs founded a great city. Here the Persian kings reveled in wealth and luxury, until the fierce invaders from Arabia came pouring down upon them like an avalanche, shouting the battle cry, "There is but one God, and Mahomet is his Prophet." As we glided past, not a human being could be seen on either shore—the picture of desolation was complete.

The rapid current bears us swiftly down the river, which is now in every direction overflowing its low banks. Sometimes for miles the country seems one vast maze of swamps, through which only the keen eye of the Arab pilot can detect the winding channel. At dark we came to anchor until the moon rose, for when the river is so high the downward trip is very liable to accidents from the increased speed of the boat, and the danger of her paddle-wheels striking the banks.

The " Dijleh " stops for an hour or two at Amarah to discharge and receive freight. This town being about half way between Bassorah and Bagdad, the owners of the steamers maintain here a coal depot. The fuel for these English boats and for all the Turkish steamers at Bassorah and Bagdad, is brought out from England. It costs at Newcastle about five dollars a ton, but when it reaches the Euphrates the freight has increased its value six-fold. Coal of poor quality, almost as soft as bitumen, has lately been discovered near the Tigris, about four hundred miles north of Bagdad, and the government are trying, with poor success, to use it on their steamers. A mine of good coal would be of great value to this country in promoting steam navigation on these rivers.

The " strong box " in the clerk's cabin contains many packages of specie remitted by native merchants. I notice the receipts taken on the delivery of these parcels are merely the seal of the consignee, impressed on the bill of lading. Every town Arab wears a seal ring for use rather than ornament, and carries in his pocket a bit of India ink. During my interview with the Pasha of Bagdad his secretary laid before him some documents for his signature; but instead of writing his name, he merely stamped upon them his official seal.

While our boat was stopping at Amarah a bright and handsome little boy, about six years old, came on board and sought out Captain Holland, with whom he seemed a great favorite. He was well dressed, and had the air and manner of one born to command. Great deference was

paid to him by the Arabs, and our genial captain filled his
pockets with nuts and bonbons. When the bell rang
to start, he was carefully set on shore in charge of his
attendant. He is the son of Abdul-Kareem, the chief
of the Shammas, the most populous and warlike tribe of
Arabs in Lower Mesopotamia. His father was a man of
independent spirit and great influence, but being suspected
of conspiring against the government, a price was set upon
his head. Last year one of his friends betrayed him to
the Turks. Having invited him to a feast, he arranged to
have soldiers placed in ambush, and he was captured in
the house of his entertainer. The chief was taken to Bagdad and tried by a court-martial, but there was not sufficient evidence to convict him. He was then ordered to
be sent under guard to Constantinople. When the party
having him in charge reached Mosul they received a telegram from the Porte ordering his immediate execution.
As they crossed the bridge over the Tigris at that place,
the unfortunate prisoner caught sight of a rope dangling
from a beam overhead, and knew that his hour had come.
The party halted, the rope was put around his neck and
his horse led from under him. He died a brave man, pro-
testing his innocence, and sending his last blessing to his
boy. But the traitor who betrayed him, though Sheik of
a powerful tribe, lives with the mark of Cain upon his
brow. He violated the most sacred rights of hospitality,
and his life is not safe for a moment. If he visits the
town, even the beggars in the streets spit upon him. It
is necessary, of course, to keep the Arab tribes in subjection, but treachery and bad faith reflect no credit upon the
Turkish government.

The second day was through a section of the country
where game was very abundant. Cranes, pelicans, herons,
ducks, and other water fowl, were always within shot, but

attracted little attention. We are on the lookout for larger game, such as wild boars, antelopes, and jackals. My friend, Mr. Finnis, had loaned me his breech-loading rifle, and supplied me with a hundred cartridges, which I was told to use unsparingly.

One morning I was awakened by the shout of " pig! pig!" from one of the officers, and glancing through the open window of my cabin, I saw a large, black, wild boar clumsily galloping along where the water, overflowing the banks, was about two feet deep. His long pointed snout, sharp, curved tusks, and back embellished with bristles, like " quills upon the fretted porcupine," gave him a savage and ferocious look, and he would have been an ugly cus-

HUNTING THE WILD BOAR.

tomer to attack single-handed on shore. Wild boars are usually hunted in this country by parties of Europeans on horseback, armed with spears and revolvers. They are very tenacious of life, and when wounded, frequently turn upon their pursuers and show fight. It becomes dangerous and exciting sport, when the enraged beast rips up a horse and goes for the dismounted hunter, with half a dozen broken spear shafts bristling from his tough hide. But now I had "piggy" at disadvantage. Quickly adjusting the sight at two hundred yards, I shoved my rifle through the window and poured five Minnie bullets into him in quick succession. There was an Arab encampment at some distance out on the plain, just in range, and a stray ball might do mischief in that direction. But at the last shot the boar went under with a great splash, and I heard a cheer from the Arab passengers who had been watching the sport from the upper deck. During the morning I had many fine shots, and at breakfast the coffee and hot rolls suddenly lost their attraction, when a bend in the river brought a prowling jackal within range.

The rivalry between the first engineer and myself was at times rather lively. While off duty, his station, Enfield rifle in hand, was on the forward deck, and my position being further aft on the wheel house, he often secured the first shot. But my superior weapon was more than an offset for his greater experience and advantage of position. There were over a hundred deck passengers, all Arabs and Persians, who took a lively interest in the sport.

When we reached Kernah, where the two rivers unite to form the "Shat-el-Arab," we made a short stop, and I improved the opportunity to set foot on the reputed "Garden of Eden." I very naturally looked about me for "apple trees"; but if that fruit ever grew in this locality it has long since disappeared. I am rather fond of *souvenirs* from interesting places, but in this dirty Arab village I could see nothing suggestive of the Paradise of our first parents, except an old fig tree, from which I brought away a few leaves as mementoes.

Before night we brought to under the walls of the *Khan* at Marghil, where I had spent a few days so pleasantly three months before. I had expected to find in the river at Bassorah, three miles below, an English steamer about to sail for Suez. But she had not arrived, and I concluded to wait here for the " Mesopotamia," a steamer belonging to my English friends, which would be due in about ten days. Captain Carter was absent, having left a few days before on a short trip to Bagdad to recruit his health. But as soon as he heard of my arrival and necessary detention, he sent the characteristic telegram: "A thousand welcomes to Marghil. Mr. C—— is instructed to do everything in his power to make you comfortable."

My life at Marghil during the next two weeks was very quiet and lonely, but by no means unpleasant. The early mornings were spent under the great mulberry tree in the garden, and a large collection of miscellaneous books afforded all the reading I could desire. During the hot hours of the day, I roamed from room to room, sometimes writing for an hour or two when so inclined, taking long *siestas*, while the servants kept the *punkah* in motion, thus creating an artificial current of air. The walls of the house were very thick and protected from the sun by wide verandas. My servant, Yusef, had accompanied me from Bagdad, bringing with him the elegant *narghileh* which had been specially appropriated to my use, and now his principal duty was to be always within call to " make," or prepare, the *chibouk* and *narghileh*, and bring coffee or tea as often as required. The light morning meal, the breakfast, luncheon, and dinner, were served with the same regularity and in as elegant style as if the house was full of guests. As it grew cooler towards evening,

A GROUP OF BEDOUINS.

*From a photograph in possession of the Author.*

the large lounging chairs were taken out into the garden, and sometimes Mr. Cadenhead, who in the absence of Captain Carter had charge of the office in Bassorah, came up to dine and spend the night.

I frequently took long solitary walks through the date groves to the edge of the desert as the sun neared the western horizon, and sometimes visited the little lonely cemetery, where several marble slabs mark the resting place of the Europeans who have fallen victims to a pestilential climate. It is neatly enclosed, planted with English roses, and tenderly cared for by Captain Carter.

After sunset, and sometimes during the lone hours of the night, I could hear the wailing cries of prowling jackals, echoing from one side of the river to the other, in *crescendo* tones, then gradually die away, to commence again a few minutes later, seeming to approach nearer and nearer. To a nervous person, such sounds would be far from soothing to quiet sleep, or promotive of pleasant dreams.

One morning I accompanied Mr C—— in his *mashoof* down the river to Bassorah. This is a peculiar boat,—a double-ender, very long and narrow, and as easily upset as an Indian birch canoe. An awning stretched over hoops fitted close to the sides, and it was paddled very swiftly by a boatman sitting astride each end. We carefully placed ourselves in the bottom, and were obliged to keep very quiet, as the sides were but a few inches above the water. The river is here more than a mile in width, very deep, with a rapid current. The *mashoof* is made of bitumen spread over a frame work of date-sticks, and if filled with water would sink like a shot to the bottom.

The boatmen, to take advantage of the current, pushed out into the middle of the river, and as the wind was blowing quite fresh, every few minutes a splash of water

would come over the side.  My companion took it quite
coolly, although he could not swim, but I never before so
fully appreciated the value of a life-preserver.  I had in my
pockets several pounds weight of silver rupees, which I
quietly unloaded into the bottom of the boat, thinking
they would not increase my buoyancy in case of an accident.  But the strongest swimmer could hardly have
reached the shore through the swirling eddies, if our boat
had swamped.  Not to be outdone in coolness, I reclined
back in the *mashoof*, holding by each hand to the gunwale,
and smoked my cheroot with apparent unconcern.  But it
occurred very vividly to my mind at that moment, that
my life insurance policies were both invalid, as I had gone
" without permit" beyond the limits of travel allowed by
Insurance Companies.  We reached the shore in safety,
but on our return, having left my friend in Bassorah, I
insisted that the boatmen keep near the banks of the river,
and have never accepted another invitation to ride in a
*mashoof*.

The climate of Bassorah is quite different from that of
Bagdad.  Everywhere near the shores of the Persian Gulf
the air is moist, and a heavy dew at night makes it necessary to sleep under a thatched awning, which is supported
by poles upon the housetop.  Miasmatic diseases are prevalent, especially during the hot weather, and European
constitutions are sure to break down after a few years' residence in this country.  One day the temperature fell in
an hour nearly twenty degrees, and the wind suddenly
changing, blew fiercely from the north, charged with fine
dust and sand.  The sky darkened and at times assumed
a peculiar violet hue, rather alarming to one unaccustomed
to such a phenomenon.  In spite of closed doors and
tightly drawn blinds, there being no glass windows here,
the fine particles of sand penetrated every crevice of fur-

niture and clothing, and the skin became dry and parched.
The *Shāmmāl* subsided as suddenly as it had arisen, and
when the sun again came out I counted over a dozen native boats and *marhallahs* driven on shore by the violence
of the gale. This dry sand storm left a very unpleasant
impression of the climate of Bassorah, and for a permanent residence I should certainly select some other locality.

At last the arrival of the " Mesopotamia" was tele-
graphed from Fāu, at the mouth of the river, after a voyage of forty-five days from London, *via* the Mediteranean
and Suez Canal. She is an iron steamer, three years old,
built expressly for this trade, and though not remarkable
for speed, is a very staunch and safe vessel. As she was
to be my home for several weeks, I looked for her arrival
with no little interest, and went down as far as Bassorah
to meet her. Here she was detained only long enough for
custom house permits, and then steamed up to the wharf
at Marghil.

The next fifteen days were full of life and excitement
at the *Khan*. Large gangs of natives were at once set to
work unloading the ship, and putting on board the freight
for her return voyage, which was stored in the large warehouses of the firm. The fifteen hundred tons of cargo
consisted of wool in closely compressed bales, several
thousand sacks of grain, and packages of gall nuts, Arabian
spices and gums. Mr. Finnis and Captain Carter soon
after arrived from Bagdad, and every exertion was made
to hasten her departure, as the south-west monsoon, which
blows steadily up the Arabian Sea and Persian Gulf from
June to October, was every day increasing in strength, and
would be directly in our teeth for nearly three thousand
miles. My unexpected detention of almost four weeks at
Bassorah was unfortunate, as I must now pass over this

route and up the Red Sea to Egypt during the hottest season of the year, when they are said to be like the fiery furnace, seven times heated. But perfect health, a somewhat *salamanderish* faculty of enduring the heat, and above all, visions of home, will cheer the traveler on his trying journey.

# CHAPTER XXVIII.

## FROM BASSORAH TO EUROPE.

THE "Mesopotamia" was to
sail at six o'clock the next
morning. In honor of our
departure the whole English
population of Bassorah, numbering but *two persons* outside of those attached to
Lynch & Co.'s establish-
ment, were invited to dine
and spend the night at Marghil. Captain Carter had
given his steward a *carte
blanche* for an entertainment of unusual brilliancy.
His harmonium had been taken up on the terraced roof,

for the night was to be made joyous with song and festivity. The dinner was served in elegant style, and my last night in Arabia was one long to be remembered. Our genial host seemed equally at home in the serious, the sentimental, and the comic. He played the accompaniment to his Negro melodies, Irish songs, and Scottish ballads, and the fun never flagged for a moment. I had seen him the day before scouring over the plain like the wind, mounted on a full blooded Arab mare given to him by the young Sheik Jarbah; and now he sung " My Arab Steed " with unaffected pathos and feeling. His experience as a sailor and officer in all parts of the world furnished an inexhaustible fund of anecdotes, some of which were located in New York, Savannah, and New Orleans. Nor were his guests far behind in story and jest. The hours of the short night sped rapidly away, and before we were aware of it the morning light streaked the eastern horizon. We adjourned to the garden below, and in the wide reclining chairs once more enjoyed our coffee under the spreading branches of the great mulberry tree. Then came the hour of parting. Captain Phillips, of the Mesopotamia, to whose care I had been commended more as a guest than an ordinary passenger, gave the signal to throw off the hawsers, the English flag was hoisted to the peak, and with ringing cheers, in which a crowd of Arabs joined with the Europeans on ship and shore, the stately vessel swung round into the stream, and we were off for Europe. While the white walls of the *Khan* remained in sight I watched through a glass the waving handkerchief of my friend Finnis, my " younger brother," with whom I had been intimately associated for so many months, signaling his good bye. His parting injunction was, " Now don't fail to go and visit my father's family when you reach England— they know all about you and will surely expect you." I need scarcely add that I fulfilled the promise then made, and met the cordial welcome and generous hospitality of an Englishman at home.

As we passed at full speed the Turkish gunboats off Bassorah we dipped our ensign, and the salute was promptly returned. Among them was a long, narrow, side-wheel steamer, with three raking funnels, very sharp in the bows, and evidently built for speed. She was a famous blockade runner during the rebellion, and made several successful trips between Nassau and Wilmington. At the close of the war she was sold to the Turks, and now looks old, dilapidated, and rusty. I was told that she was much out of repair, and no longer seaworthy. Before dark we passed the fort and telegraph station at the mouth of the river, and exchanged the yellow, turbid Euphrates for the clear blue waters of the Persian Gulf.

I was the only passenger on the "Mesopotamia," and the whole ladies' cabin was assigned to my use. If she had been my own private yacht Captain Phillips and his officers could not have treated me with more civility and attention. A double awning protected the deck, and although the sun was intensely hot, the motion of the ship produced an agreeable breeze. In a few days everything settled down to the usual routine of life at sea. The cabins were so hot that all my time was passed on deck. Fortunately no elaborate toilet was required, and, of course, the thinnest possible clothing was brought into requisition. Out of deference to the well known prejudice of Englishmen in regard to dinner costume, I once ventured to add for that occasion a collar and a black neck ribbon; but the captain good naturedly chaffed me about " putting on style." At night the steward spread my mattress on the skylight where I always slept. We stopped one day at the Persian port of Bushire, but I was glad to exchange the

21

stifling heat of the shore for the cooler and purer air on board our ship. While here I was urged to buy a white, long-haired Persian cat, which a native brought off to the ship. These animals are highly esteemed in Western lands by *cat fanciers*; but when I tested her temper, I found that she would spit, snap, and bite most savagely; so I concluded that the snarling, half wild brute would be a troublesome traveling companion before I reached America. But without my knowledge one of the sailors bought her to take home as a speculation. I had on board many valuable curiosities, antiques and relics, which I had secured at Bagdad—including bricks from Babylon and Nineveh, old coins, Persian and Arab costumes, etc. As a *souvenir* of Marghil, Yusef Marini had presented me with a pair of *buhl-buhls*, or Persian nightingales, which I found plenty of leisure during the voyage to make very tame. I kept them on deck in a date stick cage near the skylight on which I slept. Soon after leaving Bushire I awoke one morning and saw stretched out alongside the cage that white Persian cat. At one bound I " went for" the animal, but she was too quick for me, or the sailor's private venture would have gone overboard. Some feathers scattered on the deck was all that remained of one of my pets, and in a few minutes more the other would have shared the same tragic fate. But " Dickey" has survived all perils by sea and land, as well as change of climate, and reached America in safety.

We had seven days of smooth sea and fair weather from the head of the Persian Gulf to the straits connecting that sea with the Indian ocean. But here our trials began. In each of those memorable voyages of " Sinbad the Sailor," it is related that he started from Bagdad and sailed from Bassorah, after which he had a few days of fine weather. Then came the wrecks and the roc's eggs, the desert islands and the diamond valleys. My story is not an " Arabian Nights" tale, so that the most interesting part of Sinbad's adventures cannot here be narrated. But fate had in store for me an experience so near a wreck, that for a pocket full of diamonds I would not be willing to try my chances again.

We passed Ras al Hāt, a bold promontory extending out from the coast, then shaping our course to the south-west, the monsoon struck us with full force. For the next twelve days until we arrived at Aden, it blew steadily ahead, and raised a heavy sea. The square sails were unbent and the yards sent down, as all useless rigging impeded our progress. The effect of the monsoon, which in these seas blows during so many months in one direction, is to produce surface currents, the force of which cannot be calculated. These variable currents often throw a ship off her course, and cause serious difficulties in navigation. My intimate relations with the captain gave me an opportunity of studying the charts, and knowing at all times the location of the ship. The observation at noon on the third day after passing Ras al Hāt gave our exact position, which the captain pointed out to me on the chart. He said at our present rate of speed, five miles an hour by the patent log, we should pass about midnight Ras Madraka, another headland jutting out from the Arabian coast, giving it at least forty miles leeway.

That night when the twelve o'clock watch was called I was awake, and the first officer as he passed me after hauling in the log, said that we had made twenty miles during the last four hours. The sea was quite rough, and sometimes a dash of spray would reach my bed on the skylight. So I rolled up my mattress, and for the first and only night while on board, I went below and crawled into one of the berths in my cabin. Three hours later I was awakened by a rude shock, and knew, almost instinctively, that *the ship had struck.* Slipping out of my berth I was quickly on deck, and there clinging to the door of the companion way, a scene met my view that would have appalled the stoutest heart. All was darkness and confusion. Our gallant ship was thumping heavily with every receding wave, and looking ahead I could dimly see high rocky cliffs looming up through the thick haze. Both on our right and left, but a few hundred yards away, the white breakers were dashing over rocks, while astern the rough sea seemed to cut off all retreat. When the ship struck, Captain Phillips was asleep in the chart-room under the bridge, but at the first alarm he was on deck, and now I could hear his ringing voice issuing orders in loud and excited tones. Neither the officer in charge nor the look-out on the forecastle had seen the land until too late ; and the ship struck at full speed. An unknown current had carried us more than forty miles off our course since noon the day before, and we had struck on the projecting Cape of Ras Madraka. On the charts this part of the coast of Arabia is marked as inhabited by inhospitable and barbarous tribes, who would rob and murder every ship-wrecked mariner whom the sea might cast upon their shores. It needed but a single glance around to show the imminent danger of our situation.

I went down to my cabin, struck a match, slipped on a light overcoat, unlocked my trunk, put a roll of gold into one pocket and my watch into the other, and again made my way on deck, holding by the balusters, while the ship thumped and rolled, as if struggling to free herself from impending destruction. The Steward, a Maltese, came up to me, and with chattering teeth asked whether I thought we should go to pieces. I told him that it seemed quite likely ; and he dropped on his knees, devoutly crossed

himself, and muttered some prayers—the first he had said,
I fancy, for a long time. When I reached the deck the
second time there seemed no improvement in our condition. Fortunately we had struck on a spit of sand—a
short distance on either side were rocks, the first thump
on which would have punched a hole in the bottom of our
ship, and, as Captain Phillips·expressed it the next day,
" the Mesopotamia would have been *scrap iron* in half an
hour." In the meantime everything that experience and
good seamanship could suggest was done. Soundings
were taken on all sides to ascertain the depth of water,
the engines reversed, and all steam put on. I looked
about me for something that would float if worst came to

"GET READY TO PASS IN YOUR CHECKS."

worst, and started towards a life preserver lashed to the
rail near by. But it then occurred to me how little
use it would be, with the gale blowing off shore, as I

should be carried out to sea, and have not one chance in ten thousand of being picked up on this lonely ocean.

Of course, no one paid the least attention to me, but I recognized and hailed the second officer with the remark that it looked very bad—" D—d bad " was his emphatic reply. " I advise you to get ready to pass in your checks," and he disappeared in the darkness. But there was a better fate in store for us than his expressive, but somewhat profane remark indicated. It was now about twenty minutes since the first alarm,—the ominous pounding ceased ; the ship slowly drew off from the land, and turning her head towards the open sea, the rocks and breakers disappeared from sight. The pumps were sounded and it was found that no seams had started, nor any serious damage been sustained by the ship. At daylight no land was in sight, everything had resumed its usual routine, and the perilous night's experience seemed but a wild dream.

During the remainder of the voyage we often discussed the possibilities of a different result. The Captain said that for fifteen years he had been master of a ship on these seas, and never before had he come so near losing his vessel. He said if she had gone to pieces he should have launched the two life boats, and sailed back before the monsoon, five hundred miles, to Muscat. These boats are of wood and rest upon skids in the waist of the ship. They have never been in the water, and having for three years been exposed to a tropical sun, I doubt very much whether they would float. To clear them out, launch, provision, and equip them with sails, charts, and instruments for such a voyage, would be the work of hours in daylight, with a smooth sea. To accomplish this in darkness, amid the confusion of storm and wreck, would be next to impossible. Life at sea is surrounded with peculiar perils. Sailors are proverbially reckless of danger, and when the sudden emergency comes they are often found unprepared to meet it.

With the monsoon blowing directly in our teeth the average speed of the vessel was lessened from seven and a half to five miles an hour. Before we reached Aden some anxiety began to be felt about our supply of coal. Besides filling the bunkers, fifty tons had been stored on deck before leaving Bassorah. The chief engineer had each day's consumption carefully weighed, and close calculations were made as to how long it would hold out. To be caught a hundred miles from port, with the fuel exhausted, and a head wind, would be disastrous. A large steamer of the " Peninsular and Oriental Line " from Bombay, was not long ago obliged to burn all her extra spars and the mahogany wood work of her elegant cabins to reach Aden. But when the Mesopotamia sighted the high cliffs of Aden we had still about fifty tons of coal on hand.

In that harbor we found the steam yacht *Deerhound*, which rescued Captain Semmes after the destruction of the Alabama. I was curious to see this famous vessel, and was courteously shown over her by the officers in charge. She is a beautiful craft of about two hundred tons, but since the event that associated her name with the rebel pirate, she has been very unfortunate, and has several times changed owners. She was seized in attempting to smuggle arms from England to the Carlists in Spain, and is now on her way to Zanzibar, the owner expecting to sell her to the Sultan of that country. She started from this port a month ago for her destination, but being unable to make headway against the wind, she has returned to Aden to wait until the monsoon is over.

After two days stay to coal our ship, we steamed towards the entrance of the Red Sea. This last part of our voyage was especially dreaded ; but though the midsummer's heat was oppressive, it was not so uncomfortable as I had anticipated. Seven days of clear weather brought us to Suez, where I bade adieu to the Mesopotamia and her kind officers, as they were bound to London, *via* the Suez Canal and the Mediterranean. I proposed to take the shorter route across Egypt to Alexandria, and thence to Europe. Although this country during the summer months is considered decidedly tropical, I found it so much cooler than the climate from which I had come, that colored clothing took the place of white linen, and when, after a week at Cairo and Alexandria, I crossed to Brundisi and Venice, woolen garments were not uncomfortable. From Venice across Italy and France to Paris, and thence to London, is so common a journey as to require no description.

Oriental countries have their especial charms and fascinations; but life surrounded by the superior comforts of Western civilization seems never so attractive as when the traveler returns from a long journey through the East. My experiences in the "Land of the Arabian Nights" will always form some of the pleasantest pictures in my recollections of foreign travel. The happiest faculty that the wanderer in strange lands can possess, is that of making the best of everything and looking only on the bright side. And I trust the reader will see no cause for regret that the more sombre tints and the darker shadows have not been brought out with more prominence.